SMART POWER

SMART
POWER

Between Diplomacy and War

CHRISTIAN WHITON

Foreword by Ambassador Paula J. Dobriansky

 Potomac Books | Washington, D.C.

Potomac Books is an imprint of the
University of Nebraska Press.

Library of Congress
Cataloging-in-Publication Data
Whiton, Christian.
Smart power: between diplomacy and
war / Christian Whiton.
pages cm
Includes bibliographical references
and index.
ISBN 978-1-61234-619-9 (hardcover:
alk. paper)
ISBN 978-1-61234-620-5 (electronic)
1. United States—Foreign
relations—2001-2009. 2. United
States—Foreign relations—2009–
I. Title.
E902.W495 2013
327.73—dc23   2013013324

Printed in the United States of
America on acid-free paper that meets
the American National Standards
Institute z 39-48 Standard.

Potomac Books
22841 Quicksilver Drive
Dulles, Virginia 20166

First Edition

10 9 8 7 6 5 4 3 2 1

TO MARCO

Contents

Foreword

Ambassador Paula J. Dobriansky, PhD

Smart power has existed far longer as an idea than it has as a term. It began to be so described only in the previous decade. It means different things to different people but is generally a synthesizing of diverse tools of statecraft, ranging from "soft" ones like foreign aid to "hard" ones like military force. Essentially, it describes what governments do when they bring multiple forces to bear on challenges from abroad.

When I first entered government during one of the chillier periods of the Cold War, Washington was preparing to revive what today might be called smart power. The Soviet Union had been on the march and had invaded Afghanistan. Poland was soon to be under martial law, which we knew to be in advanced stages of planning in close coordination with Moscow. Its advent would reprise crackdowns behind the Iron Curtain like those in Hungary in 1956 and Czechoslovakia in 1968. I was one of two directors at the National Security Council (NSC) whose portfolio included the Soviet bloc.

Ronald Reagan's arrival at the White House brought not only a different way of seeing the world but also a way of conducting statecraft that distinguished him from predecessors of both political parties. From the beginning, his administration went to great lengths to articulate a strategy toward the Soviet Union. Reagan and his team sought clarity. We developed a series of policy options and statements that were refined into three classified National Security Decision Directives (NSDD) that Reagan signed. The first, NSDD 32, issued in May 1982, encompassed matters ranging from nuclear posture and military alliances to promoting a "well-functioning international economic system." Moreover, it laid out steps to "increase the cost of Soviet support and use of proxy, terrorist, and subversive forces," and made it policy to contain "and reverse the expansion of Soviet control." The second directive, NSDD 66, issued in November 1982, built on diplomatic efforts to limit Moscow's ability to gain economic control over U.S. allies, especially in the supply of energy. Reagan signed the third directive of note, NSDD 75, the following January. It broadly recast U.S.-Soviet relations and notably had as a key task "competing effectively on a sustained basis with the Soviet Union in all international areas."

Spirited debates between various agencies of government and those of us on the NSC staff at the White House preceded the development of each of these NSDDs. The result in each case was a strategy to use many different tools available to the United States and its allies against the various pillars of support that were enabling the dangerous conduct of America's chief adversary at the time. This fresh look highlighted many tools and techniques of national power that had been neglected during earlier stages of the Cold War. There was a prominent role for military posture, but most noticeable were the many important tasks outside the military sphere.

However, this holistic approach, while newly refined, was not new in U.S. history. From the beginning of the Cold War, many Americans realized that neither military force nor traditional intergovernmental diplomacy alone would provide for the best defense. Washington and other capitals would have to consider economic and political factors of power as well. My father, Dr. Lev E. Dobriansky, was essentially advancing this concept of smart power when he helped conceive Captive Nations Week in the early 1950s. As the son of Ukrainian immigrants, he grasped that the aspirations of those held involuntarily within the Soviet Union and Eastern Bloc could be a force for peace — and a key part of statecraft. The idea of Captive Nations Week was to ensure a focus not only on relations between governments that held power but also on average people and the impact they could have on history, as in the past. President Dwight Eisenhower made the week official by signing a 1959 law that found "the desire for liberty and independence by the overwhelming majority of the people of these [captive] nations constitutes a powerful deterrent to war and one of the best hopes for a just and lasting peace."

Of course, for these ideas and principles to become smart power in practice, they had to be followed up by concrete actions. During the George H. W. Bush administration, as the Cold War was coming to a tumultuous end, I oversaw two very different parts of this implementation. At the State Department's Bureau of Human Rights and Humanitarian Affairs, we carefully assessed and presented to the world the human rights violations of various foreign governments, both friend and foe. Subsequently, at the U.S. Information Agency, where I was the associate director in charge of policy and programs, we took steps to inform and influence foreign publics and to deepen engagement between Americans and foreigners. We also broadcast news and commentary throughout the Soviet bloc countries. All of these activities were based on the assumption that ideas and factual information can be powerful enablers of U.S. national security. This was why Allen Dulles, the director of the Central Intelligence Agency from 1953 to 1961, had a biblical verse inscribed in the entrance of that agency's original headquarters building: "And Ye Shall Know the Truth and the Truth Shall Make You Free."

Throughout this book, Christian Whiton argues compellingly that these historically successful practices need to be reprised and updated for the current world situation. He deftly explains that smart power is not a checklist of policy options or a simple mix of foreign aid and military force but a wide spectrum of actions — and a way of thinking.

Making full use of smart power requires a willingness to challenge our adversaries through peaceful means, which at times has been almost as controversial as using military means. The steps we were able to take in the Reagan administration required a decision by the president to end détente, the practice of attempting to relax tensions with the Soviet Union initiated by Richard Nixon. Many opposed ending this often one-sided policy, which involved, for example, President Gerald Ford's decision to snub and ignore Soviet dissident Aleksandr Solzhenitsyn, whose expulsion from Russia and arrival in America cast new light on an intensively repressive and dangerous system. Reagan's departure from détente, which he called immoral, was a necessary antecedent to utilizing fully smart power. While Reagan was determined to sit down with the Soviets and talk — and, in fact, negotiated with them the most effective arms control treaty of the twentieth century — he was also direct about his desire to help those under Soviet tyranny free themselves.

Whiton came to work for me when I was undersecretary of state for democracy and global affairs in the George W. Bush administration. The bureaus I managed handled the transnational issues that fall in key parts of the smart power spectrum, ranging from governance and human rights to refugees to scientific issues to international law enforcement cooperation and anticorruption efforts. During a decade of war and global political turbulence, we sought to advance U.S. interests using not only traditional diplomacy and ties with other governments but also in linking with actors outside of government, ranging, for example, from American business leaders who wanted to help women in Afghanistan obtain economic power and a political voice to those who struggled peacefully to bring about the "color revolutions" that replaced repressive regimes in their countries.

It was in this environment that Whiton began to form the assumptions about statecraft reflected in this book. The decade was also one that involved significant and ongoing reorganization of national security-related parts of the U.S. government. This remains a work in progress today. This evolution is the inevitable result from changing perceptions of the world with which Washington has had to contend. The time we described in the 1990s as the post–Cold War era is increasingly distant. That gave way to the post-9/11 period, marked by the scramble to react to terrorist attacks and grapple with multiple armed conflicts. However, with global economic turbulence and dramatic political upheaval in the Middle East, we seem to have passed yet another meridian in time and history.

Considering what the U.S. government has done right and wrong during the Arab Spring is an important antecedent to getting smart power right for the rest of the decade. So too is grasping new threats to U.S. interests brought forth by governments such as those of Iran, Russia, and China, as well as the recent success of Islamist political parties in the broader Middle East. Whiton conducts these assessments in this book and would not be true to himself if he did not describe bluntly how presidents and other policymakers have fared in his estimation and what corrective steps, ranging from modest to radical, should be taken.

Amid today's turmoil, in which the number of economic, political, and security variables is increasing, the United States likely finds itself at or near an inflection point. Events are likely to again change statecraft as we have known it in recent years. There is no time like the present to take a fresh look at where and how smart power should fit. Christian Whiton masterfully undertakes such an effort in this book.

Smart power as a phrase may still be relatively new in historical terms, but it is a practice and way of thinking for which there is now a long record. Learning from the past and preparing for the future are crucial.

Introduction

The weight of the world was on Mark Wyatt's shoulders. In some respects, so was its fate. A veteran of the Office of Strategic Services — America's World War II spy agency — Wyatt found himself at age twenty-eight on the front line of American smart power against communism. Wyatt started as a political warrior as a seventeen-year-old student, when he bicycled through Germany in 1938 and delivered letters entrusted to him by British intelligence to help anti-Nazis activists escape. Now it was 1948 and he worked for the brand-new Central Intelligence Agency (CIA).[1]

Time magazine referred that year to the "stormy battlefields of peace" that pitted communists against noncommunists in places like France, Germany, Greece, and Italy. In an April 1948 cover story, it reported: "It was as though history's heart had skipped a beat. For a brief, illusory moment, other struggles between Communism and the West seemed suspended — as if the contestants paused to watch the outcome of the stirring battle being fought in Italy. At dawn this Sunday, Italians will go to the polls to choose, in a democratic election, between Communism and the West."[2]

Luckily, Wyatt and his colleagues had been hard at work behind the scenes and knew their job. By 1948, Washington had finally begun to wake up to the political and military threat that the Soviet Union and its friends posed. Russia was a wartime ally of the United States and Britain, but it now dominated the lands it had freed from Nazi control and was in no hurry to remove the Red Army from Central Europe. Two years after

Winston Churchill had warned of an "Iron Curtain" descending over Europe, Russia's grip on the nations it held captive behind the curtain was growing tighter. Soviet dictator Joseph Stalin wanted to force the Western powers out of West Berlin and would blockade the city by mid-year, prompting the Berlin Airlift. The Marshall Plan — massive U.S. economic aid to prevent still-free European countries from going communist — was getting under way. That year also marked the turning point after which the postwar military drawdown would end and U.S. defense spending would increase.

One year before, President Harry S. Truman had signed the National Security Act of 1947. The law accomplished what seems impossible in broken Washington today: in a decisive stroke it instigated drastic reform of the U.S. defense and foreign policy apparatus for a new threat. Of the many parts of the law, the most crucial aspect for smart power was the establishment of the CIA. Also important, the law gave the new organization the ability to engage in covert action and not simply gather and collate information.

President Truman initially opposed giving America's first peacetime intelligence agency this capability, but his administration soon made use of it nonetheless. Wyatt and his fellow officers knew what had to be done. The Soviets were sparing few expenses and intrigues to support those who ironically would use the ballot box itself to shift Italy away from the free West and toward the communist Eastern Bloc. Moscow likely spent more than $50 million a year to aid Italy's communists.[3] As with America's opponents today, the Soviets were more than willing to use democratic means to kill democracy. The only realistic hope for the poorly organized and under-resourced anticommunists was similar direct assistance. Years later, Wyatt noted that he literally delivered bags of cash to the coalition that opposed communist tyranny in Italy.[4]

The day was won. In what was called the miracle of '48, the Italians, in their first postwar election with universal suffrage, elected those who would keep the country free and aligned with the West. America and its allies kept at it too. U.S. covert support to Italy's anticommunists against their Soviet-funded opponents continued until the late 1960s when democratic forces in Italy could stand on their own.

Notably, the smart power victory did not occur in a vacuum. Had the United States confined its activities to quietly disbursing some cash to anticommunists in Italy, the effort to thwart Moscow would have paled next to the relentless political tide of communism and the restive Red Army immediately to the east. However, while Wyatt and his colleagues were countering communist actions in the political campaign, they were also organizing a "stay-behind" mission in Italy similar to ones conducted in the Netherlands, France, Belgium, Luxembourg, Denmark, and even neutral Sweden. These operations involved highly secret organizations and weapons caches to resist communist forces should the Russians take control either through invasion or political subversion. While no match for the Red Army, they helped demonstrate that a clear U.S. commitment would persist through even the darkest circumstances.

They were just the beginning. Despite the passage of only three years from a world war that had left more than 400,000 Americans dead, the United States rejected a common urge after costly wars to become insular. The Marshall Plan — the ultimate example of what decades later might be called soft power — was getting started. Despite postwar demobilization, Washington made clear that substantial American forces would remain in Europe to face the new post-Nazi threat. The Western powers, including the United States, initiated talks to create the North Atlantic Treaty Organization (NATO). While it was still a year before the Soviets would test "Joe-1" — their first nuclear shot — the ruthlessly efficient Gen. Curtis E. LeMay had recently taken command of the relatively new U.S. Strategic Air Command. The move signaled that America understood it needed to be prepared for global war at short notice. To counter communist propaganda, the CIA set up Radio Free Europe to broadcast into the Eastern Bloc and would launch its programming the following year in 1949. One of its antecedents, Radio in the American Sector, was already providing an information link to those behind the Iron Curtain in East Germany.

Last but not least was the attitude of the man who sat in the Oval Office. Harry Truman assumed the presidency when Franklin Roosevelt died in April 1945. Cold War hawks would later view the Democrat as having a mixed record, especially after his handling of the Korean War. Furthermore, of his conduct after his presidency, conservative William F. Buckley Jr. wrote of Truman that he was "the nation's most conspicuous vulgarian."[5] But no one could accuse Truman of being a dove. In overseeing the final months of World War II, he had lost no sleep in ordering two nuclear weapons dropped on Japan, and before that, the even-deadlier incineration of several Japanese cities by conventional bombing.

Importantly, Truman also lacked much of his predecessor's sanguine views of communists in general and of Soviet dictator Stalin in particular. Overlooking ruthless, murderous conduct in both war and peace, Roosevelt near the end of his life mused to his cabinet that Stalin might have "something in him besides this revolutionist, Bolshevist thing." Roosevelt sensed that, despite Stalin's having become an atheist dictator and the leader of global communism, some aspect of the Soviet leader's youthful training for the priesthood "entered into his nature of the way in which a Christian gentleman should behave."[6]

The former haberdasher from Missouri lacked this nuanced — and plainly incorrect — view of Stalin and the global political insurgency he was waging. In a speech in 1947, the president laid out what became known as the Truman Doctrine — "the policy of the United States to support free people who are resisting attempted subjugation by armed minorities or by outside pressures." The United States would not acquiesce to communist advances and would instead resist them. Further, unlike so many meaningless rhetorical flourishes from politicians of both major U.S. political parties today, Truman meant it.

So when CIA officer Mark Wyatt set out to provide covert support to the anticommunists in Italy in 1948, he was one point of a multipronged smart power campaign against the rising tide of global communism. The United States and its allies had begun to fight against communism intellectually (Radio Free Europe, etc.), economically (the Marshall Plan), overtly (ending the postwar military drawdown) and covertly (direct clandestine aid to anticommunists). The many bureaucracies of government necessary to wage this effort no doubt had their inefficiencies, but with a strong leadership in the White House and Congress, a clear mission, and perhaps even a rare dash of bureaucratic imagination, the task was set.

The United States deserved victory and won it. Not only Italy but also other at-risk nations, such as Greece, Turkey, West Germany, and France, remained free and allied with the West. Washington's determination registered not only with America's friends but also with those who were not its friends. The Russians received the clear message that the United States and its allies would not be pushovers in war or peace. The United States accomplished an important foreign political objective without firing a shot — the key objective of smart power.

Of course, in Washington, few good deeds ever go unpunished.

Thirty years later, what had been one of America's finest hours in the early Cold War and the annals of smart power became a chief exhibit in what supposedly was wrong with American intelligence operations. The year 1975 was perhaps the nadir for the United States in the twentieth century. The tumult that resulted from the Watergate scandal, the unsuccessful Vietnam War, and the acrimony of the civil rights movement combined with economic chaos and a perception of America's decline to usher in a Congress with radical views. The new House of Representatives and Senate that began work in January added a large new class of liberals to existing large Democratic majorities. It marked a new turn for the Democratic Party in Congress in which foreign policy hawks such as Truman were no longer in charge.

Also gone was what more or less had been a bipartisan consensus that America was an exceptional force of good in the world — even if the nation was imperfect — and that America's cause in the world was deserving of all Americans' support. Out was the healthy nationalism known as patriotism. In was the tendency to blame America for many of the problems in the world instead of the governments and people actually causing them.

The new Congress wasted little time in putting American intelligence activities on trial. In 1975 and 1976, the Senate's Church Committee and the House's Pike Committee systematically emphasized failures and obscured great successes of American intelligence operations and political warfare — two key ingredients of smart power. New laws were passed curtailing intelligence collection. Beyond that, a new mentality was taking hold and flowed through all of Washington's institutions to one degree or another. The iconoclasts who came of age in the late 1960s while assaulting the establishment became part of the establishment themselves and began to ensnare many of the instruments of national power, including the State Department's Foreign Service and the growing ranks of law-yers and civilian "defense intellectuals" at the Pentagon. At the CIA, the Directorate of Operations, which ran the actual spies and covert opera-tions, was permanently dethroned and overtaken by the PhD-heavy Direc-torate of Intelligence. This shift was similar to telling the University of Alabama's football program it would henceforth report to the school's English department.

A direct line can be drawn from the actions of those who arrived with that Congress to the intelligence lapses that years later allowed terrorists to murder thousands of Americans on September 11, 2001. Furthermore, the changes affected far more than intelligence gathering. Lost was Amer-ica's overall capacity to conduct the full spectrum of activities that con-stitute smart power, including not only the government instrumentalities to do the job but also the frame of mind that the U.S. government should work unapologetically toward foreign objectives that favor freedom and American security.

A brief resurgence was effected during the Reagan administration in the 1980s. Washington covertly armed a proxy army fighting the Soviets in Afghanistan and successfully provided military and economic aid to those resisting communism in El Salvador, Nicaragua, and Angola. Steps taken by the United States challenged the Soviet Empire at its vulnerable points and ran up the cost of maintaining the empire. Along with Pope John Paul II's running a friendly Vatican and Margaret Thatcher the Brit-ish government, the United States and its allies helped sustain a freedom movement in Poland, brought down the Iron Curtain in 1989, and ended the Soviet Union and the Cold War in 1991.

But many of the old tools were beyond repair. The new ones created during that decade have since atrophied. The resurgence evaporated in the 1990s, when many in Washington were willing to ignore Plato's admoni-tion that "only the dead have seen the end of war," a warning that applies to international political conflict as well. Instead, many accepted the improb-able theory that Americans and others found themselves at "the end of history," as one historian argued.[7] The first indication this assertion was not so came when the United States went to war to eject Saddam Hussein from Kuwait in the 1991 Gulf War. Subsequently, the September 2001 attacks and ensuing decade of tumult should have led to the creation of new smart power tools calibrated for the challenges and opportunities of the day, but they did not. More recently, some scholars have resorted to the view that geography and demographics are destiny, conveniently excusing any role for statecraft or leadership to shape the world.[8] Through and through, Washington's foreign policy establishment is unable and unwilling to grasp or confront the major foreign threats the United States faces.

It need not be this way.

As Mark Wyatt and his colleagues proved, long before the phrase "smart power" was used, Americans mastered the tools of statecraft that fall between routine diplomacy and outright war. Smart power played a role throughout the Cold War. Political warfare — perhaps the most absent portion of the smart power spectrum today — also played a part in winning both world wars, with the notable contribution of the U.S. Office of Strategic Services and U.K. Political Warfare Executive during the latter war. Further back in history, the very act that brought the United States of America into existence in 1776 was an exercise in political warfare. America's Declaration of Independence was intended not only to rally the patriots' cause at home but also to entice new allies abroad. Combined with other actions, it helped achieve both goals.

At its most basic level, smart power should be thought of as progressing toward the foreign *political* outcome vital for American security and prosperity. Today, this effort usually means making life hard for America's enemies and chief adversaries by confronting them from outside their borders and at times helping to undermine them from within. It also entails helping those who are enemies of America's enemies, even if they are not necessarily America's friends. This work is often most effective when performed discreetly or indirectly.

Rediscovering smart power is vital to U.S. security in the years ahead. As this book outlines, political conflict is the realm in which the United States is likely to be challenged most in the next decades. It is an area in which U.S. adversaries from Iran to China play for keeps and are beating America. Furthermore, after a decade of war in Iraq and Afghanistan that has changed the domestic politics involved with national defense, the time is right for the United States to rediscover the missing middle between diplomacy and war.

Often mistaken for the narrower missions of propaganda, or "winning hearts and minds," smart power can include diverse diplomatic, political, cultural, military, technological, financial, economic, rhetorical, legal, and espionage-related tools and practices. Some seem to believe that economic sanctions are the best reaction to a foreign problem if Washington is through issuing stern warnings to its opponents but is not prepared to go to war. This option is not simply a failure of imagination by the Washington foreign policy establishment but also a byproduct of unappealing political trends on both the left and right. The neoconservative voices on the right, whose sole solution to foreign problems so often seems to be sideshow wars, are souring Americans to involvement in the world. The Obama administration's de facto policy of "leading from behind" is dangerous and inconsistent with America's character. What is missing is the middle way on foreign policy that such presidents as Truman, Dwight Eisenhower, John F. Kennedy, and Ronald Reagan pursued. They sought peace through strength, remaining stingy with the lives of American servicemen but nonetheless unabashed when U.S. security was on the line.

Smart power and its political warfare subcomponent are key tools of this missing middle. Used properly, they mesh seamlessly with espionage and operations that countries conduct with a military short of going to full war and include a nation's peacetime military posture. If U.S. espionage today is the "pull" of information that America's opponents do not want it to have, political warfare is the "push" of confrontational ideas, people, forces, and events with which America's opponents would rather not contend. That push is aided by a strong military posture, whether or not is it engaged in outright combat.

For example, smart power waged against communists in Europe during the Cold War and in support of anticommunists was made more effective in no small part by the forward deployment of the American military in Europe and East Asia. Paradoxically, even though it supposedly meant losing "hearts and minds" due to controversy and widespread protest, the West's necessary use of smart power against communism was actually enhanced when President Reagan deployed a new class of American nuclear weapons to Europe in the early 1980s and countered Soviet military advantages. Determination and a clear mission count for a great deal in foreign affairs, as elsewhere.

In defining smart power, understanding what it is *not* is equally important. It is not only sanctions. It is not only foreign aid. It is not only what the military until recently called psyops, or psychological operations intended to demoralize or manipulate the perceptions of an enemy in combat. It is neither political propaganda in its various forms nor even softer information tools directed abroad like the Voice of America. Those tools might be some of a dozen or more elements of a successful smart power strategy, but they do not make up the whole picture. Nor has any one of them worked in isolation in the past.

Most important, smart power is not the unfortunate endeavor that falls under the banner of public diplomacy today. This enterprise has been conducted from a regrettably irrelevant corner of the State Department. I saw its shortcomings firsthand as a political appointee at that plodding institution during the previous decade. As an official seeking to expand democracy and human rights abroad, I looked for help from those who fashioned themselves as warriors in the "global battle of ideas." I need not have bothered. Known sardonically as the "kumbaya approach," U.S. public diplomacy has consisted partly of winning hearts and minds, partly of attempting to put a positive spin on U.S. foreign policy, and partly of diplotourism that has sent countless U.S. officials and politicians abroad to pitch bromides about Americans' affinity for peace and tolerance. Impaired by political correctness, implied weakness, and poor leadership, U.S. public diplomacy since 9/11 has, if anything, heartened America's enemies and disappointed its friends. There is a role for this softest of smart power tools, but its proper place has eluded Washington.

Just as many policymakers and average citizens used to understand smart power intuitively, Americans used to grasp instinctively that a great country has to be clear on who its friends and enemies are. Most Americans still do. It is their government and their foreign policy establishment in Washington that have forgotten. For example, most Americans would not hesitate to name the Chinese government as an adversary of the United States. A sizable number would even consider it to be America's enemy. How else would one describe a foreign government that wages relentless cyberwar on the United States, that is building a navy to exclude the United States from the Western Pacific, that trades unfairly, and that systematically steals U.S. technology and intellectual property to improve its military and damage America's economy?

But good luck finding a mainstream foreign policy official or expert in Washington who is willing to characterize China as the enemy. Even at the Pentagon — the one province of Washington one would think would dispense with happy talk about China's "peaceful rise" — officials and military brass are often eager to avoid clear, accurate labels. Straight talk leads to one being accused of "having a Cold War mind-set," which, ironically, is a smear coined by the paranoid Chinese government itself.[9]

The same holds true for the Iranian government. Most Americans instinctively understand that this regime is an enemy of the United States. After all, in an inaugural act of foreign policy, the new Islamic Republic in 1979 condoned taking U.S. diplomats hostage. Iran was behind the kidnapping and murder of countless Americans in Lebanon and elsewhere in the 1980s. In 1996, Iranian agents bombed the Khobar Towers military dormitory in Saudi Arabia, killing seventeen American servicemen.[10] During the Iraq War, the Iranian government was responsible for the deaths and maiming of untold thousands of American servicemen in Iraq. It has bridged the Shiite-Sunni and Persian-Arab divides in violent Islamist circles, supporting terrorist groups of different stripes. And while U.S. intelligence bureaucrats have downplayed Iran's aspirations for nuclear weapons, most average Americans have no doubts about this regime's ultimate intentions. Americans do not want war, but neither do they favor fealty or incompetence in managing foreign threats.

But among our foreign policy elite, these complex issues require a nuanced approach, endless negotiations and ruminations, and tactics that most Americans learned during their early playground days are ineffective in handling a bully. In fairness to those who populate our national security bureaucracies and their counterparts at think tanks, why should they be working on ways to perturb Iran's global power aspirations if our leaders have not really identified that regime as an enemy? America cannot prevail over foreign threats if its leaders are unable or unwilling to characterize them accurately in the first place. The task is also made harder when effective options short of war are left unexplained and unutilized.

The following chapters detail the "missing middle" where smart power should be, providing options to deal with such adversaries as the governments of Iran and China, the multiplying ranks of Islamist political parties across the Middle East, and other problem states like North Korea. They outline a foreign policy that is consistent with both President Kennedy's call to "pay any price, bear any burden, meet any hardship, support any friend, oppose any foe, in order to assure the survival and the success of liberty" and the political reality explained by John Quincy Adams that "America does not go abroad in search of monsters to destroy." They explain the key events that brought the United States and its allies to this point, remind the reader of times in the past when America has done better, and show the way ahead.

Los Angeles
May 2013

SMART POWER

THE MISSING MIDDLE

CHAPTER I

The False Choice

Diplomacy or War

"Frankly, we don't want to be accused by Beijing of fanning the flames of democracy here." The words hung in the air. They came out of the mouth of a senior officer at our diplomatic outpost in Hong Kong, the one part of China that actually has an open and vibrant democracy movement. It was the fall of 2006.

I was speechless. To receive this pearl of wisdom, I had been summoned to the imposing U.S. consulate on Garden Road and led through a warren of offices and maintenance areas to a highly secure conference room. There, presumably beyond the reach of China's extensive human and electronic eavesdropping tools, I was witnessing an up-close view of what some political appointees in government such as myself regarded as "going native." Joining the concerned diplomat around the table was a number of other representatives of various consulate departments. Ostensibly they were there to brief me, but they imparted no useful or sensitive information. In reality, they were there to discourage me.

At the time, this comment seemed to be more than the usual dismaying conduct from senior members of the U.S. Foreign Service, which dominates the State Department. After all, this moment occurred not long after President George W. Bush — in whose administration I served as a political appointee — had declared in his second inaugural address that "it is the policy of the United States to seek and support the growth of democratic movements and institutions in every nation and culture."

I thought my trip to Hong Kong and nearby geographies fit neatly enough with this seemingly crystal-clear objective. At the time, I had moved from supporting the State Department's undersecretary who dealt with governance issues globally to working on the more focused issue of North Korean human rights. America had a president who personally loathed North Korea's dictator and thought that U.S. security in particular and the world in general would be better off if the Kim family's communist dynasty could be altered or replaced. In a tried-and-true method of peacefully undermining dictatorships over time Congress had passed a law calling for opening the flow of uncensored information into North Korea.[1] Using peaceful means to make life harder for the regime that had once been at war with the United States — and would soon test its first nuclear device — struck me as smart for U.S. security and consistent with the values of the American people.

The White House and Congress also wanted us to find ways for North Korean refugees to reach a free country safely. Given the difficulty of crossing the heavily guarded and mined demilitarized zone between the two Koreas, those escaping from North Korea in search of freedom or food headed for China instead. There, China's government was subjecting them to a brand-new Orwellian nightmare, in plain violation of a treaty Beijing had signed promising to treat refugees humanely.[2] The Chinese authorities forcibly sent anyone they caught back to North Korea to face fates ranging from jail, in the best case, to prison camps or execution in the worst case. To avoid these fates, those remaining in China had to elude the authorities at all cost. Some men lived in the woods and foraged for food. Many women were easy victims of what is called "trafficking in persons," often forced into prostitution and modern-day slavery.

It seemed straightforward to me to talk with those in East Asia who were helping North Korean refugees escape to freedom via a modern underground railroad. I also wanted to hear firsthand from governments and political leaders in the region what they thought about the issue and where it stood on the longer list of problems caused by the Chinese government and its clients, of which the North Korean government is one. I wanted to verify who would help beleaguered North Koreans in their quest for personal or national freedom, who would hurt them, and who would at least be willing to look the other way while others helped them.

Hong Kong seemed a natural place to conduct part of this inquiry. Despite reverting from British to Chinese hands in 1997, the former colony retained a separate local government system based on the rule of law that was a marked contrast to mainland China a few miles north. Free speech and freedom of the press were preserved, and some in the local legislature were freely elected. Those aiding North Korean defectors and refugees against the wishes of Beijing and other governments felt comparatively safer to talk in Hong Kong. Local media representatives were somewhat interested in the matter and always eager to talk about broader U.S.-China issues. Pro-democracy advocates would lend a sympathetic ear, familiar as many were with the nearby horrors of tyranny.

In short, it was a relatively opportune place to do preparatory work for smart power. One could collect better information than what was available in Washington, partner with those seeking similar goals, convey to local leaders the interest of the U.S. government, and talk to friendly media. One could also meet with various pro-freedom forces that play a role in the very serious and high-stakes political contests with China's unelected government, a contest that exists whether the United States chooses to recognize it or not.

But where I saw opportunity, the consulate saw only risk. Doing any of those things — and certainly attempting to do all of them — is utterly alien to the Washington establishment and its many outposts, of which the U.S. consulate was one. Its inhabitants sat in a coveted piece of property above Hong Kong's busy central business area, which is a key financial and media hub in East Asia and essentially the only free city in China. The consulate's six floors were filled with diplomats and other bureaucrats from the State Department and various agencies of the U.S. government. Each of those employees costs taxpayers far more than the average American household earns in a year.

Since it was not in the nation's capital city, hence its designation as a consulate instead of an embassy, its workers were not tied up with the many national-level meetings between governments that consume many embassy workers' time. Nonetheless, the consulate prided itself on being only one of two in the world that reported directly to Washington rather than through the U.S. embassy in the country. (The other independent consulate is in Jerusalem.) And yet with all of that free time and operational latitude, it seemed as though not one of these people had spoken to the men and women on America's side of the political contest with China and North Korea, nor did they appear to have the vaguest inclination to do so. In fact, they wanted desperately not to do anything of the sort.

In spite of the bemused reception I received at the consulate, I proceeded to meet with those involved in the underground railroad for North Korean refugees, making sure they knew of President Bush's specific concern about the fate of these brutalized individuals and inquiring about the obstacles they faced. I also met with democracy advocates and the media, including organizations like Radio Free Asia.

Apparently unfazed by conduct so upsetting to some of the State Department's career employees, the world did not end. Chinese tanks did not roll through the New Territories and Kowloon toward Hong Kong Island. Diplomatic receptions and cocktail parties were not angrily canceled. The perspective I gained, meanwhile, helped our office formulate plans to shape political outcomes abroad that were consistent with America's national security goals on this particular matter.

While my Hong Kong experience is only one anecdote, it will be a familiar tale to anyone in U.S. and allied governments who has really tried to have an impact on political outcomes abroad in recent decades. This experience has been true regardless of the occupant of the White House or his political party. For a town that likes to talk about smart power and diplomacy, Washington can be surprisingly amateurish about both. Furthermore, the closer one gets to some of the biggest challenges to U.S. security — especially China, Iran, and Islamism — the more one must contend with the gravity of people who can think of any number of reasons why we should do nothing.

THE MISSING MIDDLE

The net result is that U.S. presidents and others who shape policy are left with few effective tools between the softest of diplomacy and the blunt instruments of sanctions and military force. At its most basic level, the problem is that many of our experts in Washington are at a loss to understand what really constitutes smart power, or the missing middle between diplomacy and war.

This situation has been the norm since the Cold War ended in 1991. It has been said since time immemorial that armies prepare to fight the last war. This observation is a critique of their disinclination to prepare for the next war. Ironically, it would be an improvement over today if this assessment held true of contemporary American power. The United States was far more adept at smart power during most of the Cold War than in the period that has followed. The die may unfortunately have been cast during the 1991 Gulf War, from which military success beyond anyone's wildest dreams continues to shape American power and expectations for how the United States should conduct itself in the world. It is worth reviewing that episode to understand how U.S. policy and power arrived at this place.

In August 1990, Iraqi dictator Saddam Hussein rapidly overran neighboring Kuwait and annexed the country. President George H. W. Bush ordered U.S. forces to Saudi Arabia to prevent further Iraqi expansion in the oil-rich region. In January 1991, the U.S. military began an air campaign against Iraqi forces. A month later, the United States and its allies sent ground forces into Kuwait, liberating the country with stunning speed. The U.S.-led coalition also smashed Iraqi forces in southern Iraq. By the time President Bush halted the war — merely a hundred hours after the ground offensive began — what had been the world's fourth-largest army lay in ruins.

Considering it was America's first major armed conflict since the Vietnam War, the impact it had on U.S. perceptions of its military forces was significant. So too was its impact on nonmilitary action.

During the tense period between Saddam Hussein's August invasion of Kuwait and that country's liberation in February, many of the assumptions held today about using national power took hold. Intense debate in Washington and other allied capitals marked the period. As time went by, the Republican president and his administration concluded it would take military force to get the Iraqi army out of Kuwait. They also perceived the cost of waiting, including the impact of high oil prices and of uncertainty on an economy already in recession, to be prohibitive. Aligned against them was a majority of Democrats, whose party controlled both houses of Congress, each of which would have to approve an authorization to use force and appropriate funds for an offensive. Many Democrats wanted to give sanctions and diplomacy more time to potentially force Saddam to quit.

A political showdown was in the offing. In that era, when congressional hearings were a more consequential part of the legislative process, the Senate Armed Services Committee scheduled a full five days of public deliberation. American presidents never testify before Congress owing to the principle of separation of powers, but their cabinet members do when key issues come before the legislative branch. Chairing the committee was Sam Nunn, a Democrat from Georgia whom many on Capitol Hill regarded as a moderate. The deeply analytical Nunn was married to a former Central Intelligence Agency (CIA) officer, had served in the Coast Guard, and had a lawyerly demeanor with less edge than the party's other more liberal leaders.[3] During the previous decade, he had bucked his party's liberals at times and compromised on some issues with Ronald Reagan's administration in seeking to confront the Soviet Union more forcefully. His agreements with Reagan included, for example, controversial aid to Nicaragua's anticommunist Contras.[4]

At the political crescendo of the hearings, Nunn squared off against another man regarded as a relatively mild-mannered moderate at the time. Richard Cheney had left his seat as the sole congressman from Wyoming in the House of Representatives to become secretary of defense two years earlier. He was the point man representing the Bush administration's case for obtaining the authority to go to war in Kuwait.

War opponents did not call for doing nothing. Instead, they advocated giving economic sanctions imposed on Iraq more time hopefully to change Saddam's mind. Among antiwar protesters around the country, the argument was simplified to "Give peace a chance."

Cheney testified: "Given the nature of the regime, given Saddam Hussein's brutality to his own people, his very tight control of that society, his ability to allocate resources for the military, their ability to produce their own food . . . he can ride [sanctions] out."[5]

From the chairman's seat at the center of the dais in the ornate Senate hearing room, Nunn looked back, paused thoughtfully, and said: "If we have a war, we're never going to know whether they would have worked, would we? That's the major point here. The way you find out if sanctions work is to give them time enough to work."

Cheney responded: "That's a big assumption. There's a difference between saying we know if we use military force we can achieve our objectives [and] it may be, if we wait a year or two, economic sanctions will get him out of Kuwait." Cheney concluded of Saddam Hussein that "there is no guarantee that sanctions will force him out of Kuwait" and the United States could not "wait indefinitely."[6]

Ultimately Cheney and his boss, George H. W. Bush, prevailed. On January 13, 1991, the Senate adopted a resolution authorizing the use of military force by a narrow vote of 52 to 47. In the House, the vote was 250 to 183.[7]

Cheney incidentally was not the only future vice president to weigh in on the pivotal debate on Capitol Hill that winter. Joe Biden, then the junior senator from Delaware, remarked: "Even if you win today, you still lose. The nation is divided on this issue."[8]

The nation would not be divided for long. Within days, the American people would witness dazzling airpower far more precise and effective than anything in the history of war, and cable TV beamed the action's results directly into homes for the first time. Within a month, the war was over.

But in many ways the events leading up to the Gulf War still influence Americans and tacitly guide their conduct of statecraft. Essentially, the debate at that time — and often today — is when, if ever, to flip the switch from sanctions and diplomacy to war.

Smart power and political warfare beyond economic sanctions did not really enter into the debate before the Gulf War. This omission was entirely understandable. From the beginning of that crisis, the clock was ticking loudly, essentially pushing aside other options that are time-consuming or difficult to predict. The threat that Saddam might have ordered his army to advance beyond Kuwait into Saudi Arabia was real. This move would have given him a near monopoly on Middle Eastern oil and considerable influence over the world economy. Deterring such a possibility required the urgent dispatch of U.S. air, naval, and ground forces. Once such a force was in the region, it placed a strain on the military. Deployments anywhere, particularly to Saudi Arabia and nearby environs, are expensive and fatiguing. In addition to the financial burden, the war footing also put stress on American and allied troops, especially reservists, who were called up in large numbers for the first time since the Korean War. The always-menacing Soviet Union was on its last leg but still existed. Moscow had to be watched even amid other preoccupations. American and allied policymakers also had to consider that were they to invade, sooner would probably be better given the fresh outrage at Saddam's conduct in Kuwait.

What the fast-moving emergency precluded was a long-term effort to shape the political situation through means other than war. Aside from sanctions, time left little chance to use America's economic and financial might to undermine Saddam's regime. America's cultural power and the ideological appeal of America's society and system of government — often misunderstood and misapplied — could be powerful components in a strategic communications campaign. But this effort was similarly too abstract for the mission at hand. Information tools such as radio and TV broadcasts designed to foment opposition to Saddam among his remaining supporters could hardly be stood up in time. They could not be allotted the number of months or years it might take to make a measureable political impact. Furthermore, at that point, they could spotlight few examples of Arab-run democracies as an alternative model, nor could anyone conceivably envision in Iraq a workable monarchy that would care for its people, even if it did not seek their consent to govern. Free trade with the United States and other developed economies is not the political panacea its advocates claim it to be, but it can help create a middle class that later resists the corruption of repressive governments. But this endeavor too takes time, is unpredictable, and was impossible to pursue after Washington understandably had imposed a trade embargo on the country.

Other potential elements of smart power or political warfare were not applicable either. Technological war — or cyber war as it is now commonly known — was not relevant to pre-Internet Iraq, nor can it realistically be the centerpiece of a strategy once two opposing armies are fielded. The powerful financial tools that the U.S. Congress unleashed more than a decade later with the PATRIOT Act were still underappreciated in 1991.

Arming an opposition for a proxy war seemed improbable and unlikely to succeed against a massive, well-equipped army.

Thus, smart power options for our national leaders were extremely limited. This circumstance was not the fault of the practitioners of those tools, nor did it stem from negligence on the part of those focused on the most important goal a nation can have — that is, winning an imminent war. It was simply the reality of situation. But one of its consequences was that the Gulf War and its lead-up etched in the minds of many a "light switch" notion of statecraft with an enemy: one tries negotiations and sanctions and then flips the switch to war if diplomacy does not work. As America's first major war since Vietnam, and its first relatively clear-cut major victory since World War II, that the Gulf War and its preparation would become the model for crisis management from that point on was understandable. And it did.

Back in Washington, this state of mind would combine with other realities to rob policymakers of smart power options in situations that were not as imminently grave as the Gulf War. In 1999, the U.S. Information Agency (USIA), established in 1953 to coordinate overseas information programs and influence foreign publics, was shuttered.[9] Its remnants were dumped into the State Department and a newly created Broadcasting Board of Governors. Lacking a clear mission and saddled with a bizarre management structure, the board has been a case study in how not to organize a government agency. Other potential tools of smart power from the soft, aid-dispensing U.S. Agency for International Development to the notionally harder CIA generally have conducted themselves independently of the foreign political goals that the U.S. government should be seeking. Long before the State Department's Foreign Service officer in Hong Kong frowned upon my attention to a foreign political goal established by law and by the White House, his agency had largely given up on cultivating democracy advocates abroad. Over time, the State Department has proved itself extremely adept at communicating with other incumbent governments — but little else.

Ironically, and sadly, smart power did play a significant and ignominious role in the closing days and aftermath of the Gulf War. On February 15, 1991, nearly a month after the air war had started but before the allies commenced ground operations, President Bush announced: "There is another way for the bloodshed to stop: And that is, for the Iraqi military and the Iraqi people to take matters into their own hands — to force Saddam Hussein, the dictator, to step aside and to comply with the United Nations (UN) resolutions and then rejoin the family of peace-loving nations."[10]

The message was radio broadcast on the Voice of America. Saddam Hussein was not pushed aside before the ground war, but Shiites in the south and Kurds in the north rose against him immediately afterward.

Advisers to Bush had told him that Saddam was in perilous political shape. The dictator's adventure in Kuwait had not only failed, but it had also cost him most of his army. Televised images of Iraqi soldiers attempting to surrender to surprised coalition helicopter pilots were one of many signs that the esprit de corps of those on whom Saddam relied for power was limited.

But Saddam still had the will and force necessary to suppress the uprising, which he did with trademark brutality, including the mass slaughter of 30,000 to 60,000 civilians.[11] Most important, he knew the United States was not serious about using smart power against his rule after the war. Coalition armies were still on Iraqi soil, but a cease-fire had ended their major activities while allowing the Iraqi Republican Guard the mobility it required to operate throughout the country. Top Iraqi officials were undoubtedly relieved that the United States and its allies had put toppling the Iraqi ruler in the "nice to do" category but were not methodically supporting those who could make the aspiration a reality. Saddam would rule for twelve more years. Only after a change in the security calculus after the 9/11 attacks on the United States did his regime become wholly unacceptable to the American and British governments. Iraqi Shiites still regard the botched political warfare into which they were urged in 1991 as a historic betrayal. Many Americans, including some of those who walked the corridors of power at the time, agree.[12]

Twenty years later, the U.S. government was in no better position when it really mattered for national security and America's place in the world. The most remarkable political developments were about to sweep the Middle East since European colonialists were kicked out in the decades following World War II. Washington's lack of dexterity at smart power would cost it dearly.

CHAPTER 2

Arab-Persian Spring

How Not to Use Smart Power

"Big things have small beginnings, sir." The character playing a senior diplomat from Britain's Arab Bureau in Cairo offered this pithy analysis to a skeptical commander of the British Egyptian Expeditionary Force, Sir Archibald Murray, in the movie *Lawrence of Arabia*. The film was based loosely on T. E. Lawrence's book *Revolt in the Desert*, which recalled British-Arab efforts to end Ottoman Turkish domination of Arabia and the Levant during World War I. The diplomat's memorable understatement became a prologue to the eventual collapse of an empire that had lasted centuries and to the birth of the modern Middle East.

It could equally apply to the moment when Mohamed Bouazizi, a Tunisian street vendor, decided to end his life. On the morning of December 17, 2010, the twenty-six-year-old stood outside the local governor's office in the gritty town of Sidi Bouzid, raised a can of gasoline over his head, doused himself, and lit a match. Before burning himself to a degree that would ultimately prove fatal, he shouted: "How do you expect me to make a living?"[1]

TUNISIA

Earlier that day, looking for a bribe, police had harassed the produce seller. His offense was not having a vendor permit. As is typical in corrupt locales such as Tunisia, which was run by then-president Zine El Abidine Ben Ali, who was repeatedly and suspiciously reelected with nearly 90 percent or more of the vote, such permits were unobtainable or unaffordable.[2] Many routine activities were illegal, thus making most people dependent on the expensive mercy of corrupt police. Bouazizi, who had lost his father at age three and had worked since age ten to support his mother and sisters, could not afford to pay another bribe. Police harassment and arbitrary fines were common. That day, he quarreled with a policewoman who then slapped him in public and confiscated his scales. Knowing he could not afford to recover the scales, the man described by his mother as uninterested in politics went to see the governor, who in turn refused to meet him.[3]

By the time Bouazizi died from his burns on January 4, 2011, his protest and self-immolation had sparked a revolt against the government that spread to the capital city of Tunis and throughout the country. Ten days later, protesters deposed Ben Ali, who had survived in office since a coup brought him to power twenty-three years earlier. He went into exile.

Later that same month, the State Department's top official for Middle East policy, Assistant Secretary for Near Eastern Affairs Jeffrey Feltman, told a press conference: "What happened in Tunisia strikes me as uniquely Tunisian. That the events that took place here over the past few weeks derive from particularly Tunisian grievances, from Tunisian circumstances by the Tunisian people."[4] Feltman, a member of the State Department's Foreign Service bureaucracy for as long as Ben Ali was president, could not have been more wrong.[5] Protesters had already filled the streets in nearby Egypt, and they soon would be active across much of the Middle East. By late January, thousands of Egyptians demanding a change in government packed Cairo's Tahrir Square. This development was of major importance given that Egypt is the world's most populous Arab-majority state, with 84 million citizens.[6] Historically, it was also a bellwether for political trends among Arabs and Muslims elsewhere in the region. Unfortunately, Washington's conduct during the Egyptian revolution is a case study in how not to use smart power.

WASHINGTON AND MUBARAK

In Egypt, the people's grievances were nearly identical to those in Tunisia. Poverty afflicted many Egyptians, about half of whom lived on $2 a day or less.[7] Corruption was rampant. In 2012, Transparency International, which ranks countries from "very clean" at the top to "highly corrupt" at the bottom, placed Egypt at 118 out of the 176 jurisdictions.[8] The country has been a long-term recipient of U.S. military and economic aid, which exceeded $1.5 billion each year.[9] But pouring cash into the corruption-soaked Egyptian economy only made it more corrupt and helped sustain a crooked government. Aid was filtered through institutions and businesses on the take. The vicious cycle of corruption ensured that foreign investment in Egypt would always be highly limited and that wealth would accrue to a select few based on privilege and not on merit. Added to this corrupt economy was the repressive government of Hosni Mubarak, who had retained power in Cairo for nearly thirty years by allowing only sham elections in which his reelection was inevitable. Mubarak crushed all potential political opposition through harassment and incarceration, deepening most Egyptians' resentment of his regime.

What happened in Tahrir Square and across Egypt in 2011, when mostly secularist crowds took to the streets, was supposed to be impossible. The value proposition that Mubarak had offered to the rest of the world, especially Washington, was that he was the only alternative to the Islamists who were seeking power. Egypt is home to the Muslim Brotherhood, an Islamist political movement whose slogan is "Islam is the solution."

As with many Islamist groups that engage in subversive political activities, violent jihad, or both, the Brotherhood has favored the essential unification of mosque and state, the use of clerically imposed Sharia instead of democratically enacted civil law, and the creation of a unitary empire of Muslim-majority nations, or a caliphate. Long before al Qaeda was founded, before Saudi dollars were used en masse to export fundamentalist Wahhabism, and before the Iranian Revolution made Islamist government a reality in a major country, the Muslim Brotherhood was reinventing and advocating modern Islamism. Among Mubarak's opponents, the Brotherhood was not even the worst. Ever more fervent were the Salafists, adherents of an intolerant, puritanical, Wahhabi-style Islam who also wish to use the power of government for their designs on society.

During his rule, Mubarak argued that the choice in the Middle East was between undemocratic strongmen like him or his Islamist opponents. If one did not condone his style of government, then the alternative was

Iranian-style theocracy along with its specter of economic, political, and perhaps even military warfare on the United States and its allies. Certainly the United States could not hope for a more classically liberal, modern, secular, and democratic alternative to emerge. Mubarak and his apologists asserted that only the smallest portion of Egyptian urbanites supported that political philosophy. Ironically and sadistically, Mubarak did his best to make this pronouncement true by harassing, corrupting, or incarcerating any secular reformers who seriously challenged his rule.

But there they were in Tahrir Square. The crowd was not full of angry, long-bearded Islamists shouting, "Death to America!" All sorts were present, but the crowd overwhelmingly comprised Egyptians who wanted accountable government, improved economic circumstances, and — most galling to Islamists anywhere — modernity. The rallying cry in January 2011 was democracy, not Islam and certainly not political Islamism or violent jihad on behalf of that ideology. The Muslim Brotherhood was also caught off guard and initially hesitated to join protests that were dominated by those who wanted a real democracy in Egypt.[10]

Back in Washington, the foreign policy establishment was not prepared to let new facts get in the way of a long-held theory. According to doctrine, these people could not exist in massive numbers; therefore, they did not exist. Their presence and their evident readiness to begin a revolution had gone undetected not only by U.S. diplomats but also by America's intelligence bureaucracy that costs taxpayers $80 billion per year.[11] Because of this inflexible commitment to dogma, combined with an inability to understand and influence foreign political developments, a false analysis would subsequently become a self-fulfilling prophecy. Washington's ultimate embrace of a resurgent Muslim Brotherhood and inability to support real reformers worked to the advantage of the Islamists.

As indicated by Foreign Service Officer Feltman's statement that political turmoil in Tunisia was an aberration and not a harbinger, the overall belief in the impossibility of broad, secular reform was accepted widely in Washington. The belief spanned both Democratic and Republican administrations. In fact, Cairo was the place where the George W. Bush administration reached the apogee of its pro-democracy "freedom agenda" and subsequently retreated.

Condoleezza Rice, Bush's second-term secretary of state, gave a speech in Cairo in June 2005 that called for governments in the region to heed the desire for democracy on display in certain parts of the Middle East. She said, "For sixty years, the United States pursued stability at the expense of democracy in the Middle East — and we achieved neither. Now, we are taking a different course. We are supporting the democratic aspirations of all people."[12] While the speech echoed Bush's inspiring second inaugural address and was composed in part by the same White House staffer, it was more of a coda to Bush's first term than a plan for his second.

Mubarak roundly criticized the thesis in Rice's speech. Rice, a former expert on the defunct Soviet Union, was never particularly enthusiastic about freedom movements and as a junior NSC staffer had counseled against supporting the anticommunist Solidarity movement in Cold War Poland. Liberated from Bush's direct staff at the White House and given her own agency, Rice was in the process of rediscovering her roots in the "realist" branch of foreign policy that the Richard Nixon–era diplomatic supremo Henry Kissinger epitomized. She rounded up her old gang of Foreign Service officers, including Nicholas Burns and Christopher Hill, and gave them prominent positions atop the State Department's powerful regional bureaus.

An unwritten rule of thumb stipulates that no speechwriter in an administration can get in trouble for quoting the president or a cabinet secretary. It is often one of the few effective tools for countering bureaucrats with an agenda that is not in line with that of the president. In my own experience, when a bureau at the State Department thought it was too impolitic to criticize North Korea's dictator as negotiations with his government proceeded, prolonged and fruitless as they were, I needed only drop in a direct quote from President Bush on the matter. So I was surprised when Rice's staff complained about an undersecretary at the department who quoted Rice's own confirmation testimony to Congress, in which she referenced various "outposts of tyranny," including North Korea.[13] From then on, Rice's diplomats focused more on stability rather than on political reform. In other words, the notion of peacefully shaping political outcomes in foreign countries — the essence of smart power — was intentionally disregarded. Rice's Egypt speech was the last time she gave much attention to foreign democracy movements. According to a leaked State Department cable, a little more than a year later, leading Egyptian secularist Saad Eddin Ibrahim complained bitterly to American diplomats that "I thought at one time the U.S. would support democracy, but I was wrong."[14] Two years later, Ibrahim was sentenced to jail for "defaming Egypt."[15]

President Barack Obama followed Rice's footsteps to Cairo less than five months into his first term. His objective was hardly to encourage secular reformers in their struggle against both the incumbent Egyptian government and the Islamist opposition. Instead, he signaled a different kind of break with his predecessors in the White House. Obama asserted early in the speech that "Iraq was a war of choice that provoked strong differences in my country and around the world. Although I believe that the Iraqi people are ultimately better off without the tyranny of Saddam Hussein, I also believe that events in Iraq have reminded America of the need to use diplomacy and build international consensus to resolve our problems whenever possible." He continued, remarking that "Israel must also live up to its obligation to ensure that Palestinians can live and work and develop their society." Later, he oversimplified history, saying, "In the middle of the Cold War, the United States played a role in the overthrow of a democratically elected Iranian government. Since the Islamic Revolution, Iran has played a role in acts of hostage-taking and violence against U.S. troops and civilians. This history is well known. Rather than remain trapped in the past, I've made it clear to Iran's leaders and people that my country is prepared to move forward."[16]

As many journalists and governments are experts at ignoring flowery language in presidential speeches and cutting right to the news content, if any, the remarks were quickly seen for what they were: an apology for past American conduct. The speech included an implied regret for the Iraq War, a critique of U.S. ally Israel delivered in a country that had warred on Israel, and even an apology for a CIA operation undertaken eight years before Obama was born.

For reformers in the Middle East and around the world, the speech was seen as an extension of Obama's 2009 inaugural address and other soundings on foreign policy. In that first speech as president, Obama said to foreign dictators that the United States would "extend a hand if you are willing to unclench your fist." None of this message was what pro-democracy dissidents truly wanted to hear. Even though some reformers and dissidents avoid the appearance of supporting the United States for reasons of political pragmatism, none believes his or her plight will improve if the United States is diffident toward repressive or aggressive governments or looks to cut deals with adversaries. At precisely those times, dissidents can disappear into prisons or gallows without anyone taking much notice.

Regardless, back in the White House, the frame of mind of the president and his key aides was that the United States had signaled a willingness to talk and walk back the mistakes of the Bush years and more distant past. In search of diplomatic breakthroughs with governments like that of Iran, the Obama administration rejected any concept of guiding political events in ways that would be unhelpful to Middle Eastern dictators. Besides, the Washington foreign policy establishment — both its Republican and Democratic provinces — now assumed little real chance for expanded democracy in the Middle East existed.

Then the protests began. Actually, before the Arab Spring took place, a Persian Spring began in 2009. In Iran, after a sham presidential election that June, Iranians took to the streets to protest. On the same boulevards where stage-managed chants of "death to America" had been common since the late 1970s, the people were instead chanting "death to the dictator."[17] Protests persisted through the summer and fall and occurred in cities beyond the capital of Tehran. In June, a regime supporter shot dead a twenty-six-year-old woman among the protesters. While violence had become commonplace, this iconic act of brutality, caught on video and rapidly mass-distributed, galvanized the opposition further.

These events dumbfounded the White House and the broader Washington foreign policy establishment. President Obama hesitated even to encourage what he should have plainly seen as a godsend to the United States and other countries that had been targeted by the Islamic Republic's operatives and terrorist proxies since the regime came to power in 1979. A State Department official said at the time that the protesters "won't be capable of bringing down the government."[18]

This intentionally disingenuous analysis is a Washington classic. Political turmoil topples repressive governments frequently in history. Yet many of those who make it to the top of today's State Department and CIA bureaucracies convince themselves that popular movements will never succeed in the near term. This belief conveniently vindicates whatever plan those U.S. diplomats have to negotiate with a repressive regime, and such a plan is always floating around the State Department's seventh floor and in the rarified air of think tanks and foreign policy institutions that are part of the same Washington establishment. So it was with Iran.

The Obama White House took solace in the advice of some opposed to the Tehran regime who cautioned against siding with the protesters. The U.S. consulate in Istanbul was secretly in touch with Ardeshir Arjomand, a legal adviser to Mir Hossein Mousavi, one of the cheated election opponents of the Iranian president. The consulate cabled Washington that Arjomand, who had snuck into Turkey, "said the current approach, of highlighting the regime's human rights failures but otherwise 'staying out of our domestic fight,' was correct. 'Don't take the opposition's side openly,' he cautioned, as that would give the regime the concrete evidence it currently lacks that Mousavi and other leaders are committing 'espionage.'"[19]

However, the Obama administration should have ignored this advice. By that time, the Green Movement in Iran, as the protesters were collectively called, had advanced far beyond the thwarted candidacy of Mousavi. Others who were closer to the protesters in the streets called on President Obama to take a side. One group chanted: "Obama, Obama — either with us, or with them!" Its members criticized the White House's overwhelming focus on relatively fruitless negotiations with the Iranian government.[20] Furthermore, if a foreign political movement is worth supporting because it advances vital U.S. interests in a key region, then Washington should support it regardless of the tactical preferences of one segment of the movement. Historically, when American presidents have drawn attention to opposition movements in other nations, it has decreased the severity of regime crackdowns on the individuals and groups involved. For example, U.S. attention to dissidents inside the Soviet Union and the opponents of Soviet control of Poland in the late Cold War and to the adversaries of apartheid in South Africa helped leaders of those movements remain viable — and alive. President Obama's refusal to take this step, or to arrange for covert support of the Green Movement, constituted a failure in the use of smart power. By the time major protests flared again in February 2010, the Iranian regime felt at ease to crack down harshly. The mullahs were back on top. It would be nearly two more years before the Obama Treasury Department took the modest step of sanctioning only two Iranian officials involved in the violence against peaceful protesters.[21]

By the time Egyptians rose in protest, a little more than a year and a half after Iranians first took to the streets in opposition to Islamist government, the Washington foreign policy establishment was in no better shape to understand events or influence them to the advantage of U.S. national security. Protests against the Egyptian government were massive by late January 2011. Yet, Secretary of State Hillary Clinton announced that month that "our assessment is that the Egyptian government is stable." Of any statement President Obama's chief diplomat could have made, including the option of saying nothing, this observation could only have been the most obviously inaccurate and the least helpful to those striving for an end to repression and corruption. At the same moment, police were battling protesters who were gaining momentum and chanting, "Down, down, Hosni Mubarak."[22]

Two days later, Vice President Biden said of Mubarak that "I would not refer to him as a dictator." When asked if the time had come for Mubarak to go, Biden said no.[23] Biden even cast doubts on whether all of the protesters' demands were legitimate. Three days later, Secretary Clinton went on no fewer than five Sunday news shows and said, "We're not advocating any specific outcome."[24] It was an unusual flurry of press activity in order to say very little.

ECHOES OF PRAGUE SPRING, 1968

Wellsprings of people power in Egypt and Iran were hardly the first time the United States failed to predict and take advantage of events that could have transformed a region of vital importance into less of a problem for America. Another such opportunity had presented itself at the midpoint of the Cold War. No one will ever know what more decisive U.S. support for an unexpected revolution against communist rule in Czechoslovakia in 1968 could have achieved. What is known from history is that an uprising took place, that the Soviet Union eventually crushed it, and that two more decades of tyranny and dangerous military standoff in Europe resulted. Sadly, many of the same factors that marked the U.S. policy failure in 1968 were repeated during the Arab Spring. Washington did not learn from the mistakes of the past.

Czechoslovakia was never a willing participant in the Soviet-dominated Eastern Bloc. Germany had occupied the nation, which consisted of today's Czech Republic and Slovakia, in World War II. As the German forces crumbled before the advancing Allies in 1945, Czechoslovak exiles and partisans tried to arrange for their liberation by the U.S. Army instead of the Soviet Union's Red Army. It was not to be. As with other areas liberated by the Soviets, Czechoslovakia was soon added involuntarily to the Soviet bloc and saddled with a brutal communist puppet government that was servile to Moscow. But the Czechs' passion for freedom and independence endured.

Major early uprisings against Soviet rule took place in the nations it held captive in the 1950s. The largest of these rebellions took place in the city of East Berlin in 1953 and in Hungary in 1956. In both instances, Soviet military forces intervened to put them down, using tanks without hesitation against peaceful protesters. Communism led by the Soviet Union was in its heyday and supposedly ran neck and neck with the West in making technological progress. The communist bloc was growing, with trends clearly favoring Moscow in Europe, Asia, Africa, and South America. Earlier communist penetration of the most sensitive parts of the American and British governments was brought to light. The death in 1953 of Joseph Stalin engendered hope in some quarters for a less murderous form of communist government in Russia. In short, however, the communist bloc was still confident enough in itself and its future — and its opponents were facing odds far too long — for the protesters to succeed at the time.

This course would clearly change by 1989, when the Berlin Wall was torn down. The rest of the Eastern Bloc followed, and then, in 1991, the Soviet Union itself fell. By that time, the tides had turned, or, more precisely, the determined men and women inside these repressed nations had turned them. Dissidents gained strength as the flaws of communism and advantages of Western freedom became more obvious. The United States helped halt and then reverse communist expansion in Central America and Central Asia by supporting local proxies. Washington and other allied capitals waged political warfare on Moscow and its allies by supporting dissent movements in multiple communist countries. Communist authority remained extremely dangerous to its opponents until the end, but by the close of the 1980s, the contest was over.

The question remains as to whether it could have been over much sooner, especially for the people of Czechoslovakia. Unlike in today's conflicts, where the voices in Washington of neoconservatives on the right and moralists on the left call for U.S. intervention at the drop of a hat, providing overt support to Czechoslovaks revolting against Moscow was out of the question. A tacit assumption during the Cold War held that American and Russian forces directly fighting each other anywhere could rapidly lead to another world war. Direct military intervention in one of the opposing superpower's blocs was regarded as a likely trigger for a general war, which no American or Soviet leader was willing to start. But that left many other options, ranging from simple verbal expressions of support and solidarity from Washington and allied capitals to clear enumeration of the various economic and other drawbacks Moscow would face if it used violence. Also within the realm of possibility was covert provision of nonlethal resources and intelligence. More daring still could have been an effort to instigate turmoil or tension elsewhere and distract Moscow from events in Czechoslovakia.

Lyndon Johnson, whose presidency was weakened by the Vietnam War, took none of these steps in 1968. As it would in Egypt forty-three years later, Washington also missed reasonably clear signs that political turbulence was on the horizon. The first indication should have been the trouble Czechoslovak president Antonin Novotny, a hard-liner, found himself in as 1967 wore on. His demise and replacement as first secretary of the country's Communist Party by reformist communist Alexander Dubček, which occurred after a ten-week struggle in the presidium and Central Committee, came as a surprise to the West. This development was particularly odd given both the high priority that U.S. and allied intelligence agencies were ordered to place on detecting and analyzing political developments in Eastern Europe and the Soviet Union, and the fact that the contest within the Communist Party at one point required Soviet leader

Leonid Brezhnev's physical presence in Prague.[25] His involvement alone should have been detected and set off alarms in Washington.

On taking office, Dubček did not seek the ostensive end of communism or the liberation of his country from Soviet domination; rather, he sought modest reforms within the context of communism, billing the result as "socialism with a human face." Dubček curtailed the secret police and permitted the liberalization of speech and other freedoms. He propagated a new party line subtitled "The Czechoslovak Road to Socialism" and in fact made reference to the "various needs and interests of individual people," noting further that "the unity of all workers will be brought about democratically."[26] At that time, this idea was radical. But disillusioned students in Prague wanted far more. As Moscow officials and hard-liners throughout Warsaw Pact countries grew steadily more alarmed, students confronted Dubček and asked, "What are the guarantees that the old days will not be back?"

During the critical months from Dubček's assumption of office in January until April 1968, the United States did not even comment on the Prague Spring. Writing the following year, an outraged Harry Schwartz, formerly of the Office of Strategic Services and the long-serving *New York Times* specialist on communist affairs, noted:

> While Soviet suspicion and fear of Czechoslovak developments deepened, Washington remained silent for more than three months after Dubcek's coming to power. In part, the changes in Prague came too rapidly to be quickly appreciated by the Johnson Administration, whose energies were fully engaged in the Vietnam War. In part, some responsible Washington officials feared that any undue suggestion of American interest in, or help for, the Dubcek regime might backfire by increasing Soviet anxiety and leading to Soviet action against Prague. . . . Finally, in April, the State Department broke its official silence. A spokesman declared that the Department was "watching with interest and sympathy recent developments in Czechoslovakia, which seem to represent the wishes and needs of the Czechoslovak people." It was a minimal gesture and hardly even began to represent the great ride of real interest and sympathy for

Czechoslovakia then flowing through all informed sections of the American people.[27]

The fate of the Prague Spring was probably already sealed by the time Johnson's State Department issued its mild statement. By March, Moscow's concerns about reform spreading throughout its satellites came true. In Poland, masses of students took to the streets, angrily confronting authorities. In Warsaw, the Polish capital, the demonstrators yelled in solidarity, "Long live Czechoslovakia!" Turmoil spread to all major Polish cities. Authorities falsely attributed the unrest to a Zionist conspiracy, conducted a base anti-Semitic campaign designed to limit the students' appeal outside of Polish cities and intellectual circles, and crushed the protests violently.

In contrast, Czechoslovakia was peaceful during this time, its people more or less content with the promise of the reformist government. One wonders what would have happened if unrest similar to that in Poland had erupted in Czechoslovakia, East Germany, Hungary, Bulgaria, and other Eastern Bloc locales. Would the great liberation of 1989 have been accelerated by twenty years? It will never be known.

The Prague Spring ended on August 21, 1968, when the Red Army and the forces of four other Eastern Bloc nations invaded Czechoslovakia with tanks and hundreds of thousands of troops. Hundreds of Czechs and Slovaks were killed. The Soviets arrested Dubček and his colleagues. Eventually, all of the liberalizations they initiated were reversed.[28]

The world was outraged, but it was too late to matter much. The Soviet ambassador in Washington preemptively met with President Johnson two hours after the invasion began, declaring the invasion an "internal" matter of the communist world. Johnson called a night meeting of the National Security Council (NSC) but waited until the next day to issue a condemnation. Historians have speculated that Johnson felt guilty for doing so little to help the people of Czechoslovakia. His ambassador to the UN implied Johnson's reticence was because he held out hope that the Soviet Union would accept an arms control breakthrough — namely, the Anti-Ballistic Missile Treaty — which Johnson had proposed a year earlier.

Washington missed a great opportunity for a political advance. Knocking one or more countries out of the Soviet Union's orbit may have radically improved the security of the United States. Even short of that lofty goal, simply saying more and spotlighting the blood on Moscow's hands would have increased the moral and economic costs to the Soviet Union for the actions it took. No one knows for certain what a different U.S. reaction would have accomplished, but it is certain that the non-reaction let events run their own course to failure and allowed Moscow to retain its aura of inevitability.[29]

What is eerie is the symmetry of Washington's failures in the Prague Spring with those of the Arab Spring and the preceding Persian Spring in Iran. In the lead-up to both revolutionary periods, U.S. intelligence missed warnings of impending change in regions that were not only of vital importance to Washington but also had been assigned high priorities and budgets for intelligence collection. Washington was afraid to voice the obvious sentiment of the American people, who were partial to those seeking their own freedom from tyrants abroad, based on an overblown fear that public sympathy would somehow empower the protesters' oppressors. This apprehension, of course, ignores the fact that those oppressors invariably blame the United States for instigating the unrest anyway. If one is going to be judged guilty regardless of fact, why not reap the benefits of the crime?

Last but not least, in both revolutionary eras, U.S. diffidence was driven in part by the government's outsized hope for arms control agreements. In Johnson's case, it was the contemplated Anti-Ballistic Missile Treaty with the Soviet Union. In Obama's case, it was the possibility of a breakthrough in talks with Iran to give up its nuclear weapons program. In either case, the chance for radical success if the revolution had succeeded along optimal lines should have been the obviously preferable option compared to the modest improvement in relations with American enemies that was on the table. In both cases, the White House failed to see this rather simple calculus.

The crushing of the Prague Spring ended that particular chapter on U.S. shortcomings in smart power. Decades later, Washington had another chance. The initial success of the Arab Spring in toppling dictatorial governments presented Washington with the option to use smart power to shape ensuing events for the better. But in keeping with recent tradition, Washington was about to fail again.

As January 2011 drew to an end in Egypt, it became clear that the Mubarak government would not survive. While some human rights groups estimated that security forces loyal to Mubarak killed several hundred Egyptians during the uprising, the government by then lacked the will or means to extinguish the wide-scale protests.[30] The one force that could save Mubarak was the army. While the army used violence against some protesters, it became increasingly clear that the army was unwilling to conduct the massacre that would be required to preserve the old order. Once this situation was apparent, and given that the future of the world's most populous Arab-majority country is important to the United States, Washington should have considered four questions and formulated policy accordingly:

1. What post-revolution government scenarios are possible in the country?
2. Which of these scenarios best advances U.S. national security?
3. Which steps are necessary to increase the chances of the best outcome?
4. What will happen if the United States does not act?

After answering those questions, a president can set about using the tools at his disposal. This calculus does not necessarily mean ignoring the welfare and wishes of the Egyptian people. In fact, U.S. national security benefits from having a larger number of governments that are both accountable to their people and unlikely to abuse their citizens or neighbors. However, that goal should not translate to leaving to chance and accepting without question foreign political developments, including elections. When dangerous forces are involved in elections and other political processes, American presidents have a right to act to preserve critical U.S. interests. In this way, U.S. smart power can fit with the values of the American people but acknowledge the U.S. government may not always act in a manner that is pleasing to high-minded moralists. There is a middle path between acting only based on altruism on the one hand and following the cynical, self-serving (and customarily French) model of realpolitik on the other. This pragmatic middle is what most American presidents have sought throughout history.

But neither President Obama nor the broader Washington foreign policy establishment followed this course in January 2011. On the same Sunday that Secretary of State Clinton went on television repeatedly and refused to acknowledge the likely end of Mubarak's regime, her political opposition in Washington was doing little better. John McCain, the top Republican on the Senate Armed Services Committee and President Obama's 2008 opponent, appeared on one of the same shows. He too refused to say the United States should support the Egyptian people in seeking Mubarak's ouster.[31] Kissinger, keeper of the flame of the "realist" branch of foreign policy that marked the Nixon and Gerald Ford administrations, said, "We don't really know what's going on. We don't know what is meant by the people of Egypt at this particular point. We know there are big demonstrations and they must represent various elements that exist in Egypt."[32]

Kissinger's comments were a sample of what would be a common refrain from Washington analysts throughout this Middle East turbulence. They quite accurately professed imperfect information about the motives of protesters and consequences of events the protesters set in motion. But the person who waits for all of the dust to settle and for reams of empirical evidence to materialize is addressed as "Professor," not "Mr. President." Analysts on the right and left who take pride in being part of the policy community that provides presidents and other policymakers with information and options were in fact making the president's job harder.

Once Mubarak was gone, Washington did no better. The main reason for supporting Mubarak in the first place was that he prevented Islamists from controlling Egypt. Another reason included Mubarak's adherence to a peace agreement with Israel to which his predecessor in office had agreed (and had paid for with his life at the hands of an Islamist assassin). Washington wanted stability in Egypt and to avoid the ascendance of the Muslim Brotherhood or other Islamist groups that might oppose the United States, restrict the Egyptian-controlled Suez Canal, or even harbor terrorists. It would follow logically that Washington would attempt to forestall any success for these practitioners of political Islam, especially since the face of the uprising had been overwhelmingly the type of secular, pro-modern, pro-democracy Muslims who Islamists hate. But logic did not follow in Washington.

Inevitably, the State Department wanted to reach out to the Muslim Brotherhood. By June 2011, Secretary Clinton summed up the rationale:

> The Obama Administration is continuing the approach of limited contacts with the Muslim Brotherhood that has existed on and off for about five or six years. We believe, given the changing political landscape in Egypt, that it is in the interests of the United States to engage with all parties that are peaceful and committed to nonviolence, that intend to compete for the parliament and the presidency. And we welcome, therefore, dialogue with those Muslim Brotherhood members who wish to talk with us.[33]

Clinton's remarks were a cogent indication of Washington's lack of serious regard or strategy for the political future of Egypt or the rest of the Middle East. The implication — and indeed the key assumption of so much Washington policy — was that any person or group passed muster for polite company if that person or group did not outwardly profess or use violence. Thus even a group that shared a more or less common vision for the Middle East with al Qaeda warranted acceptance as long as it was not killing Americans.

Clinton and her bureaucracy were not alone. The following spring, in the lead-up to elections in Egypt, representatives of the Muslim Brotherhood were welcomed to the White House for a meeting with "mid-level" officials. The White House spokesman noted that Republican senators John McCain and Lindsey Graham both met with the Islamists while visiting Cairo on an official trip.[34]

As for the Brotherhood's opponents, official Washington did little to help would-be secular reformers, even though they constituted a viable alternative to the Islamists. Unfortunately, some had made the rounds in Washington and rubbed officials and members of Congress the wrong way. Their comments were marked by triumphalism and unrealistic expectations. But such responses are typical of disorganized liberal reformers in the wake of an era of repressive government. The challenge is to help them organize, ideally through clandestine means, and to connect the new reformers with people who have been through similar transitions before. Turning one's back on the reformers' opposition is also important: if senators or White House officials fete anyone, it should be the good guys.

Unrealistic hope also drove bad policy, which threw a lifeline to Egypt's Islamists and distanced Washington from reformers. While no one would say so on the record, analysts in the government and on Capitol Hill wanted to believe that the Muslim Brotherhood had reformed. Their theory was that the people who invented modern political Islam — which grew out of the Muslim Brotherhood in Egypt in the mid-twentieth century — were not going to implement it seriously once they had power, despite their having risked prison or worse in striving for it for so many years. This belief was reflected in Hillary Clinton's explanation that it was acceptable for the United States to deal with any group that was nonviolent. But it was hard to find proof that the Muslim Brotherhood was tamed and had become an Arab equivalent of Germany's Christian Democrats, or basically a party that favored secular government with a little moral or religious sparkle added.

Not only did few facts support this hope that the Brotherhood had reformed, but also significant evidence pointed to the contrary. When sizing up Middle Eastern leaders — or any leaders for that matter — it is crucial to see what they are telling their own people in their own language rather than what they are telling American and allied diplomats in English. For those observers who listened to what Muslim Brotherhood officials were saying, clearly the organization had not caught the reform bug. In the lead-up to the election in which Mohamed Morsi would become Egypt's first Muslim Brotherhood president, he told a mass of supporters in Arabic: "The Koran was and will continue to be our constitution; the Prophet Mohamed is our leader; jihad is our path; his nation will enjoy blessing and revival only through the Islamic Sharia."[35]

Now, jihad need not be violent and is a traditional concept within Islam that shares some similarities to Judeo-Christian notions of struggle. But when utilized in a political context, it often has another implication: a call for political conflict, including violent conflict. Sharia, or Islamic religious law, can also have different meanings. Some Arab-majority countries give a nod to Sharia in elements of their law, but they still make it clear explicitly or in practice that civil law trumps Sharia when a conflict exists. Ultra-conservative Saudi Arabia recently codified Sharia. This initiative may sound as though Saudi law took a step in the wrong direction, but the move actually took power away from the religious elite there and limited its ability to influence the law through subjective interpretation.[36] Yet Morsi and his political party did not indicate Egyptian Sharia administered by a Muslim Brotherhood–dominated government should follow a moderate path. U.S. policymakers should have viewed that as a possibility but not as a probable outcome or a certainty.

Other danger signs loomed. In the televised rally that kicked off Morsi's candidacy, Egyptian cleric Safwat Higazi declared as the candidate looked on approvingly: "We can see how the dream of the Islamic Caliphate is being realized, Allah willing, by Dr. Muhammad Morsi and his brothers, his supporters, and his political party. We can see how the great dream, shared by us all — that of the United States of the Arabs . . . will be restored. . . . The capital of the Caliphate — the capital of the United States of the Arabs — will be Jerusalem, Allah willing."

Jerusalem is, of course, the capital of another country, Israel. Egypt and Israel went to war in 1948, 1956, 1967, and 1973; thus the cleric's statements should have been all the more alarming. The rally was rounded out by the master of ceremonies leading the crowd in a chant set to music: "Banish the sleep from the eyes of all Jews. Come on, you lovers of martyrdom, you are all Hamas. Forget about the whole world, forget about all the conferences. Brandish your weapons. Say your prayers. Millions of martyrs march toward Jerusalem."[37] Onlookers in Washington typically dismiss such statements as campaign hyperbole, but surely some credence must be given to the issues on which political leaders seek office and the mandate they are expected to fulfill upon taking office. Certainly at a minimum, this rally should have been a cautionary note to those in Washington who thought the Muslim Brotherhood had abandoned willy-nilly the Islamist ideology it toiled so hard to bring into the modern era.

But Washington conducted itself with a general disregard for the post-Mubarak political outcome in Egypt. Far from methodically supporting secular reformers, reporters discovered U.S. government efforts were actually aiding the Muslim Brotherhood. One report quoted the head of the State Department's new Middle East Transitions office who proudly noted that Islamist parties such as the Muslim Brotherhood could avail themselves of training funded by U.S. taxpayers to help the people build better political parties. The only possible recipients that the official pointedly said could not receive this training were those tied to the Egyptian military, or the one secular institution that could build a moderate government in the future Egypt.[38] It was as though U.S. officials were feeling guilt for an imperialist past in which America never took part. An analogy would be if the anticommunist political warriors described in this book's introduction were told in 1948 to aid not anticommunists in Italy exclusively but anyone who applied for assistance. American taxpayers would have paid to train communists, among others, who then would have pulled Italy and other countries out of the West's sphere and into the Eastern Bloc.

In the end, Washington's poor intelligence capabilities and policy based on flawed assumptions became a self-fulfilling prophecy. Before the Egyptian revolution, many foreign policy mavens associated with both political parties and establishment institutions accepted that there was no classically liberal, secular alternative for Egypt. The choice was either Mubarak or the Islamists. When hundreds of thousands of Egyptians took to the streets seeking neither of these options and instead demanded democracy, modernity, the rule of law, and accountable government, Washington was unwilling to allow facts to interfere with long-held views and policies. Once Mubarak was ousted and the post-revolution political competition began, Washington resumed its assumption that only Islamists could prevail. Secular reformers were given little or no support. U.S. officials and senators feted the Muslim Brotherhood in Washington and Cairo. The Islamists were aided by U.S. inaction and given direct training at the expense of U.S. taxpayers. The Muslim Brotherhood won control of Egypt's parliament and then won its presidency in July 2012 by a vote of 52 percent to 48 percent. With such a narrow margin, one presumes even a semblance of U.S. and allied aid for the Islamists' opposition could have made a difference.[39] The future path of Egypt is unknown, but of the possible outcomes, the riskier one for U.S. national security came to pass.

The same disregard for the eventual political outcome in the wake of a revolution would mark U.S. policy toward yet another Arab-majority nation in North Africa. When civil war erupted in Libya, the same cast of characters in Washington took to microphones without any serious long-term objective or strategy for influencing the end state. Luckily, committed smart power practitioners entered the breach in Libya, steering matters toward a reasonable outcome for those who want a civilized order in the Middle East. They happened to be from other countries than the United States and its NATO partners, which supposedly ran the foreign contribution to the civil war.

STRANGER THAN FICTION

Muammar Qaddafi was so bizarre on the world stage, one might forget for a moment how evil he was. He rose to power in a coup in 1969 and ruled as dictator until he was killed two months after the fall of Tripoli in August 2011. In his early years in office, he typically donned military garb, consistent with his occupation as a soldier on seizing power. But conservative military uniforms gave way to extremely colorful and decidedly non-Libyan garb that resembled Hollywood's take on a nineteenth-century African king's wardrobe. His conduct was not far behind in peculiarity.

After the U.S.-led coalition ended the Iraqi regime of Saddam Hussein in 2003, Qaddafi became concerned that he might be next. When Bush administration officials confronted him with evidence of Libya's chemical weapons stockpile and efforts to develop nuclear weapons, he eventually agreed to cease all weapons of mass destruction (WMD) programs, destroying or handing over their components. In turn, the United States, Great Britain, and other nations would ease sanctions on his government and begin normalizing diplomatic relations. Qaddafi had been previously treated as a pariah given his history of supporting terrorists. For example, when Qaddafi ordered the murder of U.S. servicemen in Europe in 1986, then-president Reagan ordered a retaliatory military strike on Libya, killing Qaddafi's stepdaughter and blowing up his tent. Qaddafi's agents also bombed a Pan Am airliner over Britain in 1988.

The resumption of ties with the West beginning in 2003 brought Qaddafi's eccentricities back to the fore. Rumors in the State Department at the time said that the dictator, now in his sixties, had recently greeted visiting diplomats wearing a skimpy swimsuit. Among his elaborate personal security apparatus, he included a corps of attractive women that constituted his "Amazonian Guard." In 2005, Qaddafi treated the visiting chairman of the Senate Foreign Relations Committee to his customarily surreal hospitality. The U.S. mission in Tripoli cabled Washington about the episode:

> Qaddafi, swathed in an embroidered robe with a matching cap, greeted the entire delegation in his desert encampment at midday. Qaddafi's advisors said they had taken him from a day of rest and fasting to accommodate the delegation's tight schedule. Given the intense noontime heat, Qaddafi's advisors arranged for a water truck to spray cooling mist in the immediate area in an attempt to lower the temperature. Qaddafi, initially distracted and swatting the air with his favorite prop, a branch of desert scrub brush.[40]

In 2009, the U.S. mission, now a full embassy, felt the need to prepare official visitors to Libya more generally. It sent a cable to State Department headquarters titled "A Glimpse into Libyan Leader Qaddafi's Eccentricities."[41]

Qaddafi was particularly smitten with the secretary of state who oversaw the restoration of full relations with his government, Condoleezza Rice. He referred to the American-born chief diplomat as a "darling black African woman." After he was forced from his palace in Tripoli, fighters would find a creepy, professionally made album containing only pictures of Rice.[42]

Zany as his conduct was at times, Qaddafi remained a brutal dictator, ruling the Libyan people without their consent. In any struggle against a repressive government, long before crowds of protesters fill the streets, smaller numbers of dissidents and intellectuals choose a much lonelier and more perilous quest for their nation's freedom. Sometimes they become well known both within and outside their countries, as did Andrei Sakharov of the Soviet Union or Václav Havel of Czechoslovakia. More often they do not. Typically they are people who could have had decent, middle-class lives if they kept quiet. Instead, they risk their careers, the comforts of family, and even their lives for national freedom or a sense of justice. By putting a human face on a regime's brutality, corruption, or hypocrisy, they discourage regime supporters and galvanize opponents.

Qaddafi's Libya was no exception. Investigative journalist Claudia Rosett brought one such dissident to my attention at the State Department. He was Fathi Eljahmi, a civil engineer in his sixties who, in 2002, called for free speech and political plurality in Qaddafi's Libya. For this offense, he was thrown into Tripoli's notorious Abu Salim prison. My boss at the State Department at the time, Undersecretary Paula Dobriansky, the top U.S. official charged with democracy and human rights issues, wanted to ensure the U.S. government pressed for his freedom as it normalized ties with Libya. Newly visiting U.S. officials and congressmen intervened with Qaddafi's people and did in fact help secure Eljahmi's release for a while, but Libyan security officials soon isolated him at his home. Later he was beaten and arrested along with his wife and son.[43] He was held largely incommunicado and in solitary confinement for years, abused, and denied necessary medical treatment. Eventually, after he went into a coma, he was permitted medical evacuation to Jordan but was still watched closely by Libyan security while comatose. He died without regaining consciousness in 2009 — a victim, in effect, of slow-motion torture at the hands of Qaddafi's men.[44]

Eljahmi could have had a comfortable, long retirement had he never spoke of freedom in Libya or had he withdrawn in silence after he was initially let out of jail. His choice not to keep quiet reminded the rest of the world that Qaddafi's regime, despite having ended its WMD programs, remained brutally repressive and potentially unstable.

This issue mattered to U.S. security in general because dictatorships often act aggressively toward their neighbors and work against U.S. interests. Furthermore, it mattered specifically in the Middle East because Qaddafi's conduct risked creating an opening for Islamists and terrorists who exploit discontent generated by regimes like his. Normalizing relations with Qaddafi in exchange for his WMD was the correct decision to make. The West took advantage of the beneficial fear accrued after deposing Saddam Hussein in Iraq. Qaddafi's new stance deprived Middle Eastern terrorists of a past benefactor and decreased the chance of a terrorist-smuggled WMD going off in an allied or American city. But it is important to realize that such deals in statecraft — basically a mutual accommodation with a government whose conduct is otherwise loathsome — seldom lead to lasting amity or partnership with free nations. It is especially true of regimes that exhibit no hope of long-term reform, including those apparently terrified of an aged, mild-mannered man like Fathi Eljahmi, who occasionally spoke of freedom. America's deal with Qaddafi never said anything about protecting him from his own people.

LIBYAN CIVIL WAR

As with the Tunisians to their west and the Egyptians to their east, the Libyans took to the streets in the fateful early months of 2011 to protest Qaddafi's long-repressive rule. What followed was a finely tuned international operation that swept Qaddafi from power, restored the importance of NATO, and cost little, as no NATO combatants lost their lives. At least that is how the story is told in most of Washington. The reality was less gratifying.

In fact, Washington remained largely silent as events unfolded in the early days of the Libyan uprising, which began in the commercial city of Benghazi in eastern Libya in February 2011. Before long, protests and active resistance to government authority spread to other cities. Qaddafi faced unrest in his own capital of Tripoli. It will never be known what might have happened at that point if the United States and its allies had stated clearly to Qaddafi that he had to leave and they were going to support his opponents. Unfortunately, it would be ten full days before President Obama even took a side in the contest. During that time, rebels seeking to oust the regime forcibly had begun a full-fledged revolt.

Here, the Arab Spring began to differ significantly from the revolutions that brought down communist governments at the end of the Cold War and repressive regimes in such places as Georgia and Ukraine in the 2000s. The difference was the regime opponents in Libya took up arms when the regime refused to cede power. They were joined by defectors from the government's military and intelligence services, some of whom sided with the rebels overtly while others secretly worked on the rebels' behalf while ostensibly remaining loyal to Qaddafi.

This development was remarkable for the field of smart power. Beforehand, many analysts assumed that when pro-freedom protesters resorted to violence, they had given the repressive regime the excuse it needed to use whatever force was necessary to crush the uprising. In other words, when people spill into the streets, the crisis they presented may or may not succeed in bringing down a government, but either side's resorting to violence is usually a strong indication of the uprising's imminent failure. The Arab Spring changed this perspective — at least in that time and place. It opened up new potential for the use of smart power — that is, ways to advance U.S. national interests through proxy armies.

Back in Washington, the White House was occupied by a man who came to Washington to end wars and who had probably never previously framed his mind to supporting a ragtag proxy force against an old, relatively obscure foe of the United States. Events were also moving rapidly, contributing to policy paralysis in Washington. Qaddafi quickly regained the initiative and ordered forces still loyal to him to fight the rebels. They did with ruthless efficiency. Soon, the rebels were pushed out of Brega, the oil town that would switch hands five times before the war ended. They also looked set to be annihilated in Benghazi. An encircled rebel holdout in the central port town of Misurata also looked imperiled.

Embarrassed by criticism over slow and confused reaction during revolutions in Tunisia and Egypt, the Obama administration decided to act. British prime minister David Cameron and French president Nicolas Sarkozy, both of whom professed a willingness to commit military resources, personally pressured Obama. The Obama administration went to the UN Security Council, determined to stop a Qaddafi victory, but was unclear on how or even if it would support a rebel victory. Instead, the NATO-led effort was billed as a humanitarian mission. The subsequent UN Security Council resolution purported to authorize force "to protect civilians and civilian populated areas under threat of attack."[45]

This effort was meant to lead to a no-fly zone over Libya, but NATO-led operations quickly morphed into an air war on the rebels' behalf. The UN also enacted an imprecise arms embargo on Libya. Some governments believed the arms embargo applied only to Qaddafi and his "Libyan Arab Jamhariya," which was the name used in the resolution. Others, including some permanent members of the Security Council, thought it applied to the entire geography of Libya and all parties within. Oddly, Washington appeared to believe both. A State Department spokesman said that arming the rebels would be "illegal." But when asked if the United States could arm the rebels, White House spokesman Jay Carney said, "There was a few weeks ago a statement that the arms embargo prevented us from doing that, and in fact, there's flexibility within that to take that action if we thought that were the right way to go."[46] Meanwhile, British defense secretary Liam Fox said that the embargo applied to all of Libya, the rebels included.

But the debate in Washington over the UN embargo was essentially moot. Whether as part of a coordinated policy or not, the Obama administration refused to arm the rebels and went a step further by putting a de facto arms embargo of its own in place, dealing a serious blow to the rebels' ability to fight for themselves and go on the offensive. U.S. law requires State Department approval for the export of arms or ammunition. The Obama administration refused to issue any such approvals. Furthermore, many NATO members, especially newer ones that manufacture the Russian-designed weapons that were compatible with the rebels' equipment, looked for a nod from U.S. military attachés before allowing the export of arms or ammunition from their countries. In essence, while the United States and NATO were going to war on behalf of the rebels (despite a refusal to declare this mission clearly), the White House was inexplicably taking steps to prevent those rebels from defending themselves and taking ground, which was a necessary step to ending the war and to ensuring the no-fly zone was not another open-ended U.S. military commitment similar to the decade-long no-fly zone over Iraq before 2003. Thus Washington added another chapter to the Arab Spring case study of how not to wage political or military warfare.

Also, analysts and officials in Washington issued the constant refrain that "we don't know who the rebels are." This argument was laziness at best. The rebels were among the most knowable of any group that arose in the Arab Spring. At the political level, the rebels were led and represented by the Interim Transitional National Council seated in free Benghazi. The council listed its initial, diverse thirty-one members on its website along with their portfolios. France and Qatar quickly recognized the council as the sole government of Libya, breaking relations with Qaddafi. The council even released a manifesto titled "A Vision of a Democratic Libya," calling for many of the prerogatives in the U.S. Bill of Rights and many of the institutions and balances that mark American democracy. Importantly, it condemned "intolerance, extremism and violence." At rebel rallies in liberated cities like Benghazi, participants spontaneously waved American and French flags. One would have imagined that the U.S. intelligence bureaucracy, with its massive budget, should have been able to size up the rebels to Washington's satisfaction.

Furthermore, by March 19, 2011, the issue of "who the rebels were" should have been essentially moot. On that day, NATO operations that would soon be dominated by the United States began. Having gone to war, the government had to have already passed the threshold question of whether to side with those who will ultimately end the war successfully and defeat the enemy, regardless of how agreeable or disagreeable one's notional allies are. It is worth recalling that the Unites States and Britain, of necessity, allied with murderous Soviet leader Joseph Stalin during World War II. Successful statecraft by a world power does not always lend itself to pleasant choices. But in going to war in Libya on the basis of merely stopping a humanitarian catastrophe and by never calling the military operation against Qaddafi a war, the Obama White House all but ensured contorted and dysfunctional policy.

Luckily other governments chose not to inhibit themselves with these illusions and drawbacks. The list of enemies Qaddafi had gained during his forty-two-year rule was long, and it included key states in the Persian Gulf, such as Qatar, Saudi Arabia, and the United Arab Emirates (UAE). These nations undertook on their own volition the essential job of supplying and funding the Libyan rebels. This assistance enabled the rebels to take the fight to Qaddafi and end the stalemate that had developed by early summer of 2011. France also provided some arms.[47]

Despite operating in a gray area of a UN arms embargo, these governments did essential work. Early in the war, NATO airpower transformed Qaddafi's likely slaughter of the rebels into a stalemate. Later, the Gulf States' provision of arms and funding enabled the rebels to turn the stalemate into a victory. The Gulf States' involvement also served as a case study in successful smart power: in particular, they were thinking beyond the immediate crisis to the political and security situation that would emerge in Libya after the war. By supporting factions among the rebels with which they were most comfortable, these governments helped shape postwar Libya and rightly earned access and influence in the Libyan polity that would emerge. It is no coincidence that the government that has emerged in postwar Libya, while far from perfect, is more promising than the others to come from the Arab Spring. The involvement of allied governments working toward desirable political goals was key.

Back in Washington and in European capitals, this lesson was largely missed. On October 20, 2011, the day the rebels killed Qaddafi, his Amazonian Guard having disappeared, NATO secretary-general Anders Rasmussen remarked that "NATO and our partners have successfully implemented the historic mandate of the United Nations to protect the people of Libya."[48] That same day, President Obama said, "Without putting a single U.S. service member on the ground, we achieved our objectives. . . . Working in Libya with friends and allies, we've demonstrated what collective action can achieve in the 21st century."[49] The other governments that actually made the difference on the ground and successfully used smart power did not seek credit for their actions. Indeed, they received little in Western capitals and in the media. The one case study in the Arab Spring that demonstrated successful political warfare combined with support for a proxy army was thus lost on much of official Washington.

This failure to understand the forces at work shaping important parts of the world would extend far beyond the remote world of officials and policy wonks in Washington. As the presidential campaign of 2012 was under way in the fall of 2011, the dysfunction of the political debate over war and foreign policy became apparent. What transpired was not an appealing spectacle.

CHAPTER 3

Failed Politics of National Defense

"The Martian in chief is blanketing the state today and tomorrow." The news popped up on my e-mail from Steve Yates, Newt Gingrich's director of national security staff and, like me, a senior adviser to his presidential campaign. Yates, also my business partner and a friend since his days as Vice President Cheney's deputy national security adviser, was stumping in Idaho for the former Speaker of the House and keeping an eye on the activities of Gingrich's opponents. For the second time in as many months, Gingrich's fortunes in his quest for the 2012 Republican nomination for president were ebbing rapidly from front-runner status. I sighed when I received the e-mail, which I knew referred to Congressman Ron Paul and, inevitably, his peculiar ground troops.

No matter where you were in America, the "Ronulans" would always show up. The 2012 presidential election seemed to start not long after January 20, 2009, the day Barack Obama took office as president. From the get-go, at anything that smacked of a campaign event or beauty pageant for those who would challenge Obama in 2012, buses of eager adherents to the occasionally rambling congressman from Galveston, Texas, would arrive in force. Urban Dictionary captured the essence of the movement: "Followers of the harebrained Libertarian/Republican presidential candidate Ron Paul. Characterized by their incessant spamming of political discussion boards and blind, fervent belief that their candidate is the Savior

Of The Republic, Ronulans are reviled by both Republicans and Democrats while simultaneously drawing devotees from the ranks of both."[1]

To me, the Ronulans offered a distracting and unworkable answer to very real and understandable gripes about national defense and general political dysfunction in Washington. As an appointee in the George W. Bush administration, I supported the broad, muscular U.S. response after the terrorist attacks on 9/11. In fact, it was why I moved from California to Washington, D.C., living in that former swamp for most of the administration. But I found the handling of statecraft and related politics in Bush's administration still left much to be desired. Fixing it and restoring an approach to national defense that was prudent, competent, and firm — the kind that marked the presidencies of men like Harry S. Truman, Dwight Eisenhower, and Ronald Reagan — was what I had in mind. Attempting to turn inward from a dangerous world was not. I also had no interest in overestimating the cost of our defense to the American public or in implying that savings in that area would cure the looming fiscal problems Washington created. Those assertions are part of the fiction the Ronulans offered.

Given the choices of the Left's traditional softness on national security, the open-ended foreign commitments sought by neoconservatives, and Ronulan isolationism, I wanted a unique approach in foreign policy. This alternative would be a defense policy that is stingy with the lives of American soldiers and skeptical of new foreign commitments but nonetheless confident and clear when U.S. interests were on the line and backed with a tough, modern military and ample tools for smart power. The Right's lack of an eloquent, persuasive foreign policy alternative — from either among candidates for office or those occupying various heights within the Republican Party in Washington — was frustrating. When official Washington finally talked about defense and foreign policy in debates or during a crisis, it seemed that neither side "got it." A debate I had hoped would lead to a more appealing foreign policy based heavily on smart power never materialized during the campaign.

ROOTS OF FOREIGN FATIGUE

By the time the U.S. trudged to war again in Libya in 2011, Americans had grown measurably impatient with Washington's practice of statecraft.

Polls showed consistent opposition to U.S. involvement in Libya's civil war, even with the Obama administration carefully describing the operation as anything other than a war. This attitude was understandable after a decade of conflict in Iraq and Afghanistan, during which initial victories nearly became defeats at the hands of insurgents. Americans were also rightly wary that some of the biggest recipients of U.S. foreign aid, including such nations as Pakistan, Egypt, and Iraq, had highly visible reservoirs of anti-American hatred and pro-Islamist sentiment.

Sensing this disgruntlement, even some Republicans were starting to sound like doves. This shift was partially a response to Obama, who sought approval for the Libyan "humanitarian intervention" from the UN Security Council but never from his own country's Congress. He also never spelled out the limits of U.S. involvement in the NATO operation. Washington's portion was outsized because of the inability of Britain and France to sustain even a modest military operation without American assistance.[2] As such, President Obama, who came to power in part by criticizing his predecessor's lack of an exit strategy in Iraq, did not have an exit plan himself for the intervention he ordered in Libya. (Washington lucked out when the rebels won on the ground.)

Rather than make these points in public to erode Obama's political position, a vocal minority of Republicans in Congress took matters too far and began to muse about applying the War Powers Act. This move theoretically would have forced Obama to halt U.S. involvement. The law was passed over the veto of President Nixon in 1973, after he was substantially weakened by the Watergate scandal and amid wariness of the Vietnam War. While never tested in court, conservatives and presidents of both political parties have considered the law to be unconstitutional. (Obama did not follow suit directly with this belief; instead, he made the improbable claim that the War Powers Act did not apply because the intense bombing of Qaddafi's forces did not constitute "hostilities" and thus did not trigger the act.[3])

The law purports to require a president to withdraw U.S. troops from action after sixty days if he does not obtain congressional authorization to continue hostilities. As reasonable as that stipulation may sound, there is no surer way to harm America's security permanently than to make wars run by committee, especially if it includes an often-fickle Congress. The Constitution makes the president the commander in chief of the armed forces, and that position necessarily includes control over their dispatch to conflict zones and over the operations while there. The framers of the Constitution were wary of executive power in government but saw this presidential authority as essential if the United States was to defend itself successfully from military threats. Abridging this power requires an amendment to the Constitution, not a mere piece of legislation like the 1973 law. Furthermore, Congress is not without power to limit the use of the military, especially since the Constitution gives it the sole right to appropriate funds. Congress need only cut off funds for a war it does not wish to tolerate. Republicans in Congress — the people who talk publicly about the Constitution most frequently and see themselves as strong on defense — are supposed to know this information.

On June 3, 2011, the House of Representatives considered a bill invoking the War Powers Act that was introduced by the left-leaning representative Dennis Kucinich. It would have theoretically ordered the president "to remove the United States Armed Forces from Libya." While defeated by a vote of 148 to 265, it received more Republican "yes" votes than Democratic ones and would not have been defeated without a substantial number of Democratic "no" votes.[4] Despite its failure, the episode marked a departure for a sizable bloc of Republicans and conservatives from a long-held belief that the presidency's defense-related powers should be restored and preserved in order to protect the United States from foreign threats. The quixotic but nonetheless damaging effort in Congress served as a reminder that Washington Republicans were feckless and off message both in offering an alternative to Obama's defense policies or in making him pay a political price for unpopular moves. Instead, Washington Republicans seemed largely to be grumbling and playing games. The lesson to me was that both parties were lost in trying to find a national defense philosophy that worked and, most critically, passed muster with voters.

However, Republicans' motive in opposing new foreign commitments was easy enough to understand. By mid-2011, most Americans wanted the U.S. government to pay less attention to foreign affairs. A poll at the time found that 58 percent of the American people wanted the United

States to be less active in world affairs, representing a 10 percent increase from when the question was asked in 2004. Unlike 2004, the poll found that even self-identified conservative Republicans agreed with moderates and liberals on this point.[5]

I encountered this growing sentiment myself shortly after the end of the Bush administration. I was initially impressed with newly elected President Obama's decision to salvage America's sacrifice in Afghanistan and order a counterinsurgency mission there rather than a withdrawal. While he would later impair his own strategy by under-resourcing the effort and announcing a departure date thinly veiled as "off-ramps" to a patient enemy, Obama's initial decision was promising.[6] When I said as much to Republicans and conservatives in various venues, including in such places as traditionally conservative and pro-military Orange County, California, I was surprised by the strong resistance to any further expenditure of resources in Afghanistan. This reaction was not instinctive opposition to any initiative of a new president of the opposing party but an expression of fatigue at a foreign obligation then entering its eighth year. President Obama did little to help matters, choosing not to support his position through periodic public statements and updates, as his predecessor had. Obama presumably did not want to visibly advocate a position, although the right thing to do, that might alienate him from his progressive base among other voters.

A little more than two years later, I would get another taste of the public's fatigue resulting from this conflict. Afghanistan by then had become America's longest war. Despite considerable success by U.S. forces at securing major portions of Afghanistan — including Helmand and Kandahar Provinces in the country's south, where the Taliban had held considerable sway — many Americans wanted out no matter what. This position was increasingly apparent on the campaign trail ahead of the 2012 presidential elections. While out seeking votes, Newt Gingrich found considerable resistance to any sustained commitment in Afghanistan.

On the day of the Super Tuesday primaries, Gingrich put it bluntly to those of us on his foreign policy team: "How do I look people in the eye who come up to me and ask why we're still in Afghanistan and tell them we need to expend more American lives there?" As with my earlier experience in Orange County, Gingrich was hearing this question from voters in a part of the country not known to be fickle about defending American interests with military force — namely, the South. We were all concerned that such voter disgruntlement could hurt efforts to confront other very real threats. Standing amid noisy train announcements in New York's Penn Station with a bemused former Speaker of the House calling from the campaign bus, I argued that those decisions of Obama's that we deemed to be misguided and the ongoing failure of our political class to explain matters of national security did not alleviate the threats that our enemies posed to our troops fighting in Afghanistan. We also concluded that rapid withdrawals of huge quantities of troops and military goods existed as possibilities mainly in the minds of Washington commentators and were not based in reality. Gingrich stressed the need to develop an alternative to the status quo or the Afghanistan-related options offered by other candidates, such as they were. Clearly the voters desired one.

Earlier, Gingrich had drawn tut-tuts from experts for saying:

We're not going to fix Afghanistan. It's not possible. These are people who have spent several thousand years hating foreigners. And what we've done by staying is become the new foreigners. And this is a real problem. There's some problems where what you have to do is say "You know, you're going to have to figure out how to live your own miserable life because I'm not here — you clearly don't want to hear from me how to be unmiserable."[7]

Despite gasps from some, the statement clearly echoed the concerns and conclusions of many American voters. There was a broad sense that enough time and resources had been devoted to Afghanistan and other foreign commitments, and that the mission there had become too broad and unclear.

However, at the same time, Gingrich wrote a journalist that "I am for an intelligent strategy of engagement in seeking to defeat radical Islamists; I am for a long-term strategy of shaping Pakistan and Afghanistan; the question I am raising is whether ground forces patrolling under Obama's withdrawal schedule and with Obama's rules of engagement is an effective strategy; the next president will have to be involved with the issue of radical Islamism."[8] However, these key points seldom penetrated a media and crowded field of candidates prone to slogans and platitudes. Further, they were often unaware of the many smart power options for statecraft that exist between war and diplomacy. Fatigue at anything foreign precluded a fulsome debate on an alternative foreign policy that could feature a greater role for smart power. This weariness was partially driven by an approach to defense in Washington that had gained a most unfortunate but apt label from an unnamed White House adviser commenting to a reporter.

OBAMA PROGRESSIVES: LEADING FROM BEHIND?

On the left, most voices in the national security debate came from the liberal side of the Democratic Party, especially since 2004. This situation was not always so. Throughout much of the earlier post–World War II era, a large contingent of Democrats in Washington were unabashedly hawkish on national defense and usually made sure they controlled the Armed Services Committee in each house of the then-consistently Democratic Congress. Most but not all of them were southerners. Harry Truman, elevated to commander in chief for the final months of World War II after President Franklin Roosevelt's death in 1945, did not have much use for nuance or reticence. Truman approved the use of nuclear weapons against Japan. In his main diary entry about the new weapon immediately before its first use in combat, he described the bomb's power in ominous, biblical terms, but he never entertained any doubt as to whether it should be used to expedite the end of the war.[9] In 1960, Democrat John F. Kennedy won the presidency in part by accusing the Eisenhower-Nixon administration of neglecting a "missile gap" that was theoretically allowing the Soviet Union strategic nuclear superiority. He gave an inaugural address in which he vowed the United States would "pay any price . . . to assure the survival and success of liberty."[10]

The ascendancy of the peace wing of the Democratic Party in 1972 marked a turning point. Then, Democrats nominated an antiwar candidate, George McGovern, who went on to win only one state to Richard Nixon's forty-nine. Four years later, the dimensions of Jimmy Carter's unease with the application of U.S. power were not clear when he successfully sought the presidency; however, they were abundantly apparent by the time he was turned out of the White House in 1980. By then, the

United States had been humiliated by the new Islamist government in Iran, which sanctioned the taking of American diplomats hostage that, in turn, triggered a failed U.S. military rescue operation. The United States also seemed to be losing the Cold War to the Soviet Union, which had just invaded Afghanistan and was cheering the recent success of its political allies in Central America.

Despite losing the White House and Senate in a landslide in 1980, Democratic candidates with a left-leaning, post-modern view of American power continued to be the norm. Walter Mondale led the party to overwhelming defeat again in 1984. Other factors — especially economic ones — dominated the elections, but foreign policy also colored the campaigns, especially when the Soviet threat was obviously apparent to the electorate. In 1988, Republicans juxtaposed footage of a geeky-looking Michael Dukakis in a National Guard tank with descriptions of his progressive views on defense to help defeat the Massachusetts Democrat. Republicans had won five of the last six presidential elections.

Bill Clinton turned the Democratic Party and its fortunes around. A moderate former attorney general and governor from the southern state of Arkansas, Clinton campaigned as a "third way" Democrat who was of neither the Left nor the Right.[11] He criticized the historic economic posture of both parties. In this description of his politics, he was mirrored across the Atlantic by Tony Blair, a young British politician angling to be the standard-bearer of the Labour Party. Similar to the "New Democrat" Clinton, Blair would position his party as "New Labour," signaling a clear break with unpopular, left-leaning economics that marked the histories of both parties on each side of the Atlantic. Among the factions within the British Labour Party, Blair was oddly described in media reports as a "right-winger" upon assuming the party's leadership.[12] While neither Clinton nor Blair devoted much attention to foreign policy before taking office, each man's focus would change during his tenure.

Clinton entered the White House in January 1993. Blair entered Number 10 Downing Street in London as the new British prime minister in May 1997. His win coincided with Clinton's second term in office, when a number of events turned his attention abroad, including a Congress at home controlled by the opposing party and a string of scandals and investigations. All of these developments transpired to move the national security policies of the English-speaking world's most prominent center-left parties back to the center. Blair and Clinton cooperated closely in the Kosovo War in 1998–1999 and in Operation Desert Fox in December 1998 when U.S. and allied forces conducted a major bombing campaign on Saddam Hussein's Iraq.

Throughout his tenure, Clinton dispatched U.S. troops to dozens of hot spots around the world. While politicians debated the necessity and usefulness of this defense policy at the time — and it remains an issue of disagreement for historians and foreign policy wonks — it clearly marked a divergence from earlier Democratic icons who stressed reductions in the U.S. military and a softer stance toward America's adversaries. In office, Clinton also embraced free trade, which signaled the coming of a U.S. economy that was even more integrated with the outside world. He signed the North American Free Trade Agreement, noting, "We are on the verge of a global economic expansion that is sparked by the fact that the United States at this critical moment decided that we would compete, not retreat."[13] In economic and defense policy, the Democrats had come a long way since their years of estrangement from the White House.

As the unsuccessful Democratic nominee in the 2000 presidential campaign, Vice President Al Gore sought to continue the Clinton administration's foreign policies. He even critiqued his opponent, George W. Bush, for seeking a withdrawal from some foreign commitments. Of a Bush campaign's proposal that U.S. forces be removed from Kosovo, Gore said, "I believe it demonstrates a lack of judgment and a complete misunderstanding of history to think that America can simply walk away from security challenges on the European continent."[14] Gore diverged from Clinton on economic policy but advocated a foreign policy of relative strength and engagement.

This position would not last, especially when political opportunity showed a different path to Democrats. Four years later, Democratic senator John Kerry of Massachusetts challenged Bush for the presidency. Only three years after the September 11 attacks on the United States, most analysts perceived the national defense issue to be beneficial to Bush. Nonetheless, Kerry challenged Bush on the Iraq War, faulting him for not building a larger coalition and securing the backing of the United Nations to the degree Kerry wanted.[15] Kerry also asserted that Bush's negligence had allowed Osama bin Laden to escape allied hands at the Battle of Tora Bora in December 2001.[16] While hardly a return to McGovernesque pacifism and insularity, Kerry had tacked Democratic foreign policy in a different direction.

The big change came in 2006. By then, the Iraq War had deteriorated badly after the brilliant initial invasion. Sectarian insurgents were fighting each other and seeking to undermine the new government while expelling allied forces. U.S. casualties were mounting. At that point, it appeared the allies were losing in Iraq, and America might have a Vietnam-like catastrophe on its hands. Senator Harry Reid of Nevada voiced the Democrats' common refrain when he said, "The Iraq war has diverted our focus and more than $300 billion in resources from the war on terrorism and has created a rallying cry for international terrorists."[17] Voters agreed with the arguments that Democrats posed that year, rewarding them with control of both houses of Congress for the first time since 1994. Even though the dire situation in Iraq was reversed by the 2007 surge of military forces and adoption of a counterinsurgency mission, Barack Obama and other Democrats continued to use angst over Iraq and poor management of security in Afghanistan to their electoral advantage in 2008. Those arguing for staying the course in foreign affairs had lost the debate.

However, what emerged subsequently was not any more politically appealing. Setting aside the efficacy of Obama foreign policy, its presentation to the public left much to be desired. Early in his term, Obama embarked on what critics derided as his "apology tour." On trips to Egypt, Turkey, France, and Great Britain, he stated that America had acted with arrogance and unilateralism in the past.[18] In Strasbourg, France, while three months into his presidency, Obama said that "in America, there's a failure to appreciate Europe's leading role in the world. Instead of celebrating your dynamic union and seeking to partner with you to meet common challenges, there have been times where America has shown arrogance and been dismissive, even derisive."[19]

Inevitably foreign policy commentators attempted to divine an "Obama Doctrine," or the unifying theme that seemingly must now be imputed from every new president's actions abroad. However, it was during a period of stalemate in the Libyan Civil War when the moniker that would define Obama's foreign policy emerged. In an interview with a commentator from the *New Yorker* during the summer of 2011, an unnamed White House source described the strange path to the U.S.-led NATO intervention as "leading from behind." Neither Obama nor his aides ever embraced the term and even disputed its qualities publicly.[20] But for Obama's opponents — and a public skeptical of new wars and foreign commitments — the motto rang true. And it stuck.

On the other side of the political spectrum, Obama won few plaudits from the Left. Early in his term, Obama dropped plans to close the terrorist detention facility at Guantánamo Bay, his hand forced by a Congress then dominated by his own party. Obama also expanded the use of unmanned drones for surveillance and attack purposes in Yemen, Pakistan, and Afghanistan. In 2012, a White House source leaked the highly classified fact that Obama personally chaired meetings on efforts to capture or kill high-value foreign terrorists. The press simplified the report and said Obama possessed a yearbook-style "kill list," a revelation that seemed at odds with the progressive image he had portrayed as a candidate.[21]

Other factors work against Democrats in forming an effective national security policy that appeals to voters broadly. Most ironic was the change in Washington since the last time the more left-leaning faction had been ascendant in the Democratic Party: today it has the establishment on its side. In fact, it is the establishment.

Unlike the late 1960s and early 1970s, when student radicals admonished their comrades not to trust "anyone over thirty," the Left has come to dominate the very establishment heights — including in foreign policy — it had once vehemently opposed. The nemeses of the radicals of that earlier era ranged from university administrators to institutions like the media and the Washington defense establishment. Certainly very few would have felt anything other than deep animosity for such organizations as the Pentagon, the State Department, the CIA, and the early security-related think tanks like the Rand Corporation.

In due time, those who shared their progressive view of the world would move from outsider to insider. Since the Vietnam War era, they have generally dominated the senior ranks of bureaucrats found in the Pentagon's E Ring and the State Department's seventh floor. These new establishmentarians tend to be skeptical of the unilateral use of U.S. military power abroad except for humanitarian purposes where few U.S. interests are at stake. Rather, they are deeply wedded to the notion of an "international community," which can be made to take its cues from international organizations like the United Nations. To them, invading Haiti, as Bill Clinton did in 1994, under the authority of the UN for humanitarian reasons is acceptable. Invading Iraq to secure U.S. economic and security interests via a "coalition of the willing" is not.

Most important, those with the progressive, post-modern view of America and the world dominate the mainstream media organizations and academic institutions that deal most closely with foreign affairs, including most grant-making foundations that fund research. There are of course exceptions but not many. The result is that the potential pool of recruits for career positions at the State Department, CIA, and civilian components of the Defense Department is of like mind with the progressives. This homogeneity leads to a government bureaucracy populated by those with progressive views who act as a retardant to change for any Republican administration that comes to Washington. The same is true of major foreign policy think tanks like the Brookings Institution and the Center for Strategic and International Studies. Depending on one's political persuasion, it is a virtuous or vicious cycle that ensures domination of the Washington foreign policy establishment by those who lean toward the Left.

While this dominance might sound like a godsend for Democrats, it is not — at least not anymore. Their ideological forebears railed against the old establishment for being intellectually corrupt and politically unappealing, but today's status quo in Washington has developed the same way. The downside of having little perceptible competition is that there is no incentive to innovate. Even in Washington — that most non-entrepreneurial of American cities — this condition leads to problems. The establishment greets new ideas and suggestions for change with overwhelming hostility, which is a liability in a dynamic world. While no one expects government to be agile and highly adaptable, voters being charged more than $500 billion per year on defense ultimately expect the government to deliver.

In trying to navigate the politics of national security, Democrats are stuck with two great albatrosses around their necks — the policy of leading from behind and the bulk of the Washington establishment.

FECKLESS REPUBLICANS

For their part, Beltway Republicans are also in bad shape in advancing a politically appealing foreign policy. On Capitol Hill, the Republican sena-tor most visibly linked to national security issues has been John McCain, the defeated presidential candidate in the 2008 election. In that race, McCain convincingly demonstrated a lack of both political and policy acumen, resulting in a loss to Obama by an electoral college vote of 365–173. As that year's financial crisis set in, McCain suspended his campaign, rushed back to Washington, and attended a pivotal White House meeting where he proceeded to add . . . nothing. When President Bush called on him, he remarked, "The longer I am around here, the more I respect seniority," and gave way for another senator to speak.[22] After twenty-five years in Congress, he had no ideas to contribute on the most important issue of the day. The same political ineptitude holds for McCain's most visible part of his portfolio — namely, national defense policy and spending.

McCain is a genuine war hero. The son of the senior American com-mander in the Pacific during the Vietnam War, he was shot down and incarcerated for a grueling five and a half years. He refused early release because it would have aided enemy propaganda and was tortured as a result. Unlike most of those with whom he served, however, McCain is not shy in reminding people of his service, using it at convenient times to silence critics of his policy preferences.[23] While effective in the short term, this retort does not inspire voters who want an appealing frame-work for thwarting foreign threats. Those who think a military record alone trumps any political competition on national defense issues should revisit the failed presidential candidacies of George H. W. Bush in 1992 and John Kerry in 2004.

In the 1990s, McCain supported no-fly zones over Bosnia and Iraq. This tactic denies an enemy the ability to use some or all aircraft in a certain geography. It uses American air superiority to limit an opposing military to deploying only ground forces. When the Libyan Civil War started in

2011, McCain's solution was also to establish a no-fly zone. When Syria erupted in protest and then civil war, McCain's prescription was, yet again, a no-fly zone.[24]

Voters understandably frown on these operations, even though they theoretically promise a sterile intervention with few or no U.S. casualties. No-fly zones are basically a way of going to war without candidly informing the public of the fact or having a real debate about war. The first stage of any no-fly zone involves degrading an enemy's air defenses so American pilots can operate with less chance of being shot down. This action means bombing the country. Even if this step and subsequent patrolling and air-to-ground combat are not called war, most Americans see them precisely as instruments of war. When the country is not going to war to win but only to make life harder for an opponent — another definition of a no-fly zone — many Americans are rightly skeptical if the cause is important enough to warrant the overt use of U.S. military force. Furthermore, no-fly zones do not constitute a strategy in and of themselves. They are merely tactics. When implemented without other measures to influence developments on the ground, they represent little more than sloppy, imprecise statecraft.

Sure enough, McCain's frequent sidekick and occasional conservative in the Senate, Republican Lindsey Graham of South Carolina, took pains to explain convincingly why the United States should enact a no-fly zone over Syria. He maintained that "it's good to come to people's aid when they are being slaughtered, because that's who we are."[25]

While compassionate and perhaps compelling sounding at first, this argument is a loser with voters and one that American presidents — at least the good ones — astutely avoid. Consider what going to war to stop genocide would have required of the United States in recent decades. It would have necessitated American-led interventions in Cambodia in 1975, Rwanda in 1994, and Sudan in 2003. They alone would have entailed three wars and occupations in locales where the United States has few national interests during times when other commitments required urgent attention. In addition, Graham did not invoke only genocide as a would-be casus belli for the United States but also the much lower bar of people "being slaughtered." Unfortunately, in this cruel world, and given some of the less attractive but nonetheless indelible features of human nature, that act is hardly a rare occurrence beyond our borders. Furthermore, Graham was seeking outright U.S. military intervention without drawing on any of the other, less intrusive smart power tools available to American presidents. This recipe for potentially endless war conflicts with the sentiment of the electorate. It also goes against one of the basic, unwritten principles of American foreign policy that involves being stingy in accepting new commitments or wagering the lives of American troops. Instead, presidents commit U.S. forces to war only when vital interests are at stake. They keep their powder dry for the major threats of the day. American voters most often favor this general conservatism.

Ironically, Republican Graham's standard for the use of force puts him close to people theoretically on the other side of the political spectrum. Take, for example, Samantha Power, who has had influence over Obama since his earliest days as a senator. She is a leading advocate in the United States for what is known as the "responsibility to protect." This construct emerged in the last decade from the fraternity of UN and international law aficionados. While it deals with such issues as limits to sovereignty and the role of national governments when minorities are being attacked, in the U.S. context, it means shifting American attention abroad more toward genocide and war crimes and away from a traditional foreign policy focused on national interests. It appeals to the high-minded. Voters informed of the concept likely would be less interested, pragmatically wondering if it is wise to turn the military into a Peace Corps with guns.

Of course, the United States will always oppose genocide and war crimes, but no major state in history has been successful when its foreign policy completely throws caution and pragmatism to the wind and acts on emotion devoid of any linkage to clear national interests. American foreign policy has often held a prominent place for morality, but presidents typically reserve the more intrusive tools of statecraft leading up to war for crisis areas where clear national interests are at stake — for example, in regions of vital economic importance and when important allies are threatened.

The convergence of such figures as Graham and McCain — often labeled neoconservative — with those of Power's ilk reveal an unfortunate consensus in Washington among those who are most outspoken on national defense issues. While they identify as either Republican or Democratic, they are mainly politically androgynous in reality — at least on foreign policy — and similarly disposed on how the U.S. government should act. They also have in common a political tin ear that turns off average Americans to a serious discussion and debate on foreign policy issues.

That political androgyny was on display during the Arab Spring when Egypt's government was swept from power. Amid the political struggle to shape what would follow in Egypt, it was McCain and Graham who gave cover to the Obama White House in winking at the Muslim Brotherhood. In February 2011, the two senators met with representatives of the Muslim Brotherhood in Egypt. Graham remarked publicly, "After talking with the Muslim Brotherhood, I was struck with their commitment to change the law because they believe it's unfair."[26] This détente with Islamists created the political space for the Obama administration to follow suit. In April, representatives of Egypt's Muslim Brotherhood were invited to the White House for meetings with officials. When reporters asked about it, the White House cited the McCain-Graham trip to argue its own engagement was not out of the ordinary.[27]

Elsewhere on Capitol Hill, matters in some Republican circles were even worse in recent years. In the Senate, Richard Lugar often joined McCain and Graham. A Republican from Indiana who was born when Herbert Hoover was president, Lugar entered the Senate in 1977, carving out a niche in foreign affairs. He served as chairman of the Senate Foreign Relations Committee when Republicans controlled the chamber for a portion of the 1980s. When they regained control after the 1994 election, Lugar had to play second fiddle to Republican Jesse Helms.

Helms was different than most senators, especially those interested in foreign affairs. The North Carolina native made it plainly clear he cared nothing for the approval of the Beltway establishment and had no intention of remaining in the city past his tenure in the Senate. He held the State Department to account, whether it was run by Republicans or Democrats, by delaying or denying Senate confirmation of ambassadors and other officials until he achieved the result he wanted on an issue. He also held the United Nations to account after corruption came to light by withholding a portion of annual U.S. dues.[28] Throughout the final decades of the Cold

War, Helms was a vocal advocate for taking a harder line on the Soviets and building a bigger U.S. military.

Lugar differed from Helms in policy and tone and was part of the priesthood in Washington that prioritized arms control treaties, even with governments that have a history of duplicity and cheating on agreements. He partnered with Democratic senator Sam Nunn in creating a program to pay Russia billions of dollars ostensibly to secure and dismantle its nuclear arsenal and related military platforms. Established in 1991, the Cooperative Threat Reduction Program, also known as Nunn-Lugar, resulted in payments and expenses that eventually grew to $500 million annually. The program was supposed to share costs with Moscow and others to dismantle Soviet-era strategic systems.[29] Skeptics charged that it amounted to paying Russia to modernize its military, especially since cash is easily diverted from one use to another. Money that Moscow no longer needed to devote to managing its older military apparatus could then be spent on new weapons.

Russia in the past decade, however, has not been the cash-strapped country of the early 1990s that could not afford to mothball its nuclear arsenal safely. Since then, its economy has nearly quadrupled in size.[30] Russian president Vladimir Putin plans to increase military spending, and ministers in Russia who oppose such plans tend to be fired.[31] Meanwhile, thanks to Lugar, U.S. taxpayer dollars flowed to a government that consistently opposed U.S. interests throughout the world. How this program constituted a conservative foreign policy was unclear. Ironically, the program's demise after twenty years came not from a U.S. Congress finally deciding to cease bankrolling an adversary but from Putin's cancelling the spending as part of Russia's never-ending complaining about U.S. missile defenses.[32]

The moderate Nunn was not the only Democrat with whom Lugar made common cause. He also joined forces with John Kerry to increase massively U.S. aid to Pakistan beginning in 2010. A bill titled the Enhanced Partnership with Pakistan Act of 2009 but known widely on Capitol Hill as Kerry-Lugar tripled nonmilitary aid to Islamabad to $1.5 billion annually.[33] When combined with military and other assistance, Pakistan received more than $5.6 billion dollars in U.S. taxpayer funds in 2010 alone, a total that is more than the annual budgets of some American states.[34] This amount might seem odd to voters concerned about the U.S. federal budget deficit, which now consistently exceeds $1 trillion annually and leads the U.S. Treasury to borrow approximately forty cents of every dollar it spends. Furthermore, voters might wonder what the $30 billion the United States has given to Pakistan cumulatively since 1948 has achieved.[35]

The State Department itself has said corruption in Pakistan is "pervasive in politics and government" and concluded "the government made few attempts to combat the problem."[36] In 2011, the top military adviser to President Obama revealed that a terrorist network that targeted Americans was a "veritable arm" of Pakistan's intelligence service.[37] Pakistan also harbors other terrorists and enemies of the United States and uses terrorists as tools of statecraft against India.[38] Owing to these many reasons, by early 2011, Gallup found that 59 percent of Americans favored cutting foreign aid.[39] Ignoring this reality while shoveling more dollars at corrupt and adversarial nations in an attempt to buy friends understandably turns American voters off to a discussion about smart power and shaping the world in which they live.

My own experience with Lugar and his staff during the George W. Bush administration was revealing. When I concluded the State Department's bureaucracy and even some of its leadership were stifling what President Bush said he wanted to do — and what a law passed by Congress said the executive branch was supposed to do — to help North Koreans free themselves, I started looking for allies on Capitol Hill. When I set up a meeting with Lugar's staff members, they asked if they could invite their Democratic colleagues — essentially employees of Senator John Kerry — to join the meeting. To me, this request signaled either thinly veiled hostility or a complete lack of cognizance of bureaucratic struggle. As allies of a bureaucracy resisting Bush, the Democratic aides would have immediately reported my efforts to their like-minded friends in the State Department's Foreign Service, which would have put a stop to my efforts. They would have been frowned upon by the department's Bureau of Legislative Affairs, which seeks to control all contact with Capitol Hill. I decided I needed to keep my distance from an office that should have been a pillar of support to a Republican administration.

Voters in his home state of Indiana fired Lugar in 2012. After it emerged that he used an address in the state where he had not resided since 1977 — legal but politically unwise — and amid other concerns about the eighty-year-old seeking a seventh six-year term, he lost the Republican primary to a conservative challenger.[40] During his tenure as its top Republican, Lugar made the Foreign Relations Committee so unappealing and uninteresting to other Republicans that in a body that prizes tenure and seniority above all else, the next most senior Republican senator on the committee was only in his first term in Congress. This arrangement is a far cry from the days of Jesse Helms, as Republicans have few star players or much of a farm team on foreign affairs in Congress.

Elsewhere in Washington, matters were equally grim for Republicans as the 2012 campaign trudged on. Few figures in national security appeared to have much political skill or any capability to appeal to a broad swath of American voters. George W. Bush's first secretary of state, Colin Powell, endorsed Democrat Barack Obama in the 2008 and 2012 elections. Bush's second-term chief diplomat, Condoleezza Rice, opposed the successful surge of forces in Iraq, misled President Bush on North Korea and China during failing nuclear negotiations, made a desultory attempt to solve decades-old Israeli-Palestinian issues in the dwindling days of the administration, and improved relations with Russia to the extent that Moscow felt at ease to invade the U.S. ally Georgia in the summer of 2008.[41] She also decided to offer "carrots" in hopes of enticing the Iranian regime to abandon its long-term nuclear weapons program, prompting the bemused U.S. ambassador to the UN John Bolton to order carrot soup in her presence.[42] Earlier in her career, Soviet expert Rice completely missed the coming collapse of the Soviet Union and counseled against aiding internal opponents of the Soviet Empire. Yet during the 2012 campaign and its Republican convention, Rice remained a go-to person for candidates, journalists, and others seeking a Republican take on foreign affairs.

Stephen Hadley, Rice's deputy when she was national security adviser, took over her job when Rice became secretary of state. He was even more unappealing. Some of us in the trenches at the State Department referred to Hadley as "Heaving Sadly" and regarded the National Security Council staff under his supervision as utterly unable to enforce Bush's desires on the bureaucracy. In my sole meeting with Hadley during the administration, Hadley promised Jay Lefkowitz, Bush's North Korea human rights envoy, and me to undertake a number of steps to rectify Bush's dissatisfaction with attention to the issue. He followed through on none. Figures such as Rice and Hadley continue to opine on foreign policy from a Republican perspective and often are paid handsomely for their appearances. Other than themselves, it is difficult to grasp who benefits from these lectures.

A final redoubt of center-right thinking on foreign policy and other issues in Washington is supposed to rest with a smattering of conservative think tanks. Even when the opposing team controls the White House and Congress and even when few other eloquent voices articulate center-right thought on national defense, such organizations as the American Enterprise Institute (AEI) and the Heritage Foundation are supposed to fill the gap. Unfortunately, they too are in state of intellectual recession. They tell their donors that they have the best scholars, and their ideas are persuasive and influential. The Heritage Foundation boasts on its website that it is a "powerhouse of conservative ideas" and approvingly cites a negative media report calling it the "the Parthenon of the conservative metropolis."[43] The organization certainly rakes in contributions from conservative donors around the nation. For the year 2011, Heritage reported to the Internal Revenue Service that it received $66 million in contributions and had net assets of $143 million. Its president from 1977 until 2012, Edwin Feulner, compensated himself $1.1 million dollars annually, which is an unusual salary for a nonprofit that is not a hospital, top university, or health insurance organization. Heritage paid no fewer than sixteen employees in excess of $200,000 annually and even paid an executive assistant $109,000.[44] The arrival in early 2013 of former senator Jim DeMint as the new president hopefully foreshadows a turnaround for the think tank. Historically, revitalization of dilapidated organizations in Washington has proven almost impossible, even for the most skilled managers.

Unfortunately, on Capitol Hill and within the executive branch, these organizations have essentially no influence, even when Republicans are in charge. In an earlier time, think tanks such as Heritage and AEI cultivated young experts who were likely to go into Republican administrations and leave a mark on policy. That potential for influencing government was part of the institutions' value proposition to donors. This business began to change in the 1990s when the salaries and required level of formal credentials for experts at the think tanks increased. Instead of hiring bright, young people looking for a springboard into consequential roles in government outside of the career path taken by bureaucrats, the tanks began to retain academics more advanced in their careers but often lacking government experience. Those think tank members who did come from government were increasingly derived from the ranks of bureaucrats and were not political appointees who shaped policy or saw it made firsthand.

Consequently, the number of people who attend events at these conservative think tanks has visibly dwindled, and crowds are heavy with young interns who are happy to eat a free lunch. While each think tank has at least some appealing, committed scholars and a smaller number of people who has a media profile, the organizations increasingly resemble detached universities without student bodies. For the most part, they are neither wellsprings of conservative thought nor an influence on any of the branches of government. For those fighting in Congress or in a presidential administration, the think tanks are no longer of much help.

THE RONULANS

Taken on the whole, the political fecklessness and inattention to foreign policy by both political parties lead to broad voter disgruntlement about all foreign undertakings. For some, it even led them to Ron Paul and his supporters. Now retired, Paul left an unforgettable mark on the 2012 presidential campaign. While it was all but certain Paul would fail to receive the Republican nomination for president, his brand of "noninterventionism" — which he used to describe his ideas instead of the politically deadly label of "isolationism" — could be detected well beyond his core of supporters.

Paul called for cutting off all foreign aid, an idea that proved a winner with most voters. But he opposed even sanctions on Iran for its nuclear weapons aspirations and suggested that offering Iran "friendship" would be better.[45] He suggested the U.S. presence abroad, rather than the radical Islamist political ideology, is what drives terrorism, and he thought withdrawing all U.S. forces abroad should be the solution.[46] Paul called for terrorists to be tried in criminal courts instead of facing military action or military tribunals. Demonstrating inflexibility in his doctrine, Paul also dissented on the killing of bin Laden.[47]

A trademark of the Ronulans is to overstate the impact the U.S. military has on the dire fiscal situation the country faces. In September 2011, Paul asserted in a presidential debate that "I'm not sure I can get anybody to agree with me on this panel, but we spend $1.5 trillion overseas in wars that we don't need to be in and we need to cut there."[48] Actually, a Congressional Research Service report issued in 2011 placed total war costs through that year at $1.28 trillion.[49] It is important to keep this expenditure in perspective; it occurred during a ten-year period in which the federal government spent a cumulative total of more than $29 trillion.[50] Thus the marginal cost of the wars and related military activities in the decade after the 9/11 attacks was just 4.4 percent of total federal spending. While not immaterial, the wars were hardly the chief culprit of Washington's financial trouble. Regrettably, other Republicans failed to make this counterpoint, so the lore that the military has contributed disproportionately to the national debt has become another Washington truism that is simply not true.

A final, overarching theme that the Ronulans sounded concerns the supposed loss of liberty that has occurred in the United States since September 11, 2001. The chief culprit in this tale is always the Patriot Act, which became law the month following the September 11 attacks. The law gave the executive branch additional power to fight terrorists operating in the United States and abroad. Notably, the Patriot Act did not create the Transportation Security Administration, which is the culprit many Americans associate with their loss of freedom and convenience since the attacks. The other supposed losses of freedom for average Americans simply do not exist, unless one is trying to communicate with or channel material support to groups the U.S. government has publicly designated as terrorists. But the act remains an article of faith among Ronulans as one of the evil by-products of intervening in the outside world. Paul did himself no favors in criticizing the Patriot Act and in defending his proposed alternative of treating foreign terrorists as if they are domestic criminals who deserve civilian trials in which the burden of proof is placed on the government. In a debate before the Republican primaries began, Paul argued with Newt Gingrich about the Patriot Act. Paul unwisely cited the arrest and trial of domestic U.S. terrorist Timothy McVeigh, who bombed a federal building in Oklahoma City, as a model:

> PAUL: I think the Patriot Act is unpatriotic because it undermines our liberty. I'm concerned, as everybody is, about the terrorist attack. Timothy McVeigh was a vicious terrorist. He was arrested. Terrorism is still on the books, internationally and nationally, it's a crime and we should deal with it. We dealt with it rather well with Timothy McVeigh . . .
>
> GINGRICH: Timothy McVeigh succeeded. That's the whole point. Timothy McVeigh killed a lot of Americans. I don't want a law that says after we lose a major American city, we're sure going to come and find you. I want a law that says, you try to take out an American city, we're going to stop you.[51]

That memorable exchange successfully undermined the Ronulan alternative on that particular occasion. Yet the electorate maintains a general, well-earned dislike of foreign policy as practiced by Washington's foreign policy establishment. Both parties are inept, ceding the argument to lesser lights among their ranks. The consequence is a growing inattention to key foreign issues and methods for shaping the outside world short of war.

New leaders have an opportunity to outline the need for an active role in the world, one performed prudently and with a revised toolkit that recognizes the steps between diplomacy and war. But no one of national stature has yet sought to fill this gap with a smart power–based foreign policy.

ILLUSIONS AND BROKEN TOOLS

CHAPTER 4

Smart Power with Chinese Characteristics

A pro-German Russian expatriate conceived and executed the greatest act of smart power in modern history. His actions changed the course of a world war and influenced decades of international political turmoil.

Friend and foe alike held Alexander Israel Helphand in disrepute. He was born in Belarus, which was then part of Czarist Russia and later became part of the Soviet Union. As did other Jews, he faced the prospect of a life of persecution in Russia.[1] Helphand left his rustic home for Germany as a young man, where he went by the name "Parvus" in underground circles. In Berlin he joined the ranks of exiled communist revolutionaries who held a special animus for the Romanov dynasty that ruled Russia. He also grew generally partial to Germany at the beginning of a century where that country's wars of aggression would loom large on the world stage. For a period, Parvus had as his protégé none other than Leon Trotsky, a key Marxist theorist and future leader in the Soviet Union. Parvus's reputation, however, suffered when many of his contemporaries suspected him of embezzling a large sum from the Russian writer and Bolshevik enthusiast Maxim Gorky. He lived suspiciously large for a professional malcontent and took a break from generally non-lucrative revolutionary intellectual activity in the years before World War I. For a period he lived in Istanbul, which was still called Constantinople in that day, and profited in supplying the Young Turk faction in the Ottoman Empire with military goods for their conflicts.[2]

When that dying empire was choosing a side in World War I, Parvus agitated for the Turks' alliance with Germany that eventually came to be. The next four years were prosperous for Parvus. Approaching the German ambassador to the Ottoman Empire in January 1915, Parvus suggested that the right mixture of Russian exiles could start a revolution that would knock Russia out of the war and free Germany to focus solely on France and Great Britain (joined later by the United States). Russia's internal turbulence, marked by massive protests and occasional general strikes, made the country theoretically ripe for revolution. By March, Berlin was sold on Parvus's plan and gave him a handsome budget, which he used to live extravagantly in Berlin and Zurich. Parvus reconnected with a certain Vladimir Ilyich Lenin, who was a particularly unique man among exiled revolutionaries.

The Germans had a problem in that the internal opponents of the Russian government, including the communists, had rallied around the flag to support Mother Russia in its time of war. Parvus knew that Lenin could make the revolutionaries see matters differently. To Lenin, the war was merely a contest among governments that were nothing more than capitalistic and imperialistic — supposedly the corrupt, penultimate stages of government that Karl Marx predicted would lead subsequently to communism. Lenin's revolutionary cause gained nothing by Russia aiding France and Britain against Germany. Ruthless and doctrinaire, Lenin alone could reorient the Bolshevik faction of the communists to favor Russia's immediate withdrawal from the war, even if it meant concessions to Germany; however, living in isolation in Zurich, Lenin was in exile from Russia.

Parvus stepped in. First, he arranged for indirect subsidies from Germany to the Bolsheviks. He established a base of operations in Stockholm to channel information on developments in Russia back to Lenin. By April 1917, Lenin was on his way to the Russian capital, which before long would bear his own name. His special train was arranged and funded by Germany; the plan was hatched by Parvus.

Lenin immediately set about correcting revolutionary thought in Russia to oppose the war, and he seized power by fall. The Russian war effort lapsed, and the new communist government formally accepted peace on Germany's terms the following spring.[3]

The effort had been a masterful if treacherous exercise in political warfare. While Germany still lost the war, it was not for the lack of its Foreign Ministry's resourcefulness in making life hard for Berlin's old Romanov foe in the East.

Opponents of the United States have long been adept at political warfare and smart power, especially as those enemies increasingly have come from the ranks of political revolutionaries themselves. Communists, who today retain control of the world's most populous nation, are highly adept at the middle space between diplomacy and war as it is the ground they trod most frequently before gaining power and must continue to master to preserve their necks. The professionals of political intrigue retain their skills after taking power — at least up to a point.

The rulers of the Soviet Union certainly did. Nearly a half century after the Russian Revolution, the leadership in Moscow believed it was shaping political events in the West to its advantage. Nikita Khrushchev, who took power in the Soviet Union in 1953 after the death of Joseph Stalin and an ensuing period of political jousting, thought he personally made the difference in the 1960 U.S. presidential election between Kennedy and Nixon. Khrushchev boasted to colleagues in the Kremlin that he changed the outcome of the close election by shooting down and taking prisoner American reconnaissance pilots during the election season and refusing their return until after the election. Four months before the election, a Soviet fighter jet shot down a U.S. RB-47H aerial surveillance plane over the Barents Sea, taking two survivors prisoner. This event came only two months after a more embarrassing incident in which the Soviets shot down American pilot Francis Gary Powers in a U-2 spy plane well inside the Soviet Union. The episode cast a pall over the incumbent Eisenhower administration, in which Nixon was vice president, and possibly helped tip the scale to the challenger Kennedy. The exact impact on the race is impossible to measure, but Kennedy prevailed in the popular vote by less than a fifth of a percentage point. Khrushchev moved quickly to reap the political harvest he thought he had sewn, leading to crises with the United States over Berlin and Cuba.[4]

It was not the first or last time that those who oppose Washington and its allies would use statecraft short of war to enhance their own national interests. Today, the purveyors of the two political forces in the world that pose the greatest danger to a civilized order wage successful political warfare against America each and every day. The foremost of the two has an ideological ancestry in common with the polity Parvus helped to create.

CHINA

China uses smart power to the detriment of the United States and other democracies, but not in the way many among the chattering class of experts and political commentators describe. Over the last decade, politicians and pundits have criticized Beijing most vocally for supposedly undervaluing its currency. As this book describes in chapter 10, China pursues other policies that ought to be of greater concern: building up its military, waging cyber war, and systematically stealing intellectual property. But America's political class likes to stick mostly with the currency issue. The undervalued Chinese yuan results in Chinese goods that are cheaper than they should be, American exports more expensive than they should be, and a trade deficit between the United States and China — or so the story goes. In reality, this representation is a straw man that allows politicians to appear tough on China while ignoring the real threat that the Chinese government poses.

Democratic senator Charles Schumer of New York has made the undervaluation of China's currency a pet issue since at least 2005. In that year, Schumer introduced legislation that would label the Chinese government as a "currency manipulator" and sanction Chinese exports. Schumer declared in mid-2005 that China "conceded that pegging their currency is bad for China, bad for the U.S. and bad for the world economy." Of a modest appreciation of the Chinese yuan currency, he said, "We expect more. We don't expect just this."[5] At the time, Beijing ended its longtime currency peg whereby one U.S. dollar bought about 8.3 Chinese yuan. Six years later, the yuan had appreciated in value so that a dollar bought only about 6.2 yuan. This 25 percent appreciation made Chinese goods more expensive for Americans and theoretically enabled the Chinese to consume more American goods and services. However, it failed to reduce the trade deficit with China, which grew from $202 billion in 2005 to $295 billion in 2011.[6] Undeterred, Schumer and his colleagues refused to change their tune. In mid-2011 he remarked, "I am more convinced than ever that legislation is needed to force countries like China that manipulate their currencies to play by the rules and let their currencies freely float."[7] Later that year, on October 12, the Senate voted 63–35 in favor of a bill to sanction Beijing for its currency valuation.[8] After the vote, a triumphant Schumer said that the action "put the Chinese on notice: 'Stop your cheating that is costing our country jobs, or you will face the consequences.'"[9]

However, as with much in Washington in recent years, the joke was on the American people. Everyone on Capitol Hill knew that if the bill came to a vote in either house and members had to go on record it would easily pass by a large margin. Furthermore, both sides knew that it could safely be passed out of the Senate and then face a certain death in the House of Representatives, where the leadership would never have allowed it to come to a vote and be sent to the president for his signature. A year earlier, in the previous Congress, the same cynical maneuver was orchestrated with the houses switching roles. The House of Representatives voted 348–79 in September 2010 to sanction China for its currency.[10] The bill died when the Senate failed to take action before that Congress ended three months later. But some 348 congressmen were able to return to their districts immediately before the midterm elections and boast of being tough on China. A year later, 63 senators could do the same, knowing full well the legislation would never become law with House leaders preventing their members from voting. It was business as usual in Washington.

The travesty is not that the bill failed to become law. Fixed exchange rates are not inherently bad, and China's now long-gone peg was not the source of the U.S. trade deficit. Like China, the United States itself had what amounted to a fixed exchange rate. The dollar was tied to the price of gold until President Nixon terminated the post–World War II Bretton Woods monetary system in 1971 and allowed the dollar to float. Despite being embraced as virtuous or at least inevitable by economists of all stripes, the policy has been disastrous. Forty years after the move, the purchasing power of a 2011 dollar had declined to only eighteen cents compared to its 1971 ancestor. This drop represents essentially an 82 percent tax on every American's cash, savings, and liquid assets, falling most heavily on the poor.[11]

China presumably was not eager to replicate this clear failure of public policy. Fixed exchange rates can also be highly beneficial to emerging economies, since they require fiscal discipline from the local government and reduce one form of uncertainty known as "currency risk" for foreign investors. Furthermore, the U.S. trade deficit is the result of many factors, including decisions that have made America dependent on imported sources of energy. The value of the Chinese yuan is but a small part of this picture.

The actual travesty in this Washington game is that the currency debate is allowed to pass for a serious discussion about how to handle the Chinese government, which meanwhile threatens the United States and its allies in more serious ways: economically, politically, and militarily. This selective focus occurs largely because other topics — as a result of careful planning and work by Beijing — are off limits to debate. Indeed, whenever an issue of contention arises in Washington, Beijing can rely on a combination of corporate interests and foreign policy establishment mavens to ride to its rescue, often without so much as a cue. The currency bill never really posed a major threat since its passage was always unlikely. Nonetheless, the Chamber of Commerce, National Retail Federation, Business Roundtable, and other interests made sure their displeasure at the prospect of the bill becoming law was known on Capitol Hill.[12] To head off threats to Beijing's favorable position in Washington, the Chinese can rely on a way of thinking that the foreign policy establishment has made a part of the bedrock of Washington politics.

A good example is an August 2012 story in the *Wall Street Journal* about talks Washington was holding with allies in East Asia about expanded missile defenses. The Chinese government was more than fifteen years into a headlong military buildup that included a dramatically more capable navy and air force and thousands of new ballistic missiles. China long ago perfected compact and lightweight nuclear warheads, having stolen the design of America's most advanced W-88 thermonuclear bomb design.[13] Considering that an unelected communist government with aggressive tendencies runs China and that democratic allies in the region — such as Japan, Australia, Taiwan, the Philippines, and South Korea — are concerned about China's buildup and increasingly acrimonious territorial disputes, it would seem to be a good time to talk about updated defense systems and practices. Specifically, Washington was interested in talks with Tokyo and other allies about positioning radars necessary to track and defeat ballistic missiles launched from North Korea or China that could be headed for Japan, U.S. bases in the Pacific, or North America itself.

However, the emphasis of the *Wall Street Journal* article was not on China's aggression and unexplained military buildup but on how a prudent allied reaction might discomfort the party that was misbehaving. The authors reported that such talks among the allies "could feed Chinese fears about containment by the U.S." and noted that "a senior U.S. official acknowledged that the Pentagon faces a hard sell convincing China's People's Liberation Army that the missile-defense architecture isn't designed to encircle them." Regarding China's expanding ballistic missile inventory, the article quoted a different expert who warned that "attempting to overcome this reality would risk entering the U.S. into a race that it could not afford to wage, let alone win." Inevitably, the article also quoted another expert who referenced "America's Cold War mentality," an oldie-but-goodie charge that Beijing can be counted on to lodge when someone in Washington advises reacting to Chinese actions.[14]

What is odd is that the three journalists who wrote the story and the several sources they consulted did not notice that the Chinese government was the party most responsible for what was being reported: a prudent allied reaction to both the conduct of the Chinese and of Beijing's client state, North Korea. After all, Beijing triggered the chain of events that necessitated the allied defense talks. Why did the reporters presume that the United States needed to soothe Beijing's fears that Washington, Tokyo, and other allies might one day have the ability to defend themselves against the changing threat that China and North Korea posed?

Unfortunately, this presumption that America and its allies ought to be the ones explaining themselves has been firmly emplaced in foreign policy circles through Beijing's support of those who think this way. There is one overwhelming cause of this development: Chinese money. In 2009, a congressional commission reported bluntly that "the Chinese government seeks to shape opinion in elite policy-making circles by influencing the commentary about China and U.S.-China relations that emerges from U.S. academics and think tanks."[15] James Mann, an author and journalist who reported from Beijing for years, explained the practice in greater detail. In his book *The China Fantasy*, Mann noted the proclivity of American elites to refrain from criticizing the Chinese government:

> There are huge and growing financial incentives for prominent Americans to support the status quo in China (or to argue that the status quo need not be challenged, because trade and investment will somehow eventually make things better). In Washington, U.S. political leaders and cabinet members know that if they become involved in dealing with China and don't become identified as critics of the regime in Beijing, when they leave office they can move on to lucrative careers as advisers, consultants, or hand-holders for corporate executives eager to do business in China. This is, of course, an old story; it was blazed long ago by Henry Kissinger, who after stepping down as secretary of state set up his own consulting firm, Kissinger Associates, and began escorting American bankers and other executives to Beijing.[16]

Beijing's purchasing or at least renting of influential friends — a key tactic in smart power — does not stop there. As Mann also notes, pro-Beijing money flows to friendly think tanks in Washington and academic institutions from companies that do extensive business in China. Sources of these funds are not limited to Western companies wishing to do business in China; some of China's own state-owned enterprises undoubtedly provide funding as well. Furthermore, not only former cabinet members but also a growing number of ordinary former government employees across the foreign policy, defense, and intelligence bureaucracies benefit from this arrangement.[17]

China's government is also familiar with the goodwill that it can generate by issuing or withholding visas and related travel junkets to its territory. Analysts, journalists, and academics who favor Beijing or who at least suspend disbelief and ignore Beijing's misconduct have no difficulty getting visas to enter China and get invited on paid junkets to make the trip. Those who do not cooperate can be denied a visa or, more annoyingly, be given a visa only to be denied entry on arrival. An inability to visit China also can hurt the career prospects of some experts.

These examples are only some key methods by which a repressive government with little intellectual appeal can rely on support from a diverse group of opinion influencers. The end product goes beyond the occasional newspaper article that gives prominent feature to Beijing's perspective. Far more significant, it is a reason that successive presidential candidates have talked tough on China during campaigns only to lead administrations that were weak on China. For example, Bill Clinton ran for president in 1992 criticizing incumbent George H. W. Bush for coddling the "butchers of Beijing" who three years earlier had ordered their army's tanks and machine guns turned on their own people at the Tiananmen Square massacre and other gatherings across the country. Yet Clinton paved the way for Beijing to receive most-favored-nation trading status permanently, ending what had been a valuable annual debate on the activities of the Chinese government. (Clinton also benefitted from illegal Chinese contributions to his campaign in a scandal dubbed Chinagate.)[18]

Similarly, as a candidate George W. Bush talked of getting tougher on China and recognizing the country's government as a "strategic competitor."[19] By Bush's second term, his deputy secretary of state and informal China policy supremo was Robert Zoellick, who was widely regarded as one of the more pro-Beijing voices of the Republican foreign policy establishment. By the end of his term, Bush would enjoy the Olympic Games in Beijing without bothering to bring up Chinese human rights abuses, including a brutal crackdown in Tibet that had occurred a mere five months earlier.

The net effect is that the executive branch has never seen making life harder for the Chinese government as one of its missions, even though it could do so by peaceful means. Since the end of the Cold War, presidents of both parties have tacitly accepted the soothing theory of China's "peaceful rise," a term Beijing actually coined itself. The theory began to take hold not long after Chinese leader Deng Xiaoping called for "socialism with Chinese characteristics" in a tack away from the nation's past to allow for some market-based economic activity.

Certainly some in the U.S. and allied governments have taken a tough line on Beijing and wanted to press back harder. Each morning, the admiral in charge of U.S. Pacific Command at Pearl Harbor is briefed on "indications and warnings" that assess the condition of China's military. He commands a force sprawled around the world's largest geographic area that comprises men and women who presumably know which government in their area of responsibility is least helpful to the United States. A similar exercise fills a portion of the day for the head of the U.S. Cyber Command, a general who concurrently runs the tech-heavy National Security Agency at Fort Meade, Maryland. Neither man can trust in Beijing's serene promises, especially since they see evidence to the contrary each and every day.

However, even in these provinces of government, where men and women are paid to focus on the China threat, the long reach of the "China hands" in the foreign policy establishment is felt. The man selected to run Pacific Command is often pointedly not someone who speaks in clear terms about the threat from China's unelected government and rapidly improving military. Many of today's more politically polished flag officers view the concept of a straight-talking general similar to those of the Cold War and earlier days as exotic. The four-star admiral who sits in Honolulu is often someone who talks of cooperation with China. Certainly that was the case with Adm. William Fallon, who held the job from 2005 to 2007. After retiring, Fallon told a journalist, "There were people who warned me that you'd better get ready for the shoot 'em up here because sooner or later we're going to be at war with China. I don't think that's where we want to go. And so I set about challenging all the assumptions."[20]

This account implies a false choice between being on a war footing or maintaining pleasant relations. It also deprecates both the importance of deterring bad actors with a well-equipped military and making plainly clear to other governments that actions have consequences. Furthermore, Fallon was almost certainly embellishing, as no one in a senior position in a Pentagon consumed at the time by the Iraq War would have pined for "the shoot 'em up" with China. Unfortunately, even the one U.S. government employee who should have been least interested in happy talk about China was trying to seem enlightened by Washington establishment standards. Even in what was widely regarded as a hawkish administration — that of George W. Bush — it was not acceptable to be seen devising ways to tamper with the gears of China's own smart power.

Matters at Pacific Command would grow worse still in the years after

Fallon. Adm. Samuel J. Locklear III, who assumed the position of commander in 2012, was asked in March 2013 to name the biggest threat in his area of responsibility. A logical choice for the lifelong sailor would have been China with honorable mentions for North Korea and Islamist terrorist groups in parts of Southeast Asia. Instead, America's chief warrior in Asia and the Pacific fingered climate change.[21]

Sill, at least in parts of the military, some are willing to talk realistically about Beijing and see what is a plainly visible emerging threat. The average field-grade officer (i.e., senior but below the rank of general or admiral) typically lacks a sanguine view of the Chinese military. Elsewhere in the U.S. government, matters are worse. The State Department's China desk is reputed throughout Washington as a repository of what are known in the business as "panda huggers," or analysts and operators who are loyal to the United States but awfully sympathetic to Beijing. Members of the desk are always eager for smooth relations with Beijing and generally resist statements and policies that involve getting tougher on that government. They are most effective at dulling the routine matters that make up most of diplomacy, such as daily press statements, speeches by mid-level officials, and what gets said and done in meetings below the presidential level between the two governments.

If one attempts to assert a hard line on China's abuses of human rights, intellectual property rights, or the rights of neighboring countries, a member of the China desk will reliably refuse to assent. Then one is left with the choice of either compromising or appealing to the secretary of state or other very senior officials at the department, but one can only do so sparingly if one wishes to keep access to those officials. The problem is nothing new, nor is it confined only to the China desk. Senator Jesse Helms joked as far back as 1980 "that the State Department has a 'desk' for every country in the world except for the United States of America. Ronald Reagan's first priority should be to establish an 'American Desk' at the State Department."[22]

Toward the end of the George W. Bush administration, those of us working on problems stemming from the misconduct of the Chinese government had grown bemused by the mentality that Helms lamented. The Bureau of East Asian and Pacific Affairs, of which the China desk is a part, was increasingly emboldened to oppose any negative mention of China or North Korea amid unrealistic expectations of breakthroughs with those governments. A few of us in the trenches decided to host an occasional happy hour and called it "panda spankers," meaning to bring a bit of levity to those who had to deal with the panda huggers in the building. Deputy Secretary of State Zoellick provided a nice stage prop for us when he went to China for an official visit, donned a surgical gown that presented a singularly strange image, and was photographed literally hugging a baby panda at a zoo. The panda appeared to share our bemusement at the situation. We promptly had stickers made of the picture-perfect shot and wore them on our lapels during a subsequent Panda Spankers happy hour. Some of the stickers made their way back into the State Department and onto phones and other discreet locations that might bring a smile to the occasional passerby. Some three years after leaving the agency I heard from a friend that a staffer hired in the subsequent administration asked if an event so "disrespectful of China" had indeed taken place.

High jinks aside, U.S. taxpayers ought to be concerned that so much of what they fund to keep them safe from foreign threats is so heavily compromised and not by a conspiracy but by a consensus of intellectual opinion cultivated with great care. This development is an impressive feat of smart power, especially considering Beijing lacks the fellow travelers in the West who once gave the benefit of the doubt to the Soviet Union during the Cold War. Typically they were intellectuals who refused to see the reality of communism in practice. Beijing, meanwhile, has accomplished far more with far less.

The Chinese government also does not confine its use of smart power to potentially worrisome instrumentalities of the U.S. government in Washington. It is also bent on one of the oldest and most important tasks of repressive governments seeking to maintain their power — namely, censoring independent media. Visitors to China, including some U.S. government officials, typically fail to appreciate the extent of censorship. They often stay at five-star hotels in Beijing and Shanghai that cater to foreign visitors. Guests can flip on the TV and see foreign cable news channels. On more than one occasion at the State Department, government officials cited this "openness" to me as proof that claims of censorship in China are overblown. In addition, the average man on the street in China's eastern cities is free to gripe about government officials and corruption. Is this not freedom of the press and freedom of the speech?

Certainly it is not. If one ventures beyond those foreigner-oriented hotels, access to independent media drops precipitously. Even those foreign news channels are subject to blackout when sensitive topics arise. China Central Television (CCTV), China's broadcaster, cut away from live coverage of President Obama's 2008 inaugural address during a portion of the speech of which it disapproved.[23] While complaining about the government in China through word of mouth in a small group may not get one sent to a reeducation-through-labor camp as it may have in darker days, any effort to distribute dissent to an audience of more than a few people is met with instant government opposition. This political control includes censorship of items as trivial as a blog entry or posting on an Internet comment board. Bill Clinton said in March 2000 that Chinese efforts to censor the Internet were like "nailing Jell-O to a wall." Yet by the end of that decade, China's army of web censors armed with the latest Western technology had succeeded at doing so.[24]

Beijing is particularly concerned with politically oriented content in the Chinese language. A company providing precisely that subject matter came to my attention at the State Department as the Chinese government was attempting to knock it off the air. New Tang Dynasty (NTD) TV is run by American citizens of Chinese descent and has its main newsroom in New York. It broadcasts in Mandarin Chinese and focuses on a combination of independent news and traditional, pre-communist Chinese culture — neither of which are in vogue among China's leaders. NTD also highlights corruption and other stories that embarrass Beijing. Launched in 2001, the channel is credited with breaking the news on the emergence of severe acute respiratory syndrome, known as SARS, weeks before the Chinese government admitted to the world that a new communicable disease was afoot.[25]

The attempt to censor NTD was telling of both Beijing's effort to control information and Washington's reticence in confronting Beijing directly. It proved a case study in China's prowess at smart power and America's current shortcomings in the field. Chinese authorities never would have allowed NTD to be broadcast on ordinary, terrestrial television transmitters. Instead, the nonprofit company reached audiences in China through satellite broadcasts. This technology took advantage of the shrinking size and cost of satellite-receiver dishes.

Measuring the audience NTD reached at the time was difficult, but it was significant enough to anger Beijing. NTD was carried by the W5 satellite owned and operated by Eutelsat, a French company.[26] The satellite has several steerable beams, one of which was nearly ideal for NTD to reach a broad audience across most of China. However, as a result of Chinese government pressure, Eutelsat began an effort to drop NTD. Rather than state that the reason was a corporate decision to curry favor with China's government, the company instead claimed it was moving the beam for solely commercial reasons. This change seemed improbable since it involved moving the satellite's focus from a heavily populated and increasingly wealthy area to one much less so. Furthermore, media reports noted communications indicating the Chinese government was using substantial pressure and efforts to bring lucrative Chinese state business to Eutelsat.[27] Ironically, one of the satellite company's largest customers was the U.S. government — namely, the Pentagon, which has a massive need for classified and unclassified satellite communications.

A source close to NTD informed me that an enterprising Defense Department official had reminded the satellite company of this fact to stave off a previous effort to dump the anti-Beijing broadcast in 2005. On this round, the satellite company's friends preemptively brought the issue to the State Department, going first to the agency's commercial and regional bureaus, which would have the least interest in embarrassing either the Chinese government or a powerful French company. The effort almost worked this time. However, grassroots and nongovernmental organizations' support for NTD, which echoed from Capitol Hill down to the State Department, elevated the issue out of the hands of ordinary bureaucrats.

Rather than confront the Chinese government or the French company directly, the U.S. government took the less confrontational path of calling Eutelsat's bluff. With strong congressional backing, the International Broadcasting Bureau, which handles civilian broadcasts funded by the U.S. government, simply shifted some of the content it was already placing in East Asian markets onto the satellite and thus removed the commercial argument for moving the beam. This modification bought NTD a few extra years.

By 2008, as Washington's interest in Chinese human rights generally declined, Eutelsat dumped NTD.[28] Although NTD lives on, the company and others similar to it continue to face Beijing's concerted efforts to suppress them, regardless of whether the independent media companies target Chinese inside China or Chinese expatriate populations around the globe.[29]

Throughout the saga, the satellite company maintained it was simply making commercial decisions. In an indirect way, this statement ironically was true. In mid-2012, Eutelsat announced that China's sovereign wealth fund — controlled by the Chinese government — was taking an equity stake in the company.[30] Eutelsat never admitted it was being pressured by Beijing.

In many respects, Washington refuses even to engage in the increasingly complex and effective war of ideas and information — essentially a smart power fight — that its enemies are waging. For example, China's state mouthpiece, CCTV, is welcomed on many cable, satellite, and other media platforms in the United States. Yet Beijing does not reciprocate with governmental and independent media from America and even jams the signals of some U.S. government broadcasts. Beijing limits the number of U.S. movies that can be shown in China and uses the leverage created by this restriction to force movie studios to censor content Beijing does not like.[31] Overall, this situation and the NTD episode serve as a case study in how far America's adversaries have come in the communications and information portion of the smart power spectrum. Their efforts are far more sophisticated than the simpler propaganda images and broadcasts that marked the ideological fights of the twentieth century. The Chinese are the best at this campaign in the world, but they are far from alone. Furthermore, Washington fares little better with its other opponents.

CHAPTER 5

Islamist Political Warfare

A quote often attributed to the nineteenth-century French poet Charles Baudelaire could sum up the lamentable situation with Islamists today: "The greatest trick the devil ever pulled was convincing the world he doesn't exist." More than a decade after the 9/11 attacks on the United States, many Americans and others around the world who support a civilized order do not fully grasp the political force that motivated the attackers that day. Furthermore, they do not necessarily know the important linkages between those attackers and other violent and nonviolent political actors in the Middle East and elsewhere who share a similar vision. However, most Americans still have better instincts on the nature of the problem and its possible solutions than the Washington foreign policy establishment does.

Much of the current thinking about terrorism understandably took shape in the weeks after 9/11. Almost immediately, Western leaders stressed that they were not at war with Muslims or Arabs at large. President George W. Bush said repeatedly that the effort the United States and its allies mounted was "not a war with Islam" and that "Islam is a religion of peace." At the end of September, Bush remarked, "The terrorists are traitors to their own faith, trying, in effect, to hijack Islam itself. The enemy of America is not our many Muslim friends; it is not our many Arab friends. Our enemy is a radical network of terrorists, and every government that supports them."[1] This perspective set out what would become the overriding theme of governmental efforts against terrorists for the rest of the decade. It presented a picture that was factual. However, it did not provide the whole picture.

After all, the hijackers who attacked America on 9/11 were all Muslims, and their benefactor and mastermind, Osama bin Laden, was a Muslim who believed in replacing the status quo in the Middle East with a Muslim theocratic empire, or caliphate. One of his priorities was to cleanse Saudi Arabia, the land of his birth, of infidels — namely, U.S. military forces stationed there at the time. Likewise, the Taliban government of Afghanistan that harbored bin Laden and refused to surrender him practiced a most severe form of Islam that rejected any semblance of modernity.

In retrospect, it would have been preferable if the president had explained that two distinct but overlapping elements were at work here — Islam and Islamism. The former is the religion of nearly a quarter of the world's population; the latter is a political ideology whose central tenet is unifying government and Islam and is advocated by a small subset of Muslims. The American people and allied publics, along with their governments, could have benefitted from grasping the appeal to many not only of Islam but of Islamism as well. This situational awareness is a necessary precursor of a strategy to influence Islam and undermine Islamism.

Instead, leaders across the political spectrum and around the globe essentially cast the terrorists as heretics in Islam or, more frequently, as "extremists." In his address to a joint session of Congress nine days after the attacks on New York and Washington, Bush said that "terrorists practice a fringe form of Islamic extremism."[2] Across the Atlantic, British prime minister Tony Blair took a similar approach, especially when addressing the then-common European belief that solving Israeli-Palestinian disputes would take away the causes of terrorism: "And I also believe that the extremists, the fanatics that carried out these attacks, frankly they're the enemies of the peace process."[3] A report in 2005 noted the Bush administration was going to stress the extremist angle further still, noting senior officials referencing "a global struggle against violent extremism" rather than "the global war on terror."[4]

Obviously, anyone who straps on a suicide belt or commits any of the other now-familiar acts of terrorists is an extremist. However, missing from this description is the intent and motivation of those who carry out the attacks. Also lacking is an explanation of these groups' other activities and how they might impact the United States and its allies. If terrorists are the tip of the spear, what constitutes the rest of the spear?

The leaders who cited "extremists" as culprits in the struggle that became apparent on 9/11 certainly made an understandable decision in choosing their description. From the perspective of making a succinct statement of mission to the public — an important trait among leaders of democracies in particular — politicians do not have the luxury of going on at great length about complex issues. The same holds true in the selection of the name "war on terror." The war that began on 9/11, and continues in some form, was a war on terrorism only in the sense that World War II was a war on kamikazes, buzz bombs, and U-boats. Those elements were all part of the war, but they neither served as motivating factors in the war nor encompassed the enemies' strategy or objective. They were a tactical feature of strategy. So too is terror: it is a tactic of a group that has a larger political objective. This distinction matters because while one can often hold an enemy's preferred tactic at bay, one cannot bring a conflict to a successful conclusion until the enemy's strategic objective is made impossible. Even then, much work typically remains.

What is unfortunate is that U.S. and allied leaders never succeeded at evolving this discussion with the public, especially after the turning point that was presented when the Taliban government, which was most associated with the 9/11 attacks, was deposed. Furthermore, while it is forgivable that busy leaders and the general public cannot concern themselves with highly detailed ruminations on the nature of an enemy, it is not forgivable that the national security apparatus in Washington and allied capitals failed to give this effort proper consideration. Those bureaucracies and institutions exist to do what individual Americans and senior officials cannot do by themselves. They should have illuminated in greater detail what Islamism was, how it motivated the 9/11 attackers, and how those attackers were but the terrorist vanguard of the latest despotic political ideology to challenge freedom and the rule of law.

BUSH AND KUMBAYA

Unfortunately, the part of the U.S. government theoretically most responsible for this educational effort was inherently dysfunctional. Even if senior government officials had performed to the best of their abilities — and they did not — they would have failed. Understanding and influencing political developments outside of war zones should theoretically fall to the State Department. In that agency, especially regarding the contest of ideas that takes place among foreign populations, the work falls to the undersecretary for public diplomacy and public affairs. The position was created only in the late 1990s when Congress terminated the U.S. Information Agency. On 9/11, the official inhabiting the position was Charlotte Beers, a former Madison Avenue advertising executive. This personnel decision was understandable if the job was putting an appealing or at least snazzy veneer on U.S. foreign policy but not if the job was understanding and fighting a political ideology. Beers was gone by the time a bipartisan commission reported to Congress and the secretary of state that "at a critical time in our nation's history, the apparatus of public diplomacy has proven inadequate, especially in the Arab and Muslim world."[5]

The Bush administration would have three more undersecretaries before its end. Each arrived after long gaps between service owing to personal reasons or the lengthy amount of time it often takes the Senate to act on nominations of senior officials below the cabinet level. Each had relatively short tenures. The most notable was Karen Hughes, Bush's communications director during his successful 2000 run for president. In theory, Hughes could have been great. She had the ear of the president and could thus scare the entrenched bureaucracy at the State Department. While that bureaucracy looks down upon many political appointees, whom it views as amateurs or hacks in search of stately sinecures, someone with Hughes's political skills — or a Democrat with her credentials for that matter — would generally have more sense in understanding and manipulating a foreign political movement than do the State Department lifers who work in this area.

Unfortunately, Hughes pursued what some of us at the Department referred to unofficially as the kumbaya approach. This strategy basically involves trying to put an appealing face on U.S. actions and American culture rather than looking at creative ways to put an adversary on the defensive. Hughes undertook what she called listening tours in the Middle East and in Muslim-majority countries elsewhere in the world. Before her first trip, she helpfully explained that her agenda would be based on four *E*s: "engage, exchange, educate and empower."[6] This approach basically holds that America needs to appear more mindful of interests and sensitivities of people around the globe and to overcome what is presumed to be a lack of understanding of America in these foreign cultures. A common refrain among advocates of existing government broadcasting efforts is that foreign publics — especially in Muslim-majority countries — are turned off by the coarse and corrupt America that Hollywood portrays. The U.S. government ought to undertake efforts to correct this impression, taking care to stress America's compassion, liberty, tolerance, and inclusiveness, all while somehow empowering those abroad who have more enlightened and sympathetic views. Partly at the instigation of Hughes, special care was taken to point out that Americans were free to practice Islam or any other religion without state interference or harassment.

While explaining America to the world separate from Hollywood or hostile foreign media has some utility, this tactic misses the main point. Specifically, it ignores the roots of Islamism and grossly overestimates the positive effect of statements from U.S. officials. First of all, whether they are merely adherents to the political idea of Islamism or they have taken the additional leap of supporting terrorism, Islamists generally know a great deal about America. Sometimes this impression is skewed, but other times it is accurate. Unfortunately, the more Islamists learn about America, the more they hate America. The big problem with the kumbaya approach is that it does nothing to address this issue. Generally, Islamists are merely revolted by America's liberties and libertine culture. What they find particularly enraging is the very tolerance Hughes and others were touting and especially the idea that someone can choose a religion or depart from it as if it were a hobby.

Of course, Americans should not be discouraged or dissuaded by Islamists' disapproval. However, they should understand that preaching the virtues of democratic societies and tolerance to this particular group will be ineffective. Neither the Islamists nor those flirting with the ideology are going to flip to the other side of the political spectrum as a result of knowing America better.

Furthermore, Muslims have to be the ones arguing against Islamism from within Muslim culture. English-speaking U.S. diplomats attempting this argument while also trying to put the best face on U.S. foreign policy face an impossible mission. Hughes — and by extension the State Department and Bush White House — did not appear to grasp this fact. Thus, the political force that gave rise to 9/11 and that motivates and unifies Islamic terrorists around the globe was largely off the radar of policymakers in Washington. At times, they used the terms "radical Muslims" or "fundamentalist Muslims" to describe adversaries. But even these terms miss the mark, as fundamentalist Muslims in remote areas who are not active politically and not providing support to terrorists ought to be of little interest to the U.S. government. Conversely, moderate-seeming and modern-acting Muslims who support Islamism and work to undermine allied governments ought to be of considerable interest to Uncle Sam.

It is not even clear whether Hughes understood Islamism or knew of the existence and activities of Islamist political actors beyond high-profile terrorists groups like al Qaeda. On a trip to Egypt in 2005, Hughes was asked if she would meet with the Muslim Brotherhood, a question that she should have anticipated given intense Egyptian interest about the then-banned Islamist group. Hughes looked confused, and an aide ventured that Hughes "would be respectful of Egyptian law."[7] This reply meant no. Without knowing much about the Brotherhood, it seems unlikely Hughes would have thought about how to help those who had a less repressive vision for the Middle East, including the many secularists in Egypt who opposed both Islamism and the nondemocratic Mubarak government.

Hughes and her support staff had other problems. Most undersecretaries fly commercial except in unusual circumstances. Hughes preferred government aircraft. On her initial tours she traveled on the military equivalent of Boeing 737 and 757 jetliners usually used by top military commanders, the First Lady, the vice president, or others whose positions or special missions require large staffs or security details. Later, she flew on one of only two Coast Guard Gulfstream Vs (G-Vs), which are usually used by the commandant of that service or the secretary of homeland security. It was one of few military aircraft kept at Reagan National Airport, which is more convenient to the State Department than Andrews Air Force Base in Maryland, where most of the white and robin-egg-blue aircraft emblazoned with "United States of America" were based. Her staff referred to the G-V as "our plane." Eventually, word circulated that the White House had grown wary of the requests and their associated cost and began turning them down. Hughes did not stay much longer.

Hughes had arrived full time at the State Department some fifteen months after her predecessor announced her resignation in April 2004.[8] During the long interims between Senate-confirmed undersecretaries being on the job in the public diplomacy front office — and even at times when one was on the job — noticeably not much was happening. For a job that a senator would later say should be "the supreme allied commander in the war of ideas," there did not seem to be much commanding taking place, despite the ongoing desperate struggles in the broader Middle East to which the United States was a party.[9] We used to observe consistently throughout the Bush administration that the lights in that office often went off promptly at five o'clock, which was uncommon behavior for the seventh floor, where the secretary of state and her top officials worked under a sense that the United States was at war. One weekend I was working in an annex suite that our office shared with some of the public diplomacy staff. I came across an unusually large stack of paper left on a shared printer. To my amusement, a staff member had printed off a novel he was writing and neglected to retrieve before departing on Friday. I was happy that someone found that office useful. The book was pretty good.

After another long interim period, Hughes was succeeded by James Glassman, who was the first and only undersecretary for public diplomacy to see the job as being part of a "battle of ideas," or a gentler reference to political warfare and its place in smart power. He noted after his arrival that "people frequently see my job as winning a beauty contest or an 'American Idol' vote. I disagree with that. My job is to help achieve the national interest, not necessarily by making America more popular."[10] Unfortunately, Glassman was sworn in with only six months and ten days left in the Bush administration. At that point bureaucrats with lifetime employment generally start ignoring the short-timers in political positions.

Those who have held the undersecretary position in the Obama administration reverted to the kumbaya approach. In laying out her vision in June 2012, Undersecretary Tara Sonenshine declared: "We also believe in a world without violence. We believe that personal security is linked to national security, and national security is linked to global security. And so we work every day for a world that is not torn apart by division, intolerance, hostility, and violence."[11] That vision sounds lovely, but one could infer from it that Ms. Sonenshine represented an office that did not understand basic human nature or world history, which have always been — and always will be — marked by those unfortunate things. Furthermore, her remarks shed no evidence on having any clear goals and plans to influence political forces abroad, much less the desire to command a side in a war of ideas.

POLITICAL CORRECTNESS

Unfortunately, the problems of those who should be coordinating smart power against Islamists went beyond a few poor personnel decisions and a dysfunctional office made worse by delays in getting the Senate to confirm executive branch officials — although those deficiencies certainly did not help matters. Another force was at work and remains so today. A strong feeling in Washington says that confronting Islamism sounds too much like confronting Islam. This perception is reinforced by certain groups that highlight what they perceive to be attacks on American Muslims. Chief among these organizations is the Council for American-Islamic Relations (CAIR).

Critics of CAIR assert that the group labels anyone who expresses concern over Islamic or Islamist practices as "Islamophobic." For example, they have noted instances where a CAIR chapter said the California legislature's call for state funds not to be used to advance anti-Semitism "contributes to a climate of intimidation faced by Muslim and Arab students on California campuses." This claim seems improbable on many levels, not the least of which is the California's schools' insistence on tolerating almost everything.[12] The Department of Justice listed CAIR as an unindicted coconspirator in the government's prosecution of a foundation for providing material support to the terrorist group Hamas.[13] However, in the years after 9/11, hundreds of federal law enforcement and intelligence officials were required to attend Muslim sensitivity training sessions run by CAIR.[14] The Justice Department eventually ended its linkage with CAIR's main office, but the Obama administration nonetheless responded favorably in 2011 to a call by CAIR and the closely aligned Muslim Public Affairs Council to remove all references to Islam from terror-training material used by federal officials.[15]

Despite the relative decline in fortune of CAIR, others remain willing to cast aspersions on those who would take a different approach to Islamism. For example, the Center for American Progress, a left-leaning think tank, released a report in 2011 that tried to link anti-Islamists in the United States to Norwegian mass murderer Anders Breivik and stated that "a small group of foundations and wealthy donors are the lifeblood of the Islamophobia network in America, providing critical funding to a clutch of right-wing think tanks that peddle hate and fear of Muslims and Islam." Among the foundations cited in the report was the Bradley Foundation, which is indeed regarded as conservative. The foundation also has contributed handsomely to nonconservative organizations like Boston University and Duke University.[16]

Such reports do not silence those who are already outspoken on Islamism and who already seek policies that see Islamism in a different light. However, they do send a message to career officials in the U.S. government — most of whom view controversy and public attention as detrimental to career advancement — that appearing tough on Islamism may be regarded as Islamophobic and is needlessly troublesome.

Senior government officials have also noted that political correctness has impeded better policy toward Islamists. In his memoir *Known and Unknown*, Bush's first secretary of defense, Donald Rumsfeld, wrote: "From the beginning, members of the administration worked gingerly around the obvious truth that our main enemies were Islamic extremists. I didn't think we could fight the crucial ideological aspect of the war if we were too wedded to political correctness to acknowledge the facts honestly."[17]

As a result, the major political force behind one of the biggest threats to America and its allies was largely ignored, not only in the frenzied early period after 9/11, but also in the years that followed. It continues to affect efforts today to differentiate the religion of Islam from the totalitarian political ideology that seeks to replace liberal governments with clerical governments and that includes in its ranks some people who support terrorists or who are terrorists themselves.

For those who wish to understand the struggle taking place in the Middle East and within Muslim communities around the world — a key prereq- uisite to using smart power to shape political outcomes within — it makes sense to go back to the basics. In other words, one should surmount not only inhibitions stemming from political correctness but also the emotional and distracting controversies of the past decade over such matters as the wars in Afghanistan and Iraq and how best to collect intelligence and deal with detained terrorists. Understanding how both Islam and Islamism arrived at their present condition is crucial if those who favor a civilized order in the world are to push back successfully on Islamism using nonviolent means. Grasping the nature of this ideology is equally as important as was under- standing communism and its appeal during the Cold War.

The vast majority of Muslims are peaceful, accept the idea of coexist- ing with people who practice other religions, and oppose both Islamism and terrorism. However, the Muslim religion has provided a vehicle for a revolutionary political ideology that is at once radical, totalitarian, and utopian. Why is this true of Islam in the twenty-first century, even as other religions have more or less departed from the political space?

A quarter of the world's population adheres to Islam, and Muslim- majority nations span the globe from Morocco to Central Asia to Indone- sia. While Indonesia is the world's most populous Muslim-majority state, Egypt is the most populous Arab country and was typically regarded as the intellectual and political center of what is often called the Muslim world. But the heart of Islam remains the geography from which the reli- gion sprang in the seventh century: classical Arabia, especially the Hejaz of modern Saudi Arabia and later the areas around the Persian Gulf and the Levant on the Mediterranean.

This region essentially entered the modern world during World War I. There, the British enlisted Arabs in a fight against their wartime enemy of the German-allied Ottoman Empire. After that war, in what some histo- rians refer to as the 1922 settlement, the modern Middle East took shape. One British soldier present at the creation of the new order and through- out the war was T. E. Lawrence, who was later made famous in print and film as "Lawrence of Arabia" for his exploits in aiding the wartime Arab rebellion. Lawrence was more of a historian and linguist than a soldier, although he had a notable affinity for the austerity of soldiering and certainly had a flair for adventure. In an era before modern political correctness and when those who held power in Muslim areas began radically broadening their political ambitions, Lawrence was able to capture the essence of being a Muslim in the geographic and political heart of Islam. Describing the nomadic Arabs with whom he fought, Lawrence wrote:

> In his life he had air and winds, sun and light, open spaces and a great emptiness. There was no human effort, no fecundity in Nature: just the heaven above and the unspotted earth beneath. There unconsciously he came near God. God was to him not anthropomorphic, not tangible, not mortal nor ethical, not concerned with the world or with him, not natural: but the being thus qualified not by divestiture but by investiture, a comprehending Being, the egg of all activity, with nature and matter just a glass reflecting Him.
>
> The Bedouin could not look for God within him: he was too sure that he was within God. He could not conceive anything which was or was not God, Who alone was great; yet there was a homeliness, an everyday-ness of this climactic Arab God, who was their eating and their fighting and their lusting, the commonest of their thoughts, their familiar resource and companion, in a way impossible to those whose God is so wistfully veiled from them by despair of their carnal unworthiness of Him and by the decorum of formal worship. Arabs felt no incongruity in bringing God into the weaknesses and appetites of their least creditable causes. He was the most familiar of their words.[18]

This passage is simply one description, and a florid one at that. But it captures one highly observant man's assessment of Islam's most politically consequential practitioners at a critical time and offers a type of description that probably would be off limits to academics and officials attempting to illuminate matters today. From it, one can glimpse a religion that approached God and man differently than other religions have, at least at the retail level of its rank-and-file adherents. Whether it is the result of history, geography, language, or other factors is beyond the scope of this book, but an unmistakable implication is that Muslims at this pivotal time in history were less inclined than their contemporaries of other religions to separate worldly issues from spiritual ones. Thus, far more than with Christian, Jewish, Hindu, Buddhist, or other religions, Islam was a greener pasture for a political ideology that combined temporal and spiritual issues and bucked the trend of secularization that by then had swept the rest of the world.

From this fertile ground, modern Islamism began to sprout in the twentieth century. Its true maturation came from Egypt, then the political and cultural center of Islam. There, the Muslim Brotherhood developed in opposition to successive governments. It offered an alternative to modernity and gradually westernizing society. Islamism was fueled in particular by the failure of decolonization to deliver its promises. As Great Britain and France hauled down their flags across the Middle East and Africa, local populations believed their circumstances would improve dramatically with their new self-rule. Unfortunately, progress was uneven or absent. Such cities as Cairo and Damascus grew into metropolises with modern industries and modern-looking populations; however, dictators or strongmen often replaced the colonialist governments. While the Middle East theoretically remained a bastion of market economies during the face-off between communism and capitalism, most of the economies were highly corrupt and dysfunctional. One got ahead not on merit but on privilege. This graft resulted in a political and economic disgruntlement that has been easy for Islamists to exploit.

This key point is often missed in the rest of the world. Americans and others can rightly look at life under the Taliban in Afghanistan or the clerics and morality police of Iran and conclude that only a small cohort of extremists could find this system appealing. That is true; moreover, intellectual classes around the globe do not take to Islamism in the way some did to communism or other utopian ideologies in previous times. But for some of the poor and powerless in Muslim areas, the law as meted out by Sharia courts can seem more just than what is currently on offer.

Today, one can find more instances than in the past of Muslim and Arab governments that are responsive to the will of their people. Yet this picture also remains mixed. For some, power allocated through religious systems can seem equally or more just than the status quo. Finally, for some, Islamism offers a return to a nobler state of existence than what has existed in most Muslim-majority areas for centuries. Harkening to an Islamic caliphate that once rivaled European culture and achievement but long ago passed into history, Islamism offers a false promise of restored economic, cultural, scientific, military, and artistic prosperity. Political Islam can be an avenue to respect for some. So can becoming a radical imam or other cleric. Indeed, in some Muslim-majority nations, this religious leadership position is the one of very few paths to respect for a repressed and impoverished population.

Grasping these factors is a prerequisite to effective statecraft toward the Middle East and Muslim populations elsewhere. Through this knowledge, one can see that U.S. officials sent on listening tours to preach the virtues of American tolerance and liberal culture will have an extremely limited impact. One can also see that terrorism is but the preferred tool and vanguard of a much broader political force. Dealing with that political force is what is required for lasting security. The first step — which surprisingly many among the Washington foreign policy establishment have yet to take — is recognizing and understanding the existence of Islamism.

All of the major political forces in the world that challenge the United States and its allies — the governments of China and Iran, and Islamism — are highly adept at smart power and political warfare. The Chinese government has convinced much of the world of its inevitable "peaceful rise" even as it wages cyber and economic war and conducts a stunning military buildup amid diplomatic aggression. Islamists have cowed intellectuals, officials, and others into silence or even into believing that Islamism does not exist as a potent political force in the world. The ascendancy of both threats rests on illusions held in Washington and other allied capitals. Still more illusions exist in those cities, and they can kill.

CHAPTER 6

Five Deadly Illusions

The Chinese diplomats were waiting for us at the hotel lounge. I was not enthusiastic about the meeting, which I had noticed on my calendar that morning at the State Department. When our office's special assistant had scheduled it sometime before, I had recalled previous visits to the Washington property of this particular esteemed hotel chain, where I had noticed a clientele awash in designer clothes and cologne that created an overall atmosphere that one might describe as Moscow on the Potomac. It seemed appropriately unpleasant for the conversation I was about to have.

ILLUSION I: CHINA IS NOT AN ADVERSARY

We had a serious beef with the Chinese government. At the time, I was focusing my efforts on policies and programs to help refugees fleeing North Korea's dictatorship to reach freedom and on getting independent information and news into North Korea. These difficult tasks were the major efforts of my then-boss Jay Lefkowitz. President Bush had endorsed the efforts without hesitation when Lefkowitz presented them in the Oval Office. Aside from the North Korean regime itself, the biggest obstacle was the Chinese government. Rather than allowing refugees to pass harmlessly and quietly to South Korea or other nations willing to accept them — including the United States under Bush — China forcibly expelled the refugees it caught back to North Korea. Doing so, which was in violation of an international convention China had signed, subjected the refugees to punishment ranging from imprisonment to torture and death. China also refused to cooperate with any measures to break the North Korean regime's Orwellian censorship — a key method of sustaining dictatorship — that it imposed on its people.

I was skeptical that any progress could come from the meeting with the Chinese diplomats. By that time, Lefkowitz and Undersecretary Paula Dobriansky had grown wary of making trips to China, where no real progress was likely. Beijing would tout such meetings as signs of success and recognition of Beijing's position, but China conceded little and refused even to discuss sensitive issues with any degree of candor. I too had had my fill of transpacific flights when nothing concrete was in the offing.

The Chinese political officers stood grinning as I entered the cafe with my colleague, John Kachtik. How many times had they entertained guests here who lapped up their promises of a peaceful rise and their complaints about how their government's aggressive conduct was being misunderstood or misrepresented?

As I expected, the meeting went nowhere fast. The Chinese had rehearsed their standard line that the refugees were "economic migrants" who could be sent back across the border in the same way illegal immigrants might be repatriated from the United States. We noted this description was inconsistent with any accepted definition of what a refugee really is. Furthermore, a convention Beijing had ratified allows a UN high commissioner, not the Chinese government, to decide who is a refugee.

I thought the meeting was coming to a fruitless end when the real fun began. The senior diplomat of the two asked me about comments Lefkowitz had recently made linking the mistreatment of refugees to the upcoming Beijing Olympics. Lefkowitz had simply observed, "As the world's attention turns to China for the 2008 Olympics, does anyone seriously believe a massive, abused and imperiled refugee population will go unnoticed?"[1] I knew this matter was a sensitive one for Beijing. The Olympics were to be that government's coming-out party and a symbol that China was finally a world power. Long gone would be the memories of the murderous decades of the earlier communist era and the 1989 Tiananmen Square massacre. But Lefkowitz's hitting them on a sensitive issue to get their attention was the whole point and apparently one that many at the State Department did not understand, as they preferred sweet talk despite its unimpressive record of accomplishment when Beijing was involved. When the Chinese diplomat raised Lefkowitz's comment, I knew immediately what he had in mind but waited for him to explain it in laborious detail nonetheless.

Then came the big question, which was presumably the reason they had sought the meeting in the first place: "We are curious if when Lefkowitz says this, he is speaking for himself or if this is policy, because we heard he was just expressing his own opinion." I instantly recognized the work of our China desk at the State Department, and perhaps their colleagues on the Korea desk, who had not missed the opportunity to undercut Bush's envoy on this matter by suggesting he was speaking out of turn. In crafting my response, it entered my mind that the "Chicoms," as the Chinese communists were known in a simpler time, were not completely incorrect. After all, while Bush had accepted Lefkowitz's views on dealing with North Korea, the president also had accepted a plan his second-term secretary of state, Condoleezza Rice, had devised to try to cajole and then bribe North Korea out of its aspirations to develop nuclear weapons. While it is quite possible to negotiate an arms agreement without discarding human rights issues — as Ronald Reagan proved with the Soviets — Rice tacitly rejected such an approach. Bush also seemed willing to accept insincere Chinese promises to cooperate on any number of issues, including on North Korea. Furthermore, Lefkowitz had never bothered to clear his remarks about the Olympics through the State Department's bureaucracy, knowing both that they would never be approved and that the White House would back him regardless. Of course, the latter point is what really mattered since he was there to serve a president and not a bureaucracy.

In the end, I figured there was no reason either to reinforce Beijing's belief it was winning this one by dividing the U.S. executive branch or to needlessly put my Chicom coffee hosts at ease. I replied, "Well, Lefkowitz is the president's envoy for this issue, so if he says it publicly, then it's policy."

The response was amusing. The junior diplomat turned sharply to see the reaction of his senior colleague, whose hands by that time had begun to shake — something I chalked up to reasonably good acting. His now-shrill voice cut through the genteel air of the hotel and drew glances from more than a few Russians and other transatlantic tourists in their designer clothes: "Well, if that's true, then you're going to be hearing from someone a lot more senior than me! These are not just China Olympics! They are world Olympics! They are not right place to bring up issue like this!"

To finish it off, they treated us to repetitive incantations of the slogan Beijing had chosen for the games: "One world, one dream! One world, one dream . . ." As they did, I was reminded of the Chinese government's love of big official events. Throughout the Bush administration, Beijing persistently requested that China's leader be allowed to make a formal state visit with full pomp and circumstance. Bush rightly resisted. Essentially this request was an exhibition of the insatiable thirst dictatorships have for staging events that make them look legitimate to some. We in the trenches sometimes summarized this phenomenon as "commies love pageantry."

We agreed to disagree and wound down the meeting. After I returned to the department, I sat and marveled at the position the Chinese government had achieved for itself in Washington. Essentially, Beijing could conduct itself however it pleased, misrepresent obvious facts, and yet rely on weak or sympathetic elites in Washington and other political and financial capitals to explain away its misconduct. The Chinese had some pushback from us, but they knew it mattered little. Collectively, the Washington foreign policy establishment has accepted that China's expansion will be peaceful as long as Washington and its allies do nothing to antagonize Beijing. It is an extremely dangerous illusion that might one day help bring about war on a scale thankfully not seen since the world wars. And it is not the only deadly illusion going around Washington.

ILLUSION 2: AL QAEDA IS THE ONLY REAL THREAT

The murder of U.S. ambassador Chris Stevens in Benghazi, Libya, on September 11, 2012, set off a political debate about foreign policy in the United States. It essentially was the only time foreign policy entered the 2012 presidential campaign in a major way. The Obama administration asserted from the beginning that the crisis was the product of spontaneous rage from a preview of an obscure anti-Muslim film that an ex-convict in California had made and released on the Internet. The same justification was also given for a concurrent invasion of the U.S. embassy grounds in Cairo, during which the American flag was burned and replaced by a black

Islamist flag. White House spokesman Jay Carney told gathered reporters two days after the attack that "I think it's important to note with regards to that protest that there are protests taking place in different countries across the world *that are responding to the movie that has circulated on the Internet* [emphasis in original]."[2]

Obama's opponents reacted immediately, saying the attackers were too heavily armed and well coordinated to have been the product of a spontaneous mob upset at a film clip few had seen. Some noted that the Libyan government itself promptly fingered Islamist terrorists who were a deadly minority of the remnant militias left over from Libya's civil war. Later, other information came to light that indicated the Libya attack had nothing to do with a film or an angry mob. Republican presidential candidate Mitt Romney pointed this out.

As the matter became a larger issue in the presidential campaign, some pundits and reporters began to question if al Qaeda launched the attack. On the flip side, the Obama administration appeared determined to avoid a conclusion that organized terrorists, much less al Qaeda, were involved. This possibility would have affected some of the major points of the Obama reelection effort — notably, "bin Laden is dead" and "the tide of war is receding" — that Obama's supporters often touted in the campaign.

On a news program the afternoon after the attack, I noted spontaneously that we should "wake up and smell the global jihad."[3] As President Obama's opponents looked for an organized terrorist culprit and an al Qaeda linkage, the Libyan people were one step ahead. Perhaps the most pro-American of any people in the Mediterranean outside of Israel, many ordinary Libyans were tired of lawless militias and incensed that the chief representative of the government that had helped liberate them had been murdered in their business capital. Ten days after Ambassador Stevens died, crowds of Libyans moved on the compound of the Ansar al-Sharia (Partisans of Islamic Law) brigade, which the Libyan people widely believed planned and executed the attack. Earlier, tens of thousands of Libyans had marched peacefully against the militias in general; now unarmed Libyans braved bullets to overrun the Ansar al-Sharia's compound and evict the militia from Benghazi.[4] In the following days, press reports began to indicate that the Islamist brigade was in touch with the nearest al Qaeda affiliate, known as al Qaeda in the Islamic Maghreb. Others noted that the group was basically al Qaeda rebranded for the Arab Spring.[5]

While any possible al Qaeda involvement in the assassination of a U.S. ambassador is no small matter, the search for an al Qaeda link not only missed the main point but also reinforced an illusion about terrorists and radical Islamists that has persisted since 9/11. Obviously, the group that murdered more than three thousand people on a single day and was a major element in the deadly Iraqi insurgency will always loom large in considering terrorism. However, plenty of other Islamist groups with only an incidental connection to al Qaeda are equally dangerous and detrimental to U.S. interests in the world. This myopic focus on al Qaeda is an additional by-product of Washington's failure to grasp and explain how to undermine the broader Islamist political movement. Furthermore, as the Arab Spring progressed, the nonviolent Islamists did more damage to U.S. interests, especially through political action in places like Egypt and Tunisia, than their terrorist brethren did. A hyper-focus on al Qaeda was missing the big picture.

The illusion has its convenient elements. U.S. Navy SEALS famously killed al Qaeda's founder on May 2, 2011. Numerous other al Qaeda leaders have either been killed or sent to the U.S.-run terrorist detention facility at Guantánamo Bay. What politician would not wish to tout these successes and chalk them up to progress in a conflict that has now lasted for more than a decade? Unfortunately, this emphasis can also lead some who want security and a civilized international order to lower their guard. It undercuts broader efforts to combat terrorists and causes people to ignore the political fellow travelers of terrorists. Further, any security deriving from these sanguine assumptions about progress would be illusory, and such presumptions set back the cause of U.S. smart power.

ILLUSION 3: ALLY NEGLECT SOFTENS ADVERSARIES

A frequent lamentation of those of us who worked on transnational issues — especially human rights — during the Bush administration, and perhaps throughout modern diplomatic history, concerned the extreme resistance career bureaucrats at the State Department have to criticizing adversarial foreign governments in a serious way. For example, not only was it difficult to obtain formal authorization to criticize China's government in private meetings between the two governments but also it was hard to do so in venues supposedly committed to human rights. In the now-defunct UN Human Rights Commission in Geneva, which met annually, the State Department declined in 2003 even to introduce a resolution criticizing Beijing for the dictatorship's abuse of its citizens and others.[6] The State Department repeated this performance in 2005, with a spokesman citing supposed "important and significant steps" toward reform in a decade when China actually grew worse at respecting human rights.[7]

The reason for not condemning such behavior is a die-hard belief that these difficult-to-solve and contentious issues interfere with the daily relations that most diplomats crave with any government, good or bad. This reluctance to criticize can stem from a desire among officials to maintain contacts in host governments who can provide information and approve meetings for visiting officials. Less forgivably, it can derive from what is known as "clientitis," or the condition where diplomats "go native" and take the point of view of the country they are visiting rather than the one they are being paid to represent. Weakness can also be a factor. Perhaps more than most other people, Americans have a strong desire to be liked by foreigners. It has probably always been the case and all the more so since the 1958 publication of Eugene Burdick and William Lederer's novel, The Ugly American. Set in Southeast Asia, the book highlighted supposed insensitivity toward foreign cultures and customs by traveling Americans in general and U.S. officials in particular. Since the Vietnam War era, Hollywood has repeatedly reinforced this view.

My own experience observing Americans abroad, admittedly more recent than 1958, has been the opposite. Instead, tourists, businesspeople, and officials from the United States devote more energy to appearing respectful abroad and to understanding foreigners than is typically reciprocated. But the forces that cause many U.S. officials to be meek and overly deferential still hold sway.

Unfortunately, no such reticence exists when it comes to criticizing allies. The governments that Washington elites often are most willing to doubt and treat abruptly are America's closest friends. This behavior is the result of a double standard and the illusion that keeping allies at arm's length may make adversaries behave better. Three democratic allies receive particularly bad treatment — Israel, Japan, and Taiwan — although they are not alone.

With Israel, an article of faith among the Washington foreign policy elite is that the Jewish state should be induced to make concessions in order to achieve a lasting peace with Palestinians and other countries in the region. Similarly, it is regarded as essential that the United States be the one to pressure Jerusalem to make any necessary concessions — even if they result only in the resumption of negotiations rather than a finalized peace agreement. In fact, stemming largely from this assumption, Israel is the only country in the world for which Washington refuses to recognize the local government's designated capital city. Israel's capital is Jerusalem, but the U.S. government refuses to acknowledge this fact and maintains its embassy in Tel Aviv. The reason is that the Palestinians would also like Jerusalem to be their capital. Rather than acknowledge the probability the Palestinians will never establish their capital there, Washington chooses instead to hold its ally to a double standard. When asked, White House spokesmen have refused to name Israel's capital. In 2012, a State Department announcement implied Jerusalem was not even a part of Israel.[8]

The capital city issue is only the tip of the iceberg. In 2011, Israel's prime minister paid a visit to Washington, President Obama delivered what was billed as a major speech. He called publicly for the first time for Israel to cede all the land it gained in the 1967 war, which Israel's enemies started, but Jerusalem views this land as critical to defending its tiny geography. Sandbagging an ally on the eve of a visit is a diplomatic faux pas; moreover, it is an act no recent U.S. administration would have been willing to commit even with an adversary. Furthermore, Obama did not even drive a hard bargain, as he failed to seek anything from the Palestinians or other governments in return for this new position more favorable to them. As such, his proposal amounted to charity for a group negotiating against a U.S. ally. Presumably Obama and his State Department thought the preemptive move either would prompt negotiations and lead to a peace deal or at least would make the United States look good. It accomplished neither.

The Obama administration was not the first to try this move. President Bill Clinton's administration devoted considerable time and effort to solving the Israeli-Palestinian dispute with a lasting peace agreement. The most notable round came near the end of Clinton's presidency in 2000, during a summit at the Camp David presidential retreat outside Washington. Although it had been the location of a historic peace agreement between Israel and Egypt in 1979, a repeat performance was not in the offing. Israel's prime minister Ehud Barak offered Palestinian strongman Yasser Arafat almost all of the land he demanded and some he had not, as well as generous financial assistance. Arafat rejected the proposal and made no counteroffer.[9] The obvious conclusion from this effort was that political conditions would not allow the Palestinians to achieve a reasonable settlement with Israel. As a result Washington should have seen that only two workable options existed — try to change the Palestinians' political circumstances or do nothing. Either choice meant allowing for the passage of time and refusing to get involved again in talks until political factors had clearly changed.

The George W. Bush administration held this view when it arrived in Washington. Unfortunately, administration officials gradually wavered. Less than a year before the 2008 presidential election, Secretary of State Condoleezza Rice convened the American, Israeli, and Palestinian heads of government in Annapolis, Maryland, to reach a peace agreement. At the time, Rice was groping for a positive legacy amid failures of her various initiatives involving North Korea, China, Iran, and Russia, and as the surge of U.S. forces in Iraq that Rice had opposed became a clear success.

Once again, the Israeli prime minister Ehud Olmert indicated a willingness to make new concessions. The Palestinian leader Mahmoud Abbas did not. Furthermore, foreigners understand as well as Americans how little power a two-term president has in his eighth and final year, especially one leaving office with low approval ratings of the sort Bush had. Thus, Bush's ability to cajole the parties at Rice's desultory gathering was highly limited. Predictably, despite high hopes and the august surroundings of the U.S. Naval Academy, the gathering ended with no agreement.

Many Americans are sympathetic not only to the Israeli people — willing as they are to fight for their own freedom — but to the Palestinians as well. Few can doubt the hand average Palestinians were dealt in life is lousy. But most Americans can also see that the necessary circumstances for a lasting peace do not yet exist. Furthermore, pressuring allies for concessions in the face of intransigent counterparties accomplishes little, and encouraging the other side — as has been the case in this dispute — can in fact be counterproductive.

Japan is another democratic ally to which Washington applies a double standard. This behavior is odd given Japan's importance in what is likely to be a Pacific-focused century, especially when it comes to business activity. While the United States has many allies in East Asia and the Pacific, none comes close to Japan's economic might, and this factor often tops the list in measuring U.S. economic interests and the ability of an ally to field modern military power and other tools of statecraft. Having the world's third-largest economy also enables Japan to pay the U.S. Treasury more than $2.3 billion each year to offset the cost of keeping U.S. forces there. Tokyo also finances the military improvements to the U.S. Pacific island territory of Guam.[10] No other ally is as financially generous to Washington as Tokyo is. In the eight years after 9/11, Japan refueled U.S. Navy ships in the Indian Ocean as part of its contribution to the allied mission in Afghanistan.[11] This assistance required a creative interpretation of Japan's postwar pacifist constitution, which allows only for military self-defense.

Despite these real acts of friendship toward Washington and obvious shared values between the two populations and governments, Japan is increasingly relegated to second-class status when it comes to American statecraft. For example, Tokyo should be a natural partner in dealing with the threat North Korea's nuclear-armed dictatorship presents. North Korean missiles pose a more immediate threat to Japan than they do to North America. North Korean agents invaded Japanese territory and abducted Japanese citizens, including women and children, to advance Pyongyang's espionage capabilities.[12]

While this terrorism occurred in the 1970s and 1980s, North Korea only confessed to it in 2002 and ignited Japanese outrage. In 2004, an American soldier named Charles Jenkins, who had made the unfortunate decision to desert to North Korea while drunk in 1965, was allowed to go to Japan and reunite with the abducted Japanese woman whom he had married in North Korea. His resettlement in Japan brought the abduction issue back into news headlines and presented another clear opportunity for Washington and Tokyo to confront jointly a terrorist government of mutual concern.[13]

Meanwhile, many in the Washington foreign policy establishment seem to see Japan as more of a problem than an asset. This stance was especially apparent during the on-again, off-again six-party talks that sought to denuclearize North Korea and were a major effort of the Bush administration. Some U.S. diplomats viewed Japanese officials' concern about their abducted citizens to be an obstacle to a grand bargain with North Korea's government. Ultimately, Condoleezza Rice's lieutenant in charge of the talks, career bureaucrat Christopher Hill, negotiated a side deal with Pyongyang that ignored Tokyo. To the dismay of the Japanese, Hill arranged for Bush to drop North Korea from the U.S. list of terror-sponsoring nations and then added insult to injury by remarking privately that Japan should get its own list rather than bother him about Washington's.[14] Predictably, North Korea reneged on the agreement Hill negotiated, adding to Pyongyang's long track record of selling the same deal over and over again and never delivering.

Other examples abound. Japan is the only major U.S. ally that might plausibly have to defend itself from both Chinese and Russian airpower. Yet Washington refused to sell Japan America's most advanced fighter jet, the F-22 Raptor, which would have greatly augmented allied power in the northern Pacific. After such a slight, other allies might have turned to Europe for their warplane needs. Japan still stuck with the United States, selecting the less-capable F-35 Lightning II.[15] In 2012, Washington also remained surprisingly aloof as Tokyo contended with increasingly belligerent Chinese naval activity and jingoistic claims on Japanese territory. This unfortunate silence has endured amid shrill Chinese claims to the Senkaku Islands near Taiwan that Japan has administered throughout modern history, except for a period after World War II when the United States controlled the islands. During a visit to China in April 2013, the chairman of the U.S. Joint Chiefs of Staff apparently said little when China newly described the Senkakus as one of its "core interests." This phrase is a euphemism for lands Beijing unjustly claims as its own, such as East Turkestan, Taiwan, and Tibet.[16]

Japan does have many friends in the United States, including among the ranks of officials. But those who focus on an impossible partnership with repressive, kleptomaniacal China — rather than a proven partnership with rich and democratic Japan — are the officials who most frequently rise to positions of power in Washington.

This problem can be compounded by Tokyo's refraining from lodging clear, vocal objections when Washington takes diplomatic steps that harm Japan's interests. For example, when Christopher Hill was cutting Japan out of negotiations between the United States and North Korea, I was seeking help from governments in East Asia to increase the flow of civilian radio broadcasts going into North Korea. Japan was a natural location for medium-wave radio broadcasts given its proximity to North Korea and a clear, unobstructed shot across the Sea of Japan. To my relief but also surprise, Tokyo did not ignore me, even amid ostentatious slights from its chief ally on the subject at hand. Over time, Tokyo may migrate to a new view of its long U.S. partnership and position itself as an equal rather than as a junior partner. Until then, the illusion that Japan can be treated more brusquely than are U.S. adversaries is likely to persist in Washington. This perception is unfortunate for allied smart power, since in this range of statecraft Tokyo, with its wealth, democratic values, and decreasingly diffident approach to external threats — but also its hesitancy to use military force — could be most useful to a civilized world order.

Washington also treats Taiwan poorly. The whole basis of U.S. relations with Taiwan is an illusion; in fact, it is an outright misrepresentation. Washington maintains that there is but "one China," represented by the dictatorship in Beijing, and that Taiwan is a part of China. Yet any American who visits Taiwan — or the Republic of China, as it has been known since its de facto political separation from communist mainland China in 1949 — can instantly grasp that it is a free and vibrant democracy with the rule of law and respect for individual rights that is simply not present on the mainland. Put simply, Taiwan and China are obviously two very different countries.

Beijing demands adherence to the one-China policy, and both Chinese and U.S. officials frequently incant obeisance to the concept in official meetings. The policy may have made sense when President Nixon adopted it in an attempt to isolate the Soviet Union further from China during the Cold War. Today, however, it gives Beijing cover to threaten violence against Taiwan, even in response to purely peaceful and democratic political actions that the Taiwanese people have considered in the past and may undertake at some point. Possibly they might officially recognize one day the obvious reality of their political independence from China and the existence of a separate Taiwanese nation that will never rejoin the mainland. The current situation, however, allows the notion of Beijing as a diplomatic juggernaut to permeate the rest of the Pacific, with Taiwan's condition serving as a lamentable tale of woe to other countries.

The one-China policy has severe consequences, most notably relegating Taiwan to second-class status in any diplomatic or security-related undertaking. At the State Department, had I wished, I could have met with officials from any number of odious governments that torture and kill their own citizens and pose serious risks to U.S. security. For example, inviting Sudanese, Zimbabwean, or Pakistani diplomats to my office on the State Department's seventh floor would have been no problem. Having Taiwanese diplomats anywhere in the building, however, was totally out of the question. Taiwan's representatives in Washington do not work in an embassy but in an unofficial office called the Taipei Economic and Cultural Representative Office. Going an unnecessary step beyond the basic tenets of the one-China policy, these representatives are not allowed in U.S. government buildings and U.S. officials are not to visit Taiwan's former embassy. Instead, meetings generally take place in restaurants and coffee shops around Washington, posing a countersurveillance nightmare in addition to a diplomatic slight.

Aside from being silly, the policy is dangerous. While U.S. military officers up to colonel or U.S. Navy captain can visit Taiwan for official meetings when necessary, meetings at the flag level — generals and admirals — are rare. Thus, top soldiers and sailors from the two countries cannot share information and insights seriously or form the relationships that could be critical to saving lives in a future Pacific conflict. It also impedes more routine information sharing and cooperation between the two liberal democracies.

In 2011, the Obama administration rejected a request from Taiwan to acquire new copies of the F-16 fighter jets it uses to defend its airspace from Chinese incursion.[17] It was hardly an unreasonable request. Fighting Falcons, as the F-16s are known, first took to American skies in the late 1970s. Taiwan received its first jets more than twenty years ago.[18] They are three levels of quality below America's top fighter jets (with the F-15/18, the F-35, and the F-22 each respectively a step better). Even with them, Taiwan would be badly outgunned by China. Furthermore, Taiwan must rely on purchases of advanced weapons from the United States in order to survive. European and other arms providers refuse to sell their products to Taiwan in order to preserve favor from Beijing.

The advantage of having the jets should be obvious: raising the costs of attacking Taiwan benefits not only the Taiwanese but also the Americans and others who deter and would resist Chinese aggression in the region. The move to deny the sale — and countless others like it — signals all governments that Washington is willing to see an ally's defenses degraded simply to avoid disrupting the relatively fruitless U.S.-China relationship.

This political tactic sets back American smart power and statecraft enormously. Once a military dictatorship, Taiwan is now a thriving liberal democracy with a track record of peaceful transitions of power and sustained economic prosperity. It should be the most obvious and threatening rebuke to the arguments China's unelected leaders make for maintaining power — that is, that social harmony and economic progress require deference to the communist elite. Taiwan shows that democracy works better than repression for people of Chinese heritage, language, and culture. This idea is no small matter for U.S. security and statecraft: ending the reign of China's communists would make East Asia and the world dramatically safer, freer, and richer. But Taiwan as a model for China does not work as long as Washington keeps Taiwan in the closet. Furthermore, the illusion that mistreating Taiwan helps Washington gain cooperation from Beijing remains a hypothesis for which there is no evidence, unless one thinks pleasant diplomatic meetings are a concession and an accomplishment in and of themselves. Most Americans outside of Washington do not.

ILLUSION 4: THE CIA KNOWS ALL

It is always amusing when Hollywood movies portray the headquarters of the CIA or other intelligence and security-related agencies as filled with dynamic and impeccably groomed and dressed individuals gliding purposefully between beautiful, modern offices and glass-surrounded conference rooms that evoke good taste and lavish decorating budgets. The reality is not quite so. While many government offices have ceremonial areas where senior officials can meet dignitaries, they are the exception.

Foreign ministers visiting the State Department might be received by the chief protocol on a red carpet at the front door, walked past a marble hall of flags to the one nice set of elevators in the entire building, and then escorted through the quaint treaty room to the secretary of state's outer office, tastefully adorned with colonial furniture and the like. But a few steps off of this carefully trod path would put one in a building that actually resembles a 1960s-era public school, marked mainly by endless hallways decorated primarily with a depressing color-coded stripe. The same general pattern holds at most other agencies. Furthermore, while one can find all types of people at every big agency, their attire and appearance are invariably rougher around the edges than the Hollywood-generated image. A general rule of thumb some government contract seekers teach their new hires is that the worst-dressed person in a meeting with government employees might actually be the most influential person in attendance.

A related part of this mythical image is that intelligence agency employees are competent, creative, and driven; and the agencies collectively are all knowing and all powerful when they focus their attention on particular problems. Certainly their feats and capabilities have proven impressive in many cases, not the least of which was the eventual location, identification, and killing of bin Laden. Thankfully, some elite units of government, even outside of the military, can accomplish great deeds.

However, these exploits are the exception, making the overall public impression an illusion. A part of this misapprehension arises when the American public is left with the impression in some instances that U.S. covert operatives are working assiduously and successfully when in fact they are not. These cases are hard to document given both the lack of public information about covert activities and the long periods of time that federal law and executive orders allow covert activities to remain classified after they are concluded. Furthermore, owing to the difficulty of the task or out of patriotic deference and respect for agencies that have some employees taking mortal risks for their country, many Americans, including reporters, are disinclined to search for proof when claims of intelligence operations are invoked.

However, two recent instances do shed some light on such activities. In the civil wars in Libya and Syria, historians will likely record that U.S. intelligence operations actually consisted of far less activity than was presented to the public via leaks to selected media.

Protestors in both countries took up arms against their dictators at nearly the same time in February and March 2011, respectively. However, a year later the Libyan revolution was a memory while the Syrian conflict raged on, with mounting civilian casualties and no end in sight. The Obama administration came under pressure to take some action and was increasingly criticized for its refusal even to arm Syrian rebels and improve their chances of winning. Amid this criticism, the *New York Times* broke a story in June and claimed that "a small number of CIA officers are operating secretly in southern Turkey, helping allies decide which Syrian opposition fighters across the border will receive arms to fight the Syrian government, according to American officials and Arab intelligence officers."[19]

It is entirely possible that CIA officers were, in fact, on the scene. It would not be unusual for the CIA to liaise with intelligence officials from Turkey, which joined NATO in 1952 and allows the United States to maintain a large air force base at Incirlik, located northeast of the Turkish-Syrian frontier. That the CIA maintains a large so-called station in Istanbul, Turkey's cultural and business capital — even if the agency never discusses it publicly — is also well established in literature.[20] Yet months after the story broke, rebels from nearly all factions in Syria continued to complain that they were not receiving arms or other essential military goods and training. For example, a rebel commander in Aleppo remarked in September 2012 of desired foreign-government assistance, "They told us to start the rebellion and then we would get support. . . . We don't have the ammunition we were promised. Every day the [opposing] army is pushing forwards. So we expend the one thing we have, men. Men are dying."[21]

Worse, the CIA and other parts of the U.S. government not only were failing to facilitate the flow of military goods but also were in fact discouraging other groups that were willing to do so. The same newspaper that first broke the story on supposed CIA operations reported four months later: "For months, Saudi Arabia and Qatar have been funneling money and small arms to Syria's rebels but have refused to provide heavier weapons. . . . While they have publicly called for arming the rebels, they have held back, officials in both countries said, in part because they have been discouraged by the United States."[22]

Indeed, U.S. law requires the president to issue a formal "finding" that establishes the need for covert action before the CIA or other agencies engage in activities such as clandestinely arming a rebel force. The finding is typically classified as top secret and compartmentalized, or limited to very few top officials and the field officers doing the actual work. However, because the law requires that it be disclosed to members of the two congressional intelligence committees "as soon as possible," any new operation has a political cost and invites congressional scrutiny, which is a hassle at the very least.[23] Yet it would have been unavoidable in this case given that the law specifically requires a finding for covert actions intended to influence military conditions abroad. It seems clear from the reported sequence of events that no such finding was in fact generated or issued at the time of the initial report of CIA intervention — at least not of the scope that would be required. After all, why issue a potentially controversial covert finding to arm rebels when U.S. diplomats were about to spend months discouraging others from taking that very step? And no finding means the initial leak was misleading. The reporter was used.

The same implication regarding the CIA's presence was made in the early days of the Libyan revolution. Unnamed U.S. officials leaked word of supposed covert intervention to selected media sources, one of which reported, "The CIA has sent a small, covert team into rebel-held eastern Libya while the White House debates whether to arm the opposition." The account continued, "The operatives are in Libya to gather intelligence to help direct NATO airstrikes and to help train inexperienced rebel fighters."[24] As with the previous story of the CIA's involvement in the Syrian conflict, it is entirely possible an element of this one was true. However, as a private citizen who was in touch with Americans and Libyan expatriates involved in the war — including those who returned to Libya — I do not believe this version was accurate, or at least not to the extent of media reports that hinted at major U.S. covert action on the ground in Libya to help the rebels. The Libyan rebels were so immensely grateful for U.S. and NATO air support, meanwhile, that they did not even register a complaint when a U.S. helicopter crew shot six villagers trying to welcome two downed U.S. pilots who ejected from an F-15 fighter plane.[25] However, in private, Libyans were frustrated and expressed concerns about not being afforded a coordinating capability with NATO.

After a separate friendly fire incident, in which NATO planes mistook and bombed rebel forces, a rebel commander noted he was not even in direct contact with NATO. At the same time, a NATO commander denied even the intention of having good communications and coordination with the rebels: "I have to be frank and say it is not for us, trying to protect civilians, to improve communications with rebel forces."[26] The Pentagon's spokesman remarked, "I'm not aware of any communication between the military and rebel leaders." Further, fully two months after NATO's intervention began, rebels were still trying to communicate with NATO by cell phone and Skype, including phone calls over public networks with a U.S. military attaché in far-away Germany.[27]

In other words, long after the CIA was supposedly on the ground in Libya establishing linkages with rebels and paving the way for air-ground coordination and joint targeting, any cooperation of the sort was apparently not occurring. Historians may yet unearth whether CIA operatives were there at all and, if so, what they were doing. However, it seems certain they were not engaged in the activities that officials were hyping to those reporters who wanted to know about the U.S. government's involvement.

Yet in Washington, one will find experts who insist that the CIA and its cousins in other agencies are in any hot spot where the United States has interests on the line and that they are on the job and prepared to bring the situation under control. This illusion is dangerous. It prevents the public and policymakers from having a full grasp of what tools the United States actually has its disposal to understand and influence foreign problems. In order to use smart power successfully, the United States needs capable clandestine intelligence and political warfare instrumentalities. Some powerful countries have these at present. America does not.

A final illusion that contributes to an unwarranted sense of serenity about foreign developments relates to new technology. As Iranians took to the streets in June 2009 to protest a stolen election and thirty years of political repression by the incumbent regime, the prominent liberal blogger Andrew Sullivan published a piece titled "The Revolution Will Be Twittered." Noting that Iranian protesters used social media to coordinate their plans, he wrote: "That a new information technology could be improvised for this purpose so swiftly is a sign of the times. It reveals in Iran what the [2008] Obama campaign revealed in the United States. You cannot stop people any longer. You cannot control them any longer. They can bypass your established media; they can broadcast to one another; they can organize as never before."[28]

What Sullivan did not calculate is that repressive regimes are quite capable of controlling and using social media themselves. While the Iranian government may have been slow on the uptake in the early days of the uprising, it learned quickly. Since almost all social media data still travels at some point on terrestrial cables or phone lines, which the government in repressive nations still invariably controls, it was possible to throttle back the data services and choke them off entirely at times. During the uprising, the Iranian regime itself began to use social media to monitor dissidents. Other regime tricks included sending messages stating that protesters at certain locations were being shot, whether true or not, to discourage attendance. One protester posted on Twitter: "DO NOT [retransmit] anything U read from 'NEW' tweeters, gvmt spreading misinfo."[29] The protesters were discovering that while coordinating had become seemingly easier, so had false flag operations by their opponents in power. In other words, the age-old cat-and-mouse game between dissidents and repressive regimes was not so radically different after all, even at the dawn of social media.

For inspiration, the Iranian government could easily have turned to China. There, the government has emplaced an obstacle pejoratively referred to as the "Great Firewall of China." The government in Beijing acts through telecommunications companies to limit access to virtually all Western social media outlets and carefully monitors the homegrown social media that is still allowed. Tens of thousands of censors monitor public comment boards; objectionable content is subject to immediate deletion.[30] China is also taking steps to curb anonymity on the web and in other communications, forcing Internet users — even those using public computers — to register with their real names.[31] The same steps are being applied to domestic buyers of SIM cards, a step intended to make anonymous phone calls harder to make.[32] Increasingly, other repressive regimes will see the importance of these steps and follow suit.

Sullivan was hardly alone in his optimism, though. At the time of the unrest in Iran, I had recently concluded government service where I dealt with communications matters in North Korea, China, and other countries and found myself on a conference call with the founder of several successful Silicon Valley companies. Quite admirably, he wanted to help the Iranian people in their quest for freedom and use the tools at his disposal. He described a technology that would essentially allow the passage of information into and out of Iran using a mechanism other than existing encryption. He was clearly on to a good idea, but the concept was incomplete.

Notwithstanding the foregoing, communications tools are critical to any political effort. They make the difference between lone, isolated dissidents and an organized popular movement. Czesław Bielecki, a Polish underground operative during the communist era, argued as much in an instructional pamphlet titled "The Little Conspirator." He wrote: "Newspapers do not only spread ideas; for the underground, they are the best source of information, money, and materials. An underground press serves as a training ground, it schools novices in techniques of conspiracy. It teaches them how to cope with, and overcome fear."[33]

Realizing this importance of communications, part of the Western effort to help dissident Poles behind the Iron Curtain in the 1980s involved smuggling copiers and fax machines to them. This leading-edge communications gear of the time was still simple enough that average regime opponents could use it with limited instruction. Today, the leaders of opposition groups around the world would undoubtedly be better off if they could communicate with each other and with key supporters and remain undetected or at least not traced by their opponents. Unfortunately, the hardest part of this endeavor is not necessarily developing the technology but getting it into the right hands. This effort requires first identifying promising dissidents and then contacting them, convincing them to cooperate, and ultimately providing them the tools and training required — all done clandestinely in an environment where mistakes can lead to imprisonment or worse.

On the phone call with the Silicon Valley executive, I hesitated. I did not want to come across as a typical bureaucrat, eager to think of any number of reasons why a new idea would fail. However, I did pose the question of how his group envisioned providing the new technology to the emerging leaders of the protest movement in Iran. His response was disappointing: "We're going to leave the 'last mile' to others." This reply referred to the concept much on the mind of Internet and telecommunications executives and marketers — that is, the terminal phase, or final few feet or miles, in delivering information services to customers that was typically dominated by phone or cable companies. His answer meant practically that the group had not seriously pondered the challenges of conveying evolutionary technology into the right hands in Iran to make a difference.

I wondered if the technology group thought the CIA or State Department could do this job (see Illusion no. 4). It would have been impossible given that the Obama White House had decided to avoid supporting the protesters beyond a few blithe words and given the CIA's famously poor intelligence sources and means in Iran, plus its congressionally induced estrangement from serious political warfare dating from the post-Watergate era. A participant on the call left the impression of having close ties to Israel's political leadership; however, the Israelis, while generally thought to have better intelligence means and assets in Iran than the United States does, would almost certainly never risk them for uses like this one. Furthermore, decent intelligence agencies are highly resistant to offers from amateur James Bonds and their creative ideas for saving the world. Without a nongovernmental capability of providing the right dissidents and protest leaders with ongoing support, the idea alone did not seem workable.

However, a key point is that many Americans and others around the world have the creative ideas and motivation to assist smart power directed against dangerous dictatorships. But governments that support a civilized order in the world do not have the mechanisms in place to make use of them. Furthermore, the misperception is that privately developed technology alone will make an evolutionary change in fighting dictators. Unfortunately, repressive regimes are often one step ahead, even with new technology like social media tools. What ultimately matters most is the "last mile" that exists between those who one day may bring political change and those on the outside who wish to see them succeed. This missing link is only one of many gaps in the smart power spectrum that calls for reform in Washington today.

CHAPTER 7

Washington's Broken Institutions

James Lind knew the worst of national security bureaucracy. He was an eighteenth-century Scottish physician who tried to give the Royal Navy the simple answer to one of its biggest and deadliest mysteries. In his life, he saw a tour de force of bureaucratic resistance to new ideas that would be familiar to today's reformers in Washington and allied capitals.

If all one understands of statecraft in the eighteenth century is the might of Britain's Royal Navy, one is well positioned to understand the era. After the new century dawned, Britain managed to sink much of the Spanish and French naval fleets at the Battle of Vigo Bay in northern Spain in 1702. During the rest of the first half of the century, the Royal Navy had similar success when engaging its various foes. Fortune smiled on London during that Age of Sail, which led to the peak of the First British Empire and masterful exploration like the voyages of Capt. James Cook. But every English captain who took to sea harbored a fear that he could never put too far out of mind. Far more present than the king's enemies was the gruesome disease scurvy.

Scurvy first became apparent as a menace to navies in the sixteenth century, when sailors increasingly were able to venture far from home on prolonged voyages. By the mid-1700s, some referred to it as "the plague of the sea" and the "spoyle of mariners." Scurvy might start with squishy-feeling gums, followed by tooth loss, blotches of dead and rotting skin, sore joints, and jaundice. Later it could lead to psychosis, convulsions, and death. Those afflicted not only failed to contribute to labor-intensive ship duties of the day but also burdened the remaining crew. The problem became a clear military crisis in the 1740s when a British squadron sent to raid in the Pacific lost five of six ships and two-thirds of its manpower mostly to scurvy.[1]

The Royal Navy noticed the correlation between the duration of voyages and incidences of scurvy and contemplated a host of causes and possible cures. A salty diet, bad air aboard ship, melancholy from being away from home, and other incorrect causes were considered. The navy forced sailors to eat malt as an attempted cure. The sailors themselves had the superstition that only the smell and touch of land was a certain fix.

John Lind discovered the actual cure in 1747 after providing scurvy-afflicted sailors on his ship a variety of possible cures. The ones he gave citrus fruit recovered. Lind was on to scurvy's cause — a deficiency of vitamin C — and its simple remedy.

Word did not travel fast despite the potential breakthrough to one of Britain's most sensitive military readiness problems, one that struck at the linchpin of its national might. Lind left naval service and published his *Treatise of the Scurvy* in 1753. Despite the convincing evidence he presented, his cure was ignored for decades. The naval bureaucracy, heady from its dominant position and its success at keeping threats to England at bay, refused to deviate from its incorrect official line that scurvy was caused by putrefaction. Even as late as 1781, when cholera had replaced scurvy as the chief medical menace of sailors, a British naval surgeon at sea found himself afflicted by scurvy and wrote: "About scurvy so much is to be supposed, so little known for sure."[2] Forty years after the publication of Lind's treatise, the Royal Navy finally adopted his simple and effective recommendations.[3]

By then, a major shift had happened. In the American Revolutionary War, France, Spain, and the Netherlands joined forces against Britain and dealt some of the few major setbacks to the Royal Navy during the century. A low point for London was its inability to resupply blockaded British forces at Yorktown, where their surrender ended the conflict. Scurvy contributed to British naval manpower woes.[4] Losing a war will certainly lead an entrenched bureaucracy to reexamine its ways.

The mentality at work at that time should be instantly recognizable to those who have dealt with the Washington foreign policy establishment in recent years. Through both Democratic and Republican administrations, the consistent theme in broken Washington has been overwhelming hostility toward real change, even in light of clear policy failures and a vastly changed world. Washington dispenses foreign aid to corrupt governments that hate America, and it often does not result in political or economic improvement even after decades. Washington tolerates politicized and misleading intelligence, including a near-perfect record of failing to detect nuclear breakouts by America's adversaries. In Washington's diplomatic guild members compare themselves to soldiers when it suits them, and yet "civilian surges" promised in two recent wars never materialized. Congress funds nongovernmental organizations to fill gaps in statecraft capabilities, but they coast on accomplishments from long ago. Their haughtiness rises in correlation with their budgets while they remain detached utterly from real achievement in today's world. All of these factors negatively impact a president's ability to conduct statecraft and defend the United States. It means the president has to accept a missing middle where smart power ought to be.

Congress and the executive branch enacted some reforms after the terrorist attacks of September 11, 2001, but they erred in some efforts and left much else undone. Outside of the military and a few counterterrorism provinces of the intelligence bureaucracy, the most discernable change was a bloating of budgets and little resulting improvement in output. Perversely, as the intensity of political and military turbulence in the world has increased and as policy failures have become more apparent, the Washington foreign policy establishment has resisted change and new ideas all the more. Hopefully it will not take losing a war to create the impetus for improvement.

FOREIGN SERVICE

Halloween 2007 was particularly spooky for me. On that day, I sat in my office at the State Department watching on an internal TV channel a "town hall meeting" taking place several floors below. There, a number of career department employees were embarrassing themselves before a large venue, word of which would leak instantly to the press. Members of the State Department's Foreign Service — a guild of permanent diplomats that is separate in law from those of ordinary civil servants — were complaining to their director general about the prospect of having to work in Iraq.

By this time, the surge ordered by President George W. Bush was beginning to defeat the insurgency that had exploded in Iraq in the years after the ouster of Saddam Hussein. A key part of the surge strategy was adopting a new counterinsurgency mission, which meant protecting and gaining the support of the local population. The Foreign Service was supposed to excel at such tasks as dealing with local civilians and the various nonmilitary institutions that compose civil society. In fact, some Foreign Service officers looked down on the military and believed its people were too simplistic and lacking in nuance to appreciate foreign populations and governments. However, beyond their own guild, this conceit was not to survive the Iraq War.

The State Department had a number of important but unfilled positions in Iraq. The U.S. ambassador stationed there sent a blunt cable saying he needed better-qualified people in order to succeed. He poignantly summarized: "In essence, the issue is whether we are a Department and Service at war. If we are, we need to organize and prioritize in a way that reflects this, something we have not done thus far."[5]

This request jibed with a report I had heard that a frustrated general had implored the State Department to send him "experts not dilettantes." Foreign Service officers take an oath on assuming some of the best-compensated and prestigious jobs in all of government that they will serve anywhere in the world if needed. For the first time since the 1960s, the Department was considering a tiny number of "directed assignments," where employees who did not volunteer for Iraq would nonetheless be sent. In general, the department's higher-ups wanted Foreign Service officers to serve at least one "hardship" tour for every two in cushy locales like Rome and London.

At the town hall meeting, various Foreign Service officers complained about their level of benefits and security while potentially serving in Iraq. One participant complained she had post-traumatic stress disorder from manning a desk in Basra and wanted more benefits, but she congratulated herself because she had "wanted to go to a place where I knew it was important for my country to be, even though I had a lot of questions about the origins of the war to begin with." Citing a poll of union members who apparently felt overwhelmingly that Secretary of State Condoleezza Rice was not "on their side," a representative of the diplomats' union said, "Sometimes, if it's 88 to 12, maybe the 88 percent are correct." Rather than ignore this irrelevant, impertinent assessment of the woman whom the president of the United States had appointed as their boss, the director general shot back with the odd and almost certainly incorrect statement, "Eighty-eight percent of the country believed in slavery at one time. Was that correct?"[6]

As if that display were not sufficient to cast the various speakers in a negative light, a participant decided to revisit the issue of directed assignments to Iraq. A man who identified himself as a forty-six-year veteran of the Foreign Service decried that service in Iraq was "a possible death sentence" and suggested closing the Baghdad embassy rather than sending the people necessary to do the work the U.S. ambassador and military commander thought was critical.[7] The comment received sustained applause from the audience, either unaware or indifferent to the fact that precisely zero Foreign Service officers were killed in Iraq during the entire war and aftermath.[8]

For me, the episode nicely captured the horrors of the Foreign Service. Some in the guild of diplomats frequently compared themselves to the military when it was convenient to do so, only to shrink from taking risks when they were real and apparent. There were of course exceptions, but they were exceptions that proved the rule. Many senior Foreign Service officers were consistently jealous of the resources provided to the Pentagon and felt they were undercompensated. During and after the Bush administration, they pressed successfully for higher pay and benefits. By 2011, a modestly senior Foreign Service officer assigned to Baghdad would be paid $158,850 in salary. A military officer at a comparable career level, such as an army lieutenant colonel or navy commander with sixteen years of experience, received significantly less: $116,292.[9] Furthermore, wherever they go abroad, Foreign Service officers receive free housing — often quite lavish — and such other perks as household servants and access to private schools that would be available only to the richest of Americans back home.

With these and other benefits, the total compensation for Foreign Service officers is dramatically higher than almost anyone else in government receives. They also are entitled to taxpayer-funded home leave or in-region vacations during their tours, which include postings to locations that most Americans would hardly consider to be hardships. During dreaded tours in Washington, Foreign Service officers have the rare experience of having to find their own housing. Once a Foreign Service officer in our office complained bitterly that she had to arrange for her own cable TV service to be connected while serving stateside.

Much of this prima donna conduct could be forgiven if the Foreign Service really was indispensable and effective. However, what its personnel have provided to successive U.S. presidents has been consistently deficient. In Iraq, commanders gave up waiting for the State Department to assist their critical mission of gaining the support of average Iraqis, as did the president and Congress.

As the insurgency in Iraq lurched toward its nadir in mid-decade, the administration and Congress moved to give military commanders in war zones new tools to improve security using capacities that previously were partly or wholly the province of the State Department. They became known by the section numbers of the National Defense Authorization Act of 2006 that authorized them: 1206, 1207, and 1208. Section 1206 allowed for the military to train and equip foreign military forces; previously this duty had been primarily the responsibility of the State Department and its large "foreign military forces" aid budget. Section 1207 allowed the Pentagon to transfer some funds to the State Department for "security and stabilization." Essentially it provided a way for commanders to compel the State Department to spend money on small projects critical to winning support for U.S. forces and the job they were doing.[10] In effect, it gave local commanders money to improve the lives of friendly Iraqis rapidly. Section 1208 allowed the Pentagon to reimburse foreign governments and local populations that were aiding U.S. war fighters; this key part of diplomacy to gain and keep allies was simply too critical to be left to the State Department. The authority in Section 1208 existed prior to the new act, but its authorized level was expanded from $25 million in 2005 to $1.5 billion in the 2006 law.[11]

Added to this bill was an authority called the Commanders' Emergency Response Program, which Congress first authorized in 2003. It enabled military commanders to undertake such projects as rapidly rebuilding schools and hospitals in areas where U.S. forces were expected to maintain security. The commanders did not have the luxury of waiting the years it would have taken the U.S. Agency for International Development to do the job. Gaining support from the local Iraqis was a key to the success of the 2007 surge of forces in Iraq, at the time America's highest national priority.[12]

The Foreign Service does not appear to have learned much from the episode, although the State Department ensured the Pentagon all but lost one of the authorities after the Iraqi insurgency wound down. When President Obama appointed Hillary Clinton as secretary of state and ordered the adoption of a counterinsurgency mission in Afghanistan, Clinton boasted that a "civilian surge" would be employed so key civilian counterinsurgency and counterterrorism tasks would not go unfulfilled or be left to the military. Two years later, only about a thousand civilians had been deployed, including civilian security guards to protect the other civilians, and it cost the U.S. government between $410,000 and $570,000 to position a single civilian in Afghanistan for a year.[13] For America's war fighters, the civilian surge in Afghanistan was as nonexistent as the one in Iraq had been. In these instances, a bureaucracy actually took the promising step of recognizing its deficiencies — judging from Clinton's statements about the need for a civilian surge — but then failed to implement the more important step of making the necessary the changes to fix problems.

Many good and capable people are in the Foreign Service and in the broader State Department workforce. In consulting with foreign governments over the course of the administration, I found at our own embassies many devoted, insightful, and competent diplomats who were willing to work hard to advance U.S. interests with other governments. However, many of these people tend to become frustrated with the Foreign Service and, through self-selection or the promotion of others, end up leaving the agency before they reach the senior-most levels.

On the one hand, the bureaucratic inertia of the State Department has been noticed by Republican administrations, whose members often do not share the views of what has consistently been a left-leaning workforce. Those Republicans also have noticed that department employees have given to Democratic presidential campaigns over Republicans by a ratio of fifteen to one.[14] On the other hand, Democratic presidents have also expressed frustration with the department. President Kennedy once said the agency was a "bowl full of jelly." Franklin Roosevelt was reported to have said that dealing with the department was like "watching an elephant become pregnant — everything is done on a very high level, there's a lot of commotion, and it takes twenty-two months for anything to happen."[15] Certainly the observation is true that virtually all issues of remote importance are brought to senior levels at the State Department. Whereas the military presses a tremendous amount of responsibility on many of its youngest members who do the actual fighting, the State Department does the opposite, requiring years of service before employees can write even the most mundane cables or convey minor points to counterparts in other governments.

About midway during my time in the Bush administration, a friend with long service at the White House and State Department as a civil servant summed up the situation succinctly. I asked hopefully if a Foreign Service officer appointed as the new U.S. ambassador to South Korea was good and potentially more useful to my portfolio than his predecessor was. She looked back sympathetically and replied, "Christian, you just don't get to that level of the Foreign Service without being a major asshole." As time passed, the accuracy of her assessment became apparent. The gentleman in question would warmly receive our requests to handle an issue thought to be a priority for the White House and then ignore them. It was a common occurrence in a bureaucracy that presidents of both parties have regrettably tolerated.

Last but not least, the State Department is deeply deficient in what is supposed to be its specialty, foreign political analysis, or the act of anticipating and explaining developments that affect governments abroad. For starters, many Foreign Service officers indulge the national security–related myths outlined in chapter 6, meaning their analyses are marred from the start by false assumptions about statecraft. Reviewing State Department cables that have become public, one will find analysis of foreign political events that is unremarkable and that hews closely to conventional wisdom.

Reports also arrive late due in part to the layers of bureaucracy reports must clear before reaching policymakers. Usually by the time a cable analyzing a foreign crisis arrives, several days have elapsed. Meanwhile, early wire reports and cable TV news have reported the event, and news outlets subsequently provided analysis and opinion about it. Quite frequently, while reading political assessments that arrived via diplomatic cable, I felt as though I were reading a month-old edition of the *Economist*. The vast majority of cables never make it to anyone who matters on the State Department's seventh floor. Beyond cables, the analyses that are generated in house by the department's Bureau of Intelligence and Research are generally received politely and then ignored.

One of the State Department's biggest problems with political analysis is its overreliance on information from foreign diplomats, officials, and academic experts and its suspicion and deprecation of exiles and political actors who are not in power. At one point, I relayed information from a defector from North Korea's army to department bureaucrats while making a point about political stability in North Korea. One career employee responded that the exiled Korean "had an ax to grind" and believed that perception alone was sufficient justification to disregard my point. It seemed to me that people forced to leave their homes and families to settle in a new country while bringing little more than the shirts on their backs might understandably dislike the regime they fled, but nonetheless they should be able to provide information worth evaluating. I also noticed this instinctive skepticism of exiles and similar sources seldom seemed to apply to foreign governments, even though many and perhaps all of them have a strong incentive to manipulate and distort information and perceptions held by the U.S. government.

The attitude undoubtedly contributed in an earlier time to the Foreign Service's bemusement with the Solidarity trade union and political movement that ultimately ended communism in Poland and cracked the Eastern Bloc in 1989, leading thereafter to the successful end of the Cold War. While few would confess it today, many in the Foreign Service hierarchy frowned on Solidarity as being led by ignorant, provincial shipyard workers who exaggerated their political following in the country. The career diplomats urged that Solidarity be kept at arm's length, lest it imperil U.S.

relations with Poland's unelected government, which, after all, was going to run the country forever by their estimation. Luckily for both the American and Polish people, policymakers rejected this received wisdom from the Foreign Service. In that instance, ignoring the advice of the Foreign Service helped end one of the longest and most dangerous international standoffs in modern history. Undeterred, the Foreign Service can be counted on still today to look askance at popular dissent movements and overestimate the stability and durability of repressive regimes.

In other cases, presidential administrations have not been so fortunate in escaping the bad political analysis of the State Department and its bureaucrats. One of the worst instances in U.S. history of a bureaucracy overestimating its political acumen with deadly consequences involves the Coalition Provisional Authority (CPA). This organization was established to oversee the occupation of Iraq after Saddam Hussein was deposed. In its wake, it left a country in utter political dysfunction and amid a regional proxy war layered atop a sectarian civil war. Thousands of Americans would pay for the mistakes of the CPA with their lives.

In theory, the CPA reported through the Department of Defense to President Bush. In reality, the CPA made political and security-related decisions without reference to the extensive advance planning that the Pentagon had undertaken, and it manifested a Foreign Service officer view of statecraft. Atop the CPA sat a certain L. Paul "Jerry" Bremer III who joined the Foreign Service in 1966 after studies at Andover, Yale, Harvard, and the Paris Institute of Political Studies. Bremer left government in the 1980s but remained a figure of the Washington foreign policy establishment.

The full story of the CPA's errors is beyond the scope of this book; however, in summary, the net product of its work is accepted almost universally as example of what not to do in statecraft. An early CPA error was disbanding the old Iraqi army, a move that Bremer formalized in his second order as de facto viceroy. Hundreds of thousands of young men trained in arms thus were dumped into Iraq's cities, and most were without income or job prospects. When the consequences of this decision started to become clear, Bremer frequently asserted that the army "melted away" on its own and not by his order.[16] But surely offering modest pay and removing the most brutal of Saddam's officers would have brought many soldiers back to serve. This misstep was an early sign that the CPA failed to understand the most fundamental product a successful postwar government must deliver: security.

In the closing month of the CPA's existence a little more than a year later, Bremer and his colleagues bequeathed a final poison pill to Iraq that affects that tortured nation to this day. Upon the recommendation of a UN official, Bremer decided Iraq's future democracy would be based on proportional representation effected through national "party lists" elections.[17] In other words, all eligible Iraqis would go to the polls and choose a preferred party, which in turn had already decided which of its members would be legislators. It should have been obvious that this process would further accentuate dangerous sectarian divisions in Iraq; indeed, it is precisely what happened. It also ensured a larger political role for radical parties that would have had trouble winning an outright majority anywhere in the country. Instead of legislators representing a constituency in a set geography as they do in most democracies, the party list system makes lawmakers beholden solely to their political party. In effect, the party — not voters in a set district — becomes the politicians' constituency.

Under such a system, firing unappealing legislators or recruiting new blood becomes particularly hard for voters. Bremer and his colleagues in the Foreign Service insisted that proportional representation was imperative in a country without an accurate census, which could make apportioning geographic voting districts of equal population difficult. But in a time when computers can count houses and apartments from satellite pictures, not attempting a new census was lazy. Iraq's voting system subsequently has been modified from the original UN/Bremer plan, but it retains a fatally flawed proportional representation at its heart. Even Iraq's prime minister later wrote that because of the proportional system, "the vast majority of the electorate based their choices on sectarian and ethnic affiliations, not on genuine political platforms," and "this gave rise to our sectarian Parliament, controlled by party leaders rather than by the genuine representatives of the people."[18]

The unappealing Iraqi polity that the CPA created is an example of what happens if the Foreign Service and related luminaries of the Washington foreign policy establishment are allowed to run amok. Some have tried to smear the Pentagon with the errors of the CPA, but many in government clearly saw that the CPA reported directly to the White House and a National Security Council staff directed by Condoleezza Rice, who was then angling for the job of secretary of state.[19] As such, an archetypal Foreign Service officer, Bremer, sat atop an agency that reported to an academic, Rice, who epitomized the Kissinger branch of the foreign policy establishment. That the resulting chaos would require a second American invasion — the 2007 Iraq surge — to avoid a repeat of America's Vietnam War humiliation was perhaps inevitable.

Owing to an antiquated, self-congratulating workforce that fails to cultivate its best and brightest, and evidenced by a string of disturbing failures at the statecraft game of which it thinks it is master, the State Department's Foreign Service provides presidents with only a deeply dysfunctional tool for managing foreign situations short of war. Over the course of their administrations, presidents of both political parties consequently tend to sideline the State Department when implementing their top foreign priorities. This perceived need to circumvent the State Department is a shame, not only because it wastes potential resources, but also it does not address real damage done to U.S. national interests. Further, successful smart power strategy requires that the United States have a foreign affairs agency with at least some acumen at sizing up political developments and influencing them in situations outside of war. Regrettably, the State Department is not the only broken smart power agency.

SPY AGENCIES

It is important for those sizing up American statecraft to grasp the difference between intelligence operatives — actual officers in the field — and analysts back in Washington who man desks and generate reports, or "estimates," based in part on what field officers unearth from sources. Both sides of the intelligence house have distinct problems at present.

At the CIA, the operatives are part of the National Clandestine Service, which was known before 2005 as the Directorate of Operations, or Ops for short. Back in Washington, the analysts work for the Directorate of Intelligence, or DI in internal parlance. Each party views the other with a healthy, competitive degree of disdain. In 2010, a former CIA director referenced "the kind of 'fighter pilot' mystique in the National Clandestine Service, or the 'tenured faculty' mystique in the Directorate of Intelligence."[20]

With regard to the actual field operatives, the intelligence services of any government face a fundamental question of how to balance between "legals" and "illegals." Legal operatives pose as diplomats and work out of embassies. Since they have diplomatic immunity, if a hostile government detects their intelligence-related work, generally the worst consequence they face is that they are labeled "persona non grata" and expelled for "activities outside their official capacity." More often, a hostile government will simply monitor a legal operative rather than expel that person in hope of finding which sources, or "agents," the operative is utilizing. The agents, typically nationals of the foreign country targeted for intelligence collection, do the real spying. They conduct espionage against their country (or terrorist network) and pass information back through a method dictated by the intelligence officer who controls them.

Unfortunately, those police states that the U.S. government most likely has targeted for intelligence collection have tended to be adept at monitoring U.S. diplomats and willing to commit nearly limitless resources to the job. Thus, legal intelligence operatives must take extreme care in contacting, cultivating, and running agents, lest the local government arrest or induce the agents to provide worthless or misleading information. The amount of care American intelligence officers must take in handling agents necessarily limits the number and scope of operations severely. This problem was so acute during the Cold War that there were long periods of time when the American and British intelligence services were not able to run a single high-value covert agent in the Soviet Union. At times when they did have sources, the agencies had to limit their contact severely and use strict tradecraft known as Moscow Rules to reduce the chances of the source being exposed.[21]

The alternative to relying solely on legal agents is to use illegal operatives, who are also known as NOCs (nonofficial covers). Instead of posing as diplomats, such operatives might present themselves as journalists, academics, students, businesspeople, and the like. In seeking to recruit locals to commit espionage, the NOCs would have no obvious link with the government they actually served. The upside to this operation is that illegals should ordinarily draw less attention from local counterintelligence officials and police, especially if the NOCs are afforded many years to solidify their cover and build a network of contacts prior to attempting to recruit some of them to commit espionage. Employing NOCs has several downsides. First, they have less reason to meet officials of the other government, and they are often the juiciest of targets for intelligence services given those officials' access to privileged information. The NOCs also lack diplomatic immunity. Whereas the legal operative may simply be sent home if detected, the illegal one may be prosecuted and in many countries subjected to torture or execution.[22] Aside from the harm to the individual in question, the arrest of an NOC is potentially embarrassing to the government that sent the operative.

Since World War II, U.S. intelligence agencies have used both legals and illegals, but the vast majority of human intelligence (HUMINT) collection has been via legals.[23] Perhaps only 10 percent of the CIA's employees are actual operatives, with the rest comprising analysts, administrators, scientists, technicians, and the like. Of that 10 percent, it is widely rumored in Washington that few and possibly none are illegals. In 2010, the CIA director promised more "flexible and innovative deployments overseas," including "new approaches to cover." The implication was that the CIA would use more illegals to improve its collection. Of the announcement, one skeptical operational veteran told the *Washington Post*, "In response to criticism that more than 90 per cent of its officers live and work entirely within the United States, and that the remainder work within American embassies, the CIA periodically promises to get more officers under cover, on the street, in foreign countries." Another former operative told the reporter: "They are just admitting indirectly that, despite all the hype, they still have done next-to-nothing on getting out of embassies."[24]

This situation is unfortunate because an overwhelming reliance on legal officers limits the agency's HUMINT abilities. Furthermore, for the United States, whose ethnic diversity provides a pool of recruits who could blend in with targeted societies abroad, not using such operatives represents a missed opportunity and a failure to exploit national resources at Washington's fingertips. For example, Washington could send abroad

Americans of Middle Eastern descent who speak fluent Arabic to recruit foreigners with information on terrorist networks. Instead, Washington sends Americans mostly of other ethnic backgrounds who require extensive language training and could easily be picked out as U.S. government employees even if they did not report each day to the U.S. embassy as they do. Similarly, America's intelligence agencies could hire Taiwanese Americans and others of ethnic Chinese descent to act as illegals in targeting China.

Failing to take these steps has avoided the unpleasant by-product of aggressive intelligence operations, in which one's agents are occasionally exposed and either harmed or used to create embarrassing international incidents. However, it has also severely impacted intelligence collection outside of electronic eavesdropping and overhead imagery. It represents a critical lapse in HUMINT, which is important to understanding foreign political developments and having the situational awareness necessary to fight back with effective political warfare and smart power.

However, the problems of the operatives pale in comparison to those of the analysts in the intelligence community. Critics of U.S. intelligence operations often cite activities undertaken against the Castro regime in Cuba and the left-wing governments and movements in the Americas and Iran, the arming of anti-Soviet fighters in Afghanistan, and the involvement of a CIA-linked person in the Watergate scandal as proof of the agencies' malicious intent or incompetence. While important lessons can be derived from those operations, this often-invoked list misses issues that are more important to U.S. statecraft and smart power today.

A basic reason the United States constituted its first peacetime intelligence capability outside of the U.S. Navy and State Department was to avoid another surprise like the 1941 attack on Pearl Harbor. But in 1949, merely two years after the CIA was created, a smaller but nonetheless highly consequential surprise occurred when the Soviet Union tested its first nuclear bomb. The event came years before the CIA's Office of Reports and Estimates said it would, leading to that office's termination.[25] Also at that time, the agency missed China's imminent entry into the Korean War. Furthermore, the U.S. intelligence bureaucracy failed to provide warning of India's nuclear tests in 1974 and 1998, and it missed the Soviet invasion of Czechoslovakia (1968), the Iranian Revolution (1979), and Iraq's invasion of Kuwait (1990).[26] More recently, the intelligence community was surprised by the 9/11 attacks on the United States and failed to assess properly the status of Saddam Hussein's WMD program. In 2011, America's intelligence bureaucracy, which now costs taxpayers a combined $80 billion per year, failed to foresee the Arab Spring with its major consequences for the Middle East.[27]

While senior intelligence bureaucrats have a low threshold and hair trigger for accusing policymakers and political appointees of interfering with intelligence, clearly the intelligence professionals themselves are not doing an adequate job under the current management arrangement. Tension between the political layer that sits atop government and the intelligence careerists below is nothing new, nor is executive-level disappointment with the performance of intelligence bureaucrats.

One particularly candid description of disgruntlement with intelligence professionals comes from David Lloyd George, Britain's prime minister during the latter portion of World War I. Four years after the main war in Europe ended, the new Turkey created from the detritus of the Ottoman Empire was set to go to war with Greece, eventually conquering what today is the European portion of Turkey. Lloyd George was frustrated that events proved the military and intelligence estimates of Greece's capabilities were too pessimistic, at least initially. Despite being prime minister, he was at loggerheads with his own War Office and Foreign Office. After a Greek success that was contrary to their predictions, he joyfully mocked his war minister, writing, "The Staff have displayed the most amazing slovenliness in this matter. Their information about the respective strength and quality of the two Armies turned out to be hopelessly wrong when the facts were investigated, at the [insistence] of the despised politicians." He then topped it off with: "Have you no department which is known as the Intelligence Department in your Office? It appears in the [budget] at quite a substantial figure, but when it comes to information it is not visible."[28]

With such candor, it was perhaps not a surprise that Lloyd George would cease to be prime minister a little more than a year afterward. Nearly a century later, the tension he described between the political level of government and entrenched bureaucracies still remains. More recently, in the

2000s, the American public was subjected to repeated claims that political appointees in the George W. Bush administration pressured intelligence officials and manipulated intelligence themselves to justify going to war in Iraq. However, this case is difficult to prove on two counts — the U.S. intelligence community wrongly assessed that Saddam Hussein had an arsenal of WMD before Bush arrived in the Oval Office, and virtually all other major Western intelligence agencies had reached the same incorrect conclusion.

More prevalent in Washington are senior bureaucrats who want to play pretend president, regardless of who sits in the Oval Office, and manipulate intelligence estimates. These people are neither operatives in the field nor workaday analysts toiling at the CIA in Langley or the National Security Agency at Fort Meade or the Defense Intelligence Agency at Bolling Field. Instead, they are the more senior permanent staff of agencies that have a particular view of the world and statecraft and mean to alter the way information is presented to effect the policies they want.

The most egregious instance of this practice in recent history involves Iran's nuclear program. It took place at the Office of the Director of National Intelligence (DNI), which is a new layer of intelligence bureaucracy slapped pell-mell on top of other agencies in the wake of 9/11 and Iraq-related intelligence failures. In 2007, the DNI produced a whopper of a National Intelligence Estimate — basically a formal intelligence bureaucracy assessment of a major challenge facing the United States — that almost certainly misrepresented the state of the Iranians' nuclear weapons program.

On December 3, 2007, the *New York Times* reported: "A new assessment by American intelligence agencies concludes that Iran halted its nuclear weapons program in 2003 and that the program remains frozen, contradicting judgment two years ago that Tehran was working relentlessly toward building a nuclear bomb."[29] This appraisal was almost certainly false. Two years later, the International Atomic Energy Agency released a report that would all but say explicitly that Iran's nuclear weapons–related program continued after 2003 and had progressed to an alarming stage in the interim.[30] However, at the time, the senior intelligence officials were little concerned with the facts or the reputations of their respective agen-

cies given their political objective: stopping President Bush from direct-
ing military action against Iran's nuclear program. Prior to the false intelligence estimate, Bush, Vice President Richard Cheney, and other senior
administration officials had been sounding occasional warnings about the
consequences of a nuclear-armed Iran. Bush had even suggested the situation was so dire it could lead to "World War III."[31]

The Washington foreign policy establishment has generally opposed
becoming tough on Iran since the Islamist regime there came to power in
1979. Washington forever sees moderates poised to gain power in Tehran
if only Washington could cultivate them, notwithstanding three decades
of evidence to contrary. Despite the impressive record of allied military
force in preventing Middle Eastern aggressors from realizing their nuclear
weapons capabilities — Israel halted the Iraqi and Syrian programs through
bombings in 1981 and 2007, respectively, and without sparking wider
wars — Washington's experts view the idea of using the air force against
Iran as uniquely horrifying.

Thus the timing of the faulty intelligence estimate was suspicious. It
was also a complete reversal from an estimate concerning the same issue
two years earlier. Journalists soon uncovered that the two primary authors
of the estimate, Thomas Fingar and Vann H. Van Diepen, came not from
the CIA but from the State Department's in-house intelligence bureau.
They had been opponents of Bush's decision to go to war in Iraq and felt
vindicated when intelligence related to Saddam Hussein's WMD turned
out to be faulty. By 2007, both men had been "detailed" — or temporar-
ily loaned — to the DNI, where they were in a position to coordinate the
opinions of various intelligence analysts from sixteen different agencies
and synthesize them into a single, false estimate.

Although estimates are generally top secret and compartmentalized,
someone — presumably with the concurrence of the staff at the NSC, which
is equally flush with bureaucrat "detailees" — decided to release the main
summary points of the report to journalists but to keep the overall report
classified. Fingar and Van Diepen had written this summary to overem-
phasize the incorrect conclusion about Iran ending its nuclear program.
Only later did the administration leak word that the whole report painted
a more damning picture of the Iranian program than the summary had led

the public to believe. Even with the false information about Iran's halting its nuclear program, the report detailed continued Iranian progress on its nuclear fuel cycle. This suspicious development called into question the report's simplistic conclusion.[32]

No matter, the damage was done by then. While critics immediately began pointing out the weak logic and intelligence value of the estimate, as well as the presumed political motivation of the authors, the release effectively precluded military action against Iran's nuclear program in the remaining year of the Bush administration. By that point, despite the success of the 2007 surge of allied forces in Iraq, Bush's approval rating was low, and his party had lost control of both houses of Congress. Bush would have faced a political firestorm had he chosen to strike Iran despite all of these factors and was understandably focused on the turnaround in Iraq for the remainder of his term. Furthermore, the Bush administration was influenced enough by the internal bureaucratic processes it supposedly commanded that the president could not take military action when his administration had ostensibly said a perceived threat was no longer real. There was no will in the administration to recant the assessment, for Bush's political opponents would have instantly labeled the action as manipulating intelligence to justify war.

Whether one agrees with the ultimate result of the faulty intelligence assessment — that is, undermining possible military action against Iran — the process by which the result was achieved should be concerning. The Constitution empowers the president, as one of only two elected officials in the executive branch, to direct foreign policy. When intelligence bureaucrats with their own political agenda usurp this arrangement, it is bad for democracy.

The story of Fingar and Van Diepen serves as a warning to anyone who wants to change Washington and challenge the Washington foreign policy establishment. Through the process of detailing officials from such agencies as the State Department and CIA to such coordinating bodies as the NSC and DNI, the bureaucratic establishment is able put its own people in position to influence and undermine the policies of presidents. Far from doing their jobs of implementing the policies set by a president and his cabinet, this guild seeks at times to become the policymaker itself.

The result is not only an affront to democracy but also has left a legacy of failure in properly handling the many threats facing America and its allies.

More broadly, the failure of the U.S. intelligence bureaucracy to provide the president and his aides with accurate information — information that is developed through clandestine sources who are recruited aggressively and is analyzed by experts who either disclose or control their personal political beliefs — is a major impediment to U.S. smart power. While military and other intelligence that can be derived primarily from electronic means (e.g., satellites and eavesdropping) will continue to be important, the most vital intelligence for the United States and its allies in the coming decade is likely to be political intelligence. Washington needs to know what various political actors on the world stage, be they leaders of governments or political actors outside of government, are thinking and whether their power is accreting or depleting. The U.S. government also needs to know whether these actors are friends to be cultivated or adversaries to be stymied. Little about these qualities can be divined by photographing the subjects from space or other technical means of intelligence collection. Instead, the United States needs functioning intelligence instruments of a type it does not currently possess.

THE NON-AGENCIES

If intelligence is the "pull" of information that America's adversaries do not want it to have, political warfare is the "push" of ideas, people, and events that America's adversaries would prefer to avoid. Throughout much of the Cold War, policymakers in Washington and allied capitals realized that activities like political warfare required the resources of government but were best performed by civilians outside of government and often outside of the United States entirely. For this work, Washington used instrumentalities that were independent of U.S. government agencies in fact or appearance, or what might be called "non-agencies."

One person who needed no convincing about the need for activities and organizations in this part of the smart power spectrum was Carmel Offie, one of the most colorful individuals ever to walk the halls of the modern U.S. government. A historian described Offie as physically ugly with "bulging eyes, fleshy lips and a swollen face; an open homosexual at a time when most stayed in the closet, Offie liked to disconcert other men by pinching his nipples in the midst of conversation." Entering the Foreign Service in the early 1930s and serving in Moscow and Western European capitals, Offie stretched the rules, even using the diplomatic pouch for illegal currency transfers and other modestly lucrative smuggling activities. Depending on the source one consults, he was forced out of the Foreign Service either for this misconduct or because Senator Joseph McCarthy singled him out as an undesirable and security risk. Kermit Roosevelt Jr. — the grandson of Theodore Roosevelt and a senior officer in a CIA then dominated by courtly and conventional white Anglo-Saxon Protestants (who were called WASPs) — described Offie as "an oily little jerk who talked oddly and did odd things."[33]

However, Offie was a genius of sorts. Despite modest origins, Offie had gained the confidence of hoity-toity people linked to senior levels of government ranging from ambassadors to future president John F. Kennedy. He had a large network of contacts in Europe in particular. One person who knew of his genius was Frank Wisner, a senior operations executive with the Office of Strategic Services in World War II who went on to lead the CIA's clandestine service in its early years. A CIA historian would later describe Offie as Wisner's "flamboyant and ubiquitous aide." Ostensibly pushed out of both the State Department and the CIA into private practice, Offie in fact still worked for Wisner directly in 1949.[34]

Offie and his colleagues were concerned with the activities of front groups that the Soviets were using to leverage American and European intellectuals, especially literary and artistic individuals of note, into both denouncing "U.S. warmongering" and claiming negative reports about the Stalin-led Soviet Union were fabrications. The Soviet leaders referred to these people as "useful idiots." The CIA and military strongly feared Moscow was winning the information war in Europe and possibly in the United States. A case in point was a major gathering in 1949 at New York's Waldorf-Astoria Hotel that the Soviet-dominated Communist Information Bureau (Cominform) supported as part of an effort to shape Western opinion. The attendees advocated peace with Stalin on his terms, whatever they may be. However, what impressed Offie most was the presence of a countermovement at the Cominform's "peace conference." Liberal and socialist writers led by a philosophy professor and reinforced by intellectuals and others who leaned left but hated Stalinists formed a group called Americans for Intellectual Freedom. They stole the show, asking embarrassing questions of the Soviet representatives in attendance. Pro-labor, anticommunist media covered it all in detail.[35]

Observing this development from the new CIA-linked Office of Policy Coordination (OPC) in Washington, Offie and Wisner began to formulate some of the most potent ideas and smart power organizations of the early Cold War. Specifically, they helped forge the tactic of supporting a left-leaning alternative to communism through the U.S. government's covert activities.[36] In other words, instead of unabashed free marketers touting the virtues of American-style classical liberalism and launching a frontal assault on communism, the U.S. government would instead take the more practical path of offering up socialists, social democrats, and the like to those in the key ideological battlefields of the day who might otherwise be tempted by communism. CIA Soviet expert Harry Rositzke later described this program to a historian: "It was a visceral business of using any bastard as long as he was anti-communist."[37]

Operationalizing the concept was difficult, but Offie, the wheeler-dealer not particularly concerned about the rules, was up to the task. Immediately after the Waldorf-Astoria confab ended, planning began with an eye toward undermining the next communist-influenced peace conference in Paris that same spring of 1949. While the OPC undertook to fly anticommunist intellectuals to perturb the Paris gathering, the results were unimpressive, with those attending on Washington's dime still striking a tone that was too anti-American and neutralist in the East-West confrontation. Wisner memorialized to colleagues in language one cannot use in government today that a better plan was needed to prevent decay "into a nuts folly of miscellaneous goats and monkeys whose antics would completely discredit the work and statements of the serious and responsible liberals."[38]

The solution was to turn to Berlin, where the close proximity of the Red Army and the citizens' gratefulness for the Berlin Airlift presented a more fertile ground than Paris did. American and German ex-communists and socialists were already discussing the idea of an international congress of the noncommunist Left. When the OPC caught notice of the proposal, most officials were unimpressed, but Offie knew better and saw potential. American occupation officials in Berlin were well aware that anything too closely associated with the U.S. government would lose its appeal with European intellectuals. On the flip side, back in Washington, a Truman administration being criticized as soft on domestic communism was not enthusiastic about publicly funding ex-communist intellectuals for a gabfest in Europe. As the organizers broadened what had been an idea for a mainly political conference into a much more inclusive and interesting "Congress for Cultural Freedom," the OPC arranged for covert funding. The State Department would overtly support the travel of American delegates, but the CIA would quietly handle the long-term basic support for the congress.[39]

Coincidentally, the congress opened the day after North Korea — at that time a Soviet client state — invaded South Korea, undermining any claim of Moscow's peaceful intentions. The congress turned out to be an unmitigated success. While there was fervid debate over how best to oppose communism, this tumult added significantly to the event's appeal to intellectuals. The Congress for Cultural Freedom thrived for many years, and its activities, which included meetings and publications, spread to dozens of countries. While funded in part by the CIA, the group's activities were substantially independent — and needed to be — considering the covert source of funds. In other words, the congress was not a mirror of the stage-managed Soviet Cominform but a vibrant movement that simply happened to have an unseen assist from U.S. taxpayers. Eventually, rumors of CIA funding began to spread, but the effort and its broader intellectual mission were well under way by then.

The Congress for Cultural Freedom was far from the only smart power and political warfare tool that the U.S. government put to work to undermine communism ideologically. The Office of War Information established and managed the Voice of America in 1942 to broadcast "white," or officially acknowledged, propaganda and repurposed the organization after World War II to combat communism. Its operators believed that basic, uncensored news alone would help undermine America's ideological foes.[40]

More effective was Radio Free Europe, which the CIA established and funded through a front organization in 1949 to broadcast a "muscular brand of political warfare" to Eastern Europe and Russia. Unlike the Voice of America, Radio Free Europe focused on news that was highly relevant and localized to the targeted populations. It was journalism with a cause and intended ultimately to encourage noncooperation with the Soviet Union at a minimum.[41] Radio Free Europe was later joined by Radio Liberty, which focused on the Soviet population itself.

The U.S. government topped this effort off in 1953 with the creation of the U.S. Information Agency (USIA), known abroad as the U.S. Information Service. USIA controlled the Voice of America for the rest of the Cold War and managed cultural exchanges, exhibits, and libraries at U.S. embassies and other overt actions aimed at the strategic communications and information warfare portion of the smart power spectrum. After the Cold War ended, freed people formerly held captive by communism confirmed earlier accounts from exiles and defectors as to the efficacy of these broadcasts. For some they simply boosted morale. For others, they afforded a glimpse at a better world from the dismal local environs their captors had assured them were a "socialist paradise."

After Poland's communist government was brought down, Lech Walesa, the triumphant leader of the Solidarity movement who became the newly free nation's president, was asked to what degree the U.S.-backed broadcasts of Radio Free Europe were effective. He responded, "Ladies and gentlemen, the degree cannot even be described. Would there be earth without the sun?"[42]

Unfortunately much of this broad intellectual effort collapsed in the late 1970s. It was revived somewhat in the 1980s but ended with the Cold War. Worse, not only the apparatus was killed off but also the entire way of thinking about a battle of ideas and the intellectual part of the smart power spectrum. Even as the threats facing the United States have become more numerous and multifaceted, Washington has dismantled or impaired its ability to understand and manage complexity.

In 1999, Congress terminated the USIA, its primary Soviet foe having been vanquished in 1991. Voice of America and Radio Free Europe lived on but under the control of a new Broadcasting Board of Governors, which, despite the efforts of many fine people, is basically a case study in how not to organize a smart power agency. As its name suggests, it is run not by an executive decision maker but by a board that is typically long on commercial media executives and short on smart power practitioners. Some of its members have at times rejected the notion that the organization is even a part of the U.S. national security apparatus.

As this book's introduction notes, the CIA began to be pushed out of the political warfare business with gusto in the 1970s, when Congress deeply undermined America's ability to engage in covert activities. In the 1980s, governments in Washington and London attempted to field a creative response to fill this gap in capabilities. On June 8, 1982, President Reagan addressed the British Parliament and made headlines by outlining a "plan and a hope for the long term — the march of freedom and democracy which will leave Marxism-Leninism on the ash-heap of history." Specifically, he sought "to foster the infrastructure of democracy, the system of a free press, unions, political parties, universities, which allows a people to choose their own way to develop their own culture."[43] To operationalize the effort, the U.S. government established the National Endowment for Democracy (NED) plus four subsidiary organizations. All are quasi-independent in that their actions are not necessarily directed by executive agencies of government. However, the flow of funds from government does influence their actions, and none can afford to undertake any project that the State Department directly opposes.

The idea has been for NED and related organizations to issue grants and at times directly cultivate pro-democracy activists around the world. Some of NED's work has been laudable. Many credit NED, its subsidiaries, and private pro-democracy nongovernmental organizations with augmenting the many "color revolutions" — for example, the Orange Revolution in Ukraine and the Rose Revolution in Georgia — that in the 2000s swept parts of former the Soviet bloc that had initially retained repressive governments after the Soviet Union fell. However, the non-agencies are now "blown," or fully exposed, with Russia in particular being wise to their political activities and related risks. In July 2012, Russian president Putin signed a law requiring rights groups funded from abroad to register with the Justice Ministry and file quarterly reports on their activities.[44] Such requirements will make any overt external support for political change difficult. Similarly, Egypt in 2012 halted the activities of NED subsidiaries and prevented the departure of operatives, including the son of a member of President Obama's cabinet.[45]

Ironically, the NED operatives in Egypt were not even engaged in hard-hitting activities and had opted instead for taking light-touch actions such as election monitoring and general political training for any interested parties, including anti-American Islamists.[46] (NED's founding president, Carl Gershman, who remains on the job three decades later with the Beltway equivalent of tenure, is among those who believe Islamist parties can be enticed to accept liberal democracy.[47]) The non-agencies are not only impeded by the lack of an ability to conduct covert operations but also suffer from a greatly diminished willingness to support dissidents, defectors, and others who are the key agents of potential political change. Some NED subsidiaries operating in China have the full approval of its government, thus clearly signaling their extremely limited potential to aid real dissidents or to foster political change.

NED's appropriation from the U.S. government was $31 million in fiscal year 2001.[48] By the end of the decade, this figure had quadrupled to $118 million.[49] However, NED's activities did not demonstrate any correlating quadrupling of output or even potential output. Indeed, many frontline dissidents found dealing with NED and its subsidiaries to be frustrating. I had a similar experience when trying to assist North Korean defectors who wanted to challenge the Pyongyang regime, ideally with the help of funds from NED and from their private supporters.

In 2004, Congress authorized small funding for such activities as aiding North Korean refugees and augmenting the flow of uncensored information into North Korea. In the following years, Senator Sam Brownback of Kansas and Congressmen Ed Royce of California and Chris Smith of New Jersey successfully fought for some money to be appropriated to fill out the authorization. (Explaining this frustrating Washington two-step to domestic and foreign audiences was always a painful exercise in disappointing the hopeful.) Once the money was appropriated and our office felt it would be best if NED ran the operation instead of the State Department's in-house bureaucracy, a NED officer sniffed, "We're deciding if we will accept the funds." It was my first experience but certainly not the last with NED's haughtiness. After interminable deliberations inside and outside the U.S. government that required worker hours of an expense to taxpayers that must have greatly exceeded the cost of the underlying program, some money began to make its way to independent radio stations with modest broadcasts going into North Korea. The government also funded other direct human rights work pertaining to North Korea.

Importantly, these projects included some hard-hitting defectors who could speak directly and empathetically to those left behind in the prison state, as defectors and ex-communists did in Europe a generation earlier. The impact of this program was clear enough, judging from the regime's reaction. The Kim government is suspected of multiple attempts to assassinate one of the radio station founders and frequently demanded of Washington and Seoul that the organization be put out of business.[50] Ironically, NED and Washington bureaucrats proved to be far more worrisome and deadly: they cut funding for the stronger programs. They disliked such irrelevant accounting infractions as using pseudonyms for paid stringers to protect them from assassination, tactics that were formerly known as good tradecraft skills. Meanwhile, Washington's funding of such government broadcasters as Radio Free Asia that target North Korea and China, while better than nothing, does little to foster the overall organization of opposition movements that real underground media does.

The net result of all of these lapses is that the United States has neither the tools nor even the serious inclination to engage in a war of ideas against Washington's adversaries, negating the main reason for having the non-agencies in the first place. This deficiency represents a no-show for a major part of the smart power spectrum. There is no updated Congress for Cultural Freedom for China today. While the idea of such a congress is outdated, Washington and its allies could develop modern venues for diverse opponents of Beijing to find common ground. Likewise, the same types of activities could be undertaken to undermine radical Islamists. Similarly, Radio Free Europe has not been re-created for countering Islamists, although that organization still exists along with a panoply of U.S. government–funded broadcasts. While communications technology has changed much since American-funded shortwave radio programs began crackling to life on the sets of captive Europeans and Russians behind the Iron Curtain, new tools and messages can be tailored to the information needs of those held captive by America's enemies today. Unfortunately, the old tools are broken, and little serious effort has yet gone into creating new ones.

From faulty intelligence to feckless diplomacy to non-agencies of limited use, the toll of having some of the most entrenched and inflexible national security bureaucracies, engorged with funding but short on productivity and supremely hostile to new thinking, ought to be apparent. At some point this situation will change. The Royal Navy bureaucracy, which ignored James Lind's solution to one of the key threats to British security in the eighteenth century, eventually embraced change. A U.S. military that did not adapt to emerging threats before World War II also had to change. The only real question now is whether the political level in the United States will force a change in smart power before or after experiencing a deep shock from a foreign foe.

SMART POWER SOLUTIONS

CHAPTER 8

Organizing for Victory

Once upon a time, decisions were made in Washington. Officials in the executive branch and members of Congress ruminated over problems of the day, debated the possible solutions, and then made decisions. They held hearings. Congressmen took votes. Presidents signed or vetoed legislation. No one thinks the right choices were always made, but at least a course was charted, and its merits could later be judged based on results. Corrective action could be taken when results fell short.

George W. Bush thought he had this kind of administration, but, for the most part, he did not. He once famously declared himself "the decider." When asked why he was not heeding calls upon him to fire a cabinet secretary, he responded, "I listen to all voices, but mine is the final decision. . . . I'm the decider, and I decide what is best."[1] The moniker stuck, especially with detractors who thought Bush was flippant in making decisions with long-lasting consequences. Certainly his administration made some big decisions, including decisions of war and peace, but they were exceptions to a management style that was often indecisive.

In his first term, Bush had as his national security adviser Condoleezza Rice, who favored "bridging" solutions that were intentionally constructed to avoid having the president make a decision between competing ideas. Rice wanted to generate consensus from disparate agency opinions and then inform the president that the team had reached an agreement. Some attributed this approach to her academic background of mollifying faculty members.[2] Others, who saw Bush up close, thought it was he who wanted subordinates to reconcile differences without him.[3] Whatever the cause, the result was unfortunate. As every painter knows, if one does not pick from different assortments of vivid colors and merely mixes them all, the result is mud.

So it was with some major issues in the Bush administration. The lack of clear decisions on strategy, tactics, agency roles, and how to measure success led to such fiascos in the hawkish administration as its eventual attempts to appease and bribe North Korea out of its nuclear weapons program, throwing the dangerous and brutal regime a lifeline in the process. The success of that de facto strategy was at least easy to measure: more than twenty seismic stations around the world and one radionuclide test of material that had drifted over the Pacific to Yellowknife, Canada, confirmed that North Korea became a nuclear weapons power on October 9, 2006.[4] Less spectacularly, the Bush administration's managerial lapses also led to muddling through rather than making firm and clear decisions on such matters as how to administer Iraq after Saddam Hussein's ouster and how to coordinate the many tools theoretically available to the government for Bush's vaunted "freedom agenda."

Not surprising, a system that could not make clear choices also had difficulty enforcing decisions and policies. In earlier administrations, the truest of true believers in the causes of a president — often centered around White House speechwriters — would fight strongly to include policy statements in presidential addresses. Their enemies were the bureaucrats. Inserting and preserving the portion of President Reagan's 1987 speech at the Berlin Wall where he said, "Mr. Gorbachev, tear down this wall!" was a major victory for the true believers. They beat not only the "mattress mice" (lower-level bureaucrats) of the foreign policy agencies who wanted the passage deleted for the sake of diplomatic comity but also some senior Reagan officials who thought it brash. And once the president said it, it became unquestioned policy to be followed, thus representing a major bureaucratic precedent. That desired outcome is what made the fight so important.

Not so with Bush. His public remarks were regarded increasingly as background noise as his administration progressed. For example, Bush publicly declared numerous matters to be "unacceptable," including Iran's nuclear program, Russia's invasion of Georgia, North Korea's nuclear and ballistic missile programs, Iran's tampering in Iraq, and so on; meanwhile, his administration on the whole was tacitly accepting those developments as inalterable realities. Other publicly declared presidential priorities, including the lofty goals of his second inaugural address about the spread of freedom, remained ambitions only for a small band of loyal officials. The rest of the bureaucracy knew it could do as it liked — and it did not like much of what Bush wanted.

These management breakdowns, however, were not the worst consequences from a system that sought consensus by attempting to mix insoluble policy options. Rather, the most damage came from never stepping back from day-to-day matters both to develop a comprehensive strategy for a new war and new world that emerged after the 9/11 attacks and to make the necessary consequential decisions to fight that war with some degree of clarity and cohesion.

Some in business and government refer to this myopia as being "driven by your inbox." In other words, leaders need to step back from the daily grind of routine matters and small crises and take the time to consider the bigger picture. At that time and subsequently, the White House and broader national security apparatus did not function in a way that allowed them to use a whole-of-government approach to the key security threats America faced and to produce a grand strategy. The result was a mixed bag.

Some very wise decisions were made nonetheless. The Bush administration ended without another major terrorist attack on the United States. Terrorists were put on the defensive globally thanks to a mix of intelligence, special operations, overt force, and revived legal tools and authorities. However, the Bush administration erred in knee-jerk decisions to create new bureaucracies like the Department of Homeland Security, its Transportation Security Administration, and the Office of the Director of National Intelligence. But worse than making any of those decisions was not devising a more comprehensive strategy to attack all of the pillars of radical Islamism. It meant the administration's overall approach to statecraft was desultory. Sometimes it worked; sometimes it did not.

Thankfully presidential national security planning was not always so haphazard and unimaginative. When Dwight D. Eisenhower assumed the presidency on January 20, 1953, it was apparent that the national security strategy needed to be revised and clarified. The Korean War was in its third year and stuck in a deadly stalemate that ultimately would cost thirty-seven thousand Americans their lives. Joseph Stalin, the Soviet dictator since Lenin's death, was himself at the end of his life, foreshadowing political instability in the world's most dangerous power. Investigators were bringing to light deep communist penetration of some of the most sensitive areas of the U.S. and British governments. Early steps to fight communism peacefully were either faltering or had yet to bear fruit.

Eisenhower's predecessor in White House, Harry Truman, had worked with a Republican-controlled Congress (one of only two such Congresses from 1931 to 1994) to pass the National Security Act of 1947. The law dramatically remade the U.S. national defense apparatus to take into account the lessons of World War II. The air force was created as an independent service, and four of the service branches were unified under a new command, the National Military Establishment, that was soon renamed the Department of Defense. Previously the services had fallen under the Departments of War and of the Navy, the latter of which encompassed the U.S. Marine Corps. The army and its air corps had been under the secretary of war.

This new unification was intended to overcome deficiencies in coordinating among the services during the war. For example, the U.S. Navy commander in the Philippines had failed to share with the commander of the U.S. Army Forces in the Far East, Lt. Gen. Douglas MacArthur, the news that the Japanese had bombed Pearl Harbor. In turn, the general later neglected to tell the navy that he was evacuating Manila ahead of the invading Japanese.[5] But the most important item in the 1947 legislation was the creation of the CIA and the National Security Council.

The NSC was set up to help the president manage the increasingly sprawling defense apparatus, which henceforth in the Cold War would have much to do even in times of relative peace. While the council was established under Truman, Eisenhower really institutionalized the NSC process. He held weekly meetings. During his eight years in office, he personally chaired 329 of the 366 meetings the council held.[6] (Today, when the president is not in attendance, an NSC meeting is usually called an interagency meeting instead.) Eisenhower also began the practice of having a powerful chief of staff to assist with managing both the White House and broader government, a practice every subsequent president has replicated with an occasional variation in title.

Eisenhower used a supplement of this framework to develop what would become his Cold War strategy. In what was dubbed Project Solarium, Eisenhower looked on as three teams of top national security officials debated options for grand strategy. The name "solarium" came from the part of the White House where most of the debates would take place; the corpulent William Taft had installed a solarium, or sleeping porch, at 1600 Pennsylvania Avenue to snooze away hot Washington afternoons in the summer.[7] Over the years, it evolved into a more prominent part of the White House's residence and offered a conducive place for a collegial but high-stakes debate.

Three months into his term, Eisenhower met with Secretary of State John Foster Dulles in the solarium to begin the project that would involve an intensive examination of Cold War strategy options. Eisenhower chose two generals and another senior official, asked each to put together a team, and sent them off to prepare for six weeks at the National War College. They were to address the issue of how hard to push back on Soviet aggression and under which circumstances the United States would go to war. The first team argued for building up allied forces and deterring expansion but seeking to avoid war unless directly provoked. The second team contended that a geographic red line should be drawn, and any attempts to expand communist influence beyond that boundary would trigger war. The third team sought a vigorous rollback of the Soviet Empire, including near-term military efforts to liberate captive nations. In the end, Eisenhower chose the first team's option: containment, deterrence, and a healthy dose of peaceful political efforts to perturb the Soviet bloc — essentially a smart power strategy. The product was eventually enshrined in a document numbered NSC 162/2 and simply titled "Basic National Security Policy."[8]

Perhaps most important was what Eisenhower did not do: seek consensus. Despite having been the senior general who held together the complicated Allied coalition — a hodgepodge of American, British, Canadian, Free French, and numerous other forces — in the European theater in World War II, the skilled diplomat, politician, and general preferred nonetheless to have the teams' different options presented to him in stark relief. The presenters engaged in spirited debate. Eisenhower himself chaired the proceedings, with the other members of the NSC, the military's Joint Chiefs of Staff, and a few other senior officials present. At the end of the day, Eisenhower summarized the three positions at length, demonstrating a full grasp of each, and decided then and there on the national security policy that would guide U.S. conduct for the next three and a half decades, the one most reliant on smart power.

No equivalent effort has taken place in Washington during recent political and military turning points, be they the Arab Spring, the growing danger signs from China, the removal of Saddam Hussein, the 9/11 attacks, or even the end of the Cold War. Serious planning and reform has taken place after some of these events, but nothing of the scale, seriousness, and impact of Project Solarium.

Part of the problem begins at the NSC, which is supposed to help presidents grasp complicated issues, make decisions, and then enforce them on the sprawling bureaucracy. Today, the NSC is often mistaken for the bureaucracy that staffs the president's national security adviser and other senior White House officials. They nearly constitute an in-house State Department within the Executive Office of the President with its plethora of deputy national security advisers, senior directors, directors, and miscellaneous staff. However, the real NSC, as set in law, simply comprises the president, vice president, and secretaries of state and defense. Administrations are free to enlarge this group, and often do, depending on the topic considered at an NSC meeting. Frequent attendees also include the treasury secretary and attorney general. The chairman of the Joints Chiefs of Staff and the top U.S. intelligence official have typically been advisers to the NSC, but at times, unfortunately, they have acted as de facto equal members.[9] It is always a temptation for new administrations to announce they are enlarging the NSC to encompass new issues and functions of government.[10] This expansion is unfortunate as the larger the NSC becomes, the more it begins to resemble the president's cabinet.

In the early days of the republic, the cabinet consisted of the president and his five key department executives. It was a primary tool for managing the executive branch. Today, cabinet meetings draw fully fifteen agency heads plus a half-dozen other officials designated as having "cabinet-level status," including, for example, the head of the Small Business Administration. As such, cabinet meetings now are only of ceremonial use and serve mainly as stage props so a president can appear to be guiding his top men and women for the reporters and photographers ushered in and out of the Cabinet Room for the occasion. This bloat is unfortunate for managing national security or anything else for that matter.

As recently as the Reagan administration, the NSC staff — the bureaucrats beneath the national security adviser — numbered a few dozen accomplished, skilled people in key positions. The organization was relatively flat as it lacked the stifling hierarchy of other bureaucracies. Through successive administrations, though, the number of NSC staffers has ballooned while their stature and influence have declined. Most government agencies have a single deputy director who serves as the alter ego of the agency head. As recently as the end of the Clinton administration, the NSC had two positions that came with the title of deputy national security adviser.[11] In the Obama administration, the number has grown to five.[12] As a result, officials and diplomats see lower-ranked NSC senior directors as having limited importance, and they ignore mere directors.

Numerous interagency meetings take place below the level of a full-blown NSC meeting. Each administration labels them differently. They typically follow the three-tiered hierarchy of gatherings of cabinet-level participants without the president in attendance, followed by meetings of the deputy secretaries or equivalent of relevant agencies, and then by meetings that involve lower-level officials like undersecretaries and assistant secretaries. Decisions theoretically can be made at any level where consensus is reached, or issues can be prepared for a decision by the higher levels.

Unfortunately, this arrangement only works well with a president willing to have disputes brought to him for a decision. Even the threat of this move can resolve an issue. But in the George W. Bush administration, some White House staffers joked that the conference room in the Situation Room area of the West Wing, where the top levels of meetings typically were held, was "the room in which no decisions shall be made."

The NSC should be taken back toward its original function and size, with some inevitable nods to expanded government. This step is key to enabling and cajoling presidents to make decisions and set strategy actively. Otherwise, policy is arrived at de facto by the decisions presidents do and do not make or by the collective actions of dozens or hundreds of officials answering their inbox irrespective of an overriding strategy.

Beyond that change, all of the smart power agencies of government need varying degrees of reform, retirement, or revival in order to give presidents more smart power tools.

STATE DEPARTMENT

There are different ways to run the State Department, each with its own pros and cons. During the George W. Bush administration, insiders occasionally referred to the "Powell" and "Baker" models. The Powell model was of course based on that of Colin Powell, Bush's first-term secretary of state, and was often described as "making the org chart work." In other words, when it came time to assign responsibility to someone or receive input from appropriate parts of the bureaucracy, Powell believed in turning to the assistant secretaries or other officials in charge of that issue — typically a combination of the regional bureau (e.g., East Asia, Near East) and functional bureau (e.g., democracy, economic affairs). While this approach seems obvious, it involves a conscious decision to empower the bureaucracy at the State Department, but many secretaries from both political parties wisely have been reluctant to do so. For example, Washington insiders regarded Powell's predecessor in the Clinton administration, Madeleine Albright, as being at loggerheads with the State Department bureaucracy. However, the pro-bureaucracy model was understandable for Powell. The administration in which he served arrived in Washington with the view that it would co-opt and work with the national security bureaucracy despite the predictable disinclination that bureaucracy would have for the policies Bush wanted to pursue, ranging from reforming the military to stepping away from climate and arms control treaties.

A former chairman of the Joint Chiefs of Staff, Powell had risen through the military hierarchy and adopted its management style. Typically, although there are exceptions, senior military officers in charge have their commands for about three years. During their tours, the officers who want promotions need to distinguish themselves and have operations run smoothly. This relatively short time frame does not lend itself to comprehensive or long-term reform. Instead, many military leaders focus on making do as best as possible with the tools at their immediate disposal. True to this model, Powell focused more on process and on ensuring various actors at the State Department performed their assigned roles. Less important to Powell was whether the product of that process was consistent with the president's priorities.

The Baker model — named for George H. W. Bush's first secretary of state, James Baker — is the opposite. This model presumes that the State Department bureaucracy cannot be trusted with issues of great importance to the president, especially if that president is a Republican. As a result, key issues and presidential priorities are taken away from the bureaucrats in whose portfolio they would technically fall and are handled by a small cadre of trusted advisers on the State Department's seventh floor.

Two months after James Baker was sworn in, the *New York Times* reported, "To hear some State Department veterans describe them, Mr. Baker's aides are a secretive, tightly knit family of foreign policy ingenues who seem intent on trying to run the department in isolation from the professional bureaucrats."[13] This observation overstated the case, especially since many of Baker's "outsiders" were bona fide members of the Washington foreign policy establishment, if not the State Department's Foreign Service. But the concept — more or less adapted from Henry Kissinger, who as Nixon's foreign policy consigliere served concurrently in the roles of secretary of state and national security adviser — remains one of seizing important issues and generally ignoring the bureaucracy's routine churn of lesser matters.

The downsides of the Baker model are that it demoralizes the State Department's workforce and that the president's view of the world is unlikely to be applied to the lesser issues, which still constitute an important component of statecraft. Furthermore, it theoretically fails to leverage professionals within the State Department who share the president's politics or at least are able to separate their personal preferences from their performance on the job.

George Shultz, who was Reagan's secretary of state and immediately preceded Baker, hewed closer to what would become the Powell model but with one important variation: he more actively managed the bureaucracy. This effort included taking a number of actions to impose Reagan's views of foreign policy on to the bureaucracy. After his tenure, Shultz described one symbolic action he took repeatedly that marked his different approach to managing diplomats. Upon meeting with American ambassadors who were set to leave for their new postings or upon receiving ones visiting Washington for consultations, Shultz would end their meetings by asking the ambassador to point to his or her country on the globe in his office. Invariably, the person pointed to the country to which he or she was accredited as the U.S. ambassador. Once, the new U.S. ambassador to Japan placed his finger instead on the United States, saying to Shultz, "That's my country." Shultz told this story in subsequent meetings with ambassadors, reminding them, "Never forget: you're over there in that country, but your country is the United States. You're there to represent us. Take care of our interests and never forget it, and you're representing the best country in the world."[14]

While this speech may sound quaint and even patronizing, it was an important and effective message to the bureaucracy. It was also a message that Shultz, the statesman who had served in two previous cabinet positions and as White House budget director, was uniquely positioned to deliver at a time when the United States was still recovering from the foreign humiliations of the previous decade.

While each management style has pros and cons, what is missing from these models is the radical reform that the State Department needs. Today, Foggy Bottom, as the agency is called in reference to the Washington neighborhood where it is located, remains in many ways an anachronism. As detailed in chapter 7, the agency's problems are manifold, but, in general, the department remains good at accomplishing its originally intended mission — that is, talking to other governments. This communications function remains important to smart power. Understanding the overt but sometimes opaque actions and messages from foreign governments is as critical as explaining Washington's views to those foreign governments. Giving an official line to foreign publics is also useful, although this audience now has access to nearly infinite sources of information to supplement official channels when trying to gauge what the United States is doing.

Where the State Department has run into trouble is when it steps too far beyond this basic purview. As outlined in preceding chapters, this overreach has included instances in which the agency was asked to produce a "civilian surge" in war zones or wage a "battle of ideas" leveraging nongovernmental actors. Advice that the State Department should keep in mind comes from the character Clint Eastwood played in his second Dirty Harry film, *Magnum Force*. Dirty Harry advised more than once that "a man's got to know his limitations." The State Department should apply this excellent guidance as part of a broad reorganization. Government planners should realize that the U.S. government's senior cabinet department is basically a giant, expensive telegraph machine. There is nothing particularly wrong with this reality beyond the expense. Indeed, every government has a foreign ministry, and no one has figured out how to conduct statecraft without one. When politicians begin speaking of having the government engage in "capacity building" or supporting civilian institutions abroad, though, they should understand that those people who are drawn to traditional diplomacy simply do not have the skill set for that work.

Meanwhile, Foggy Bottom should not escape major reform. To begin, the department's bifurcated workforce, which basically consists of Foreign Service officers and civil servants, should be unified. The split is a remnant of an era when living abroad was exotic and arduous. Today, in many posts where Washington sends most of its diplomats, they are no longer hardships. Diplomats living in such places as Lisbon or Shenyang undoubtedly face inconveniences unique to the localities but nothing that American businesspeople have not been able to surmount for decades. Further, as businesses generally do not have completely separate workforces to conduct their activities abroad, neither should the State Department. There is no reason a civil servant who meets objective qualifications should not be able to serve at any U.S. embassy or consulate. In fact, the same is true of many civil servants outside of the State Department, whose talent and skills ought to be tapped for diplomacy, including up to the job of ambassador.

In recent years, pay and benefits for employees who worked abroad for the State Department has exceeded what is necessary to attract the required talent, especially if the workforce were deregulated. Dethroning the Foreign Service guild would also avail U.S. statecraft of the large number of Americans in the private sector with deep experience and networks abroad. Many of these people would be open to taking a tour of a few years in government and serving their country abroad, but the opportunity now is all but impossible unless they wish to start their careers over and at the bottom of the Foreign Service hierarchy.

Going beyond workforce reform, the State Department should also be stripped of any military responsibilities or foreign police-training oversight. These jobs are the natural province of the Defense Department, which should assume the State Department's existing responsibility for doling out foreign military aid and support for foreign police forces. Further, the State Department should also lose what is known in the government as "chief of mission authority." This principle holds that an American ambassador has ultimate control of all U.S. government employees in the host country and can regulate all of their activities. An ambassador also can send anyone home at any time. Giving an ambassador this oversight was understandable in the time before instant communications; then an ambassador really had to act as the president's plenipotentiary envoy. Today, this outdated authority permits ambassadors who lack relevant training to interfere unnecessarily into spheres of intelligence and military issues.

Demoting the role of ambassador may sound counterproductive to enhancing smart power, but limiting the role of the State Department and allowing for some bureaucratic competition and tension can actually provide a president with more tools for statecraft. More important, as with intelligence collection, political warfare activities should be beyond the veto of any one U.S. ambassador abroad, even if they involve the embassy. This protocol is essential to protect both the role of the ambassador as chief diplomat (standing apart from nondiplomatic activities) and the mission of political warfare.

The State Department believes it guards against clientitis — the act of going native and taking the point of view of the local government instead of Washington's — by limiting the duration of tours abroad. Some postings run as few as two years, and some tours in dangerous areas are even shorter. This cap is highly inefficient: diplomats may spend as much time learning language skills and transitioning to and from a new posting as they do in producing effective work in their posting. Furthermore, it actually makes clientitis more likely.

Two years or less in a new country is too little time to develop a local network and assess the quality of information and insight from various sources and interlocutors. Thus, America's diplomats rely too heavily on officials from the host government and others whose introductions are arranged by local nationals who work for U.S. diplomatic missions. All of those people are easy for a newly arrived diplomat to meet, but this system does not enable the diplomat to avail himself or herself of local voices whose opinions and information run contrary to conventional wisdom. The alternative is longer tours with other mechanisms and leadership providing a disincentive for clientitis.

Next, the State Department should get out of the business of issuing visas and passports. The department famously issued visas to the 9/11 terrorist hijackers. It also gave one to Umar Farouk Abdulmutallab, a Nigerian Islamist later known as the "underwear bomber" for his attempt to destroy a Northwest Airlines flight with 289 innocent people aboard on Christmas Day 2009. Abdulmutallab's own father had warned the local U.S. embassy that he had become radicalized and absconded to Yemen "for the course of Islam" and "some kind of jihad." A senior administration official later said this highly specific information was still not specific enough for the State Department to revoke his visa. His murderous plot was foiled in part by alert and brave crew members and passengers who subdued him.[15]

The State Department almost lost its ability to issue visas when the Department of Homeland Security was created in the wake of 9/11. However, the Foreign Service objected because it viewed the prospective move as a loss of power and budget and because the service subjects its new employees to a tour on the visa line at U.S. diplomatic posts abroad. A joke at the department held that one could be a fluent Arabic speaker and the dean of an international studies graduate school but would still be sent to stamp visas in Jamaica for two years if joining the Foreign Service. In today's world, visas and passports are the work of law enforcement and should naturally rest with the Department of Homeland Security and its Customs and Border Protection agency. In Great Britain, visas are satisfactorily handled not by the Foreign and Commonwealth Office (that country's State Department equivalent) but by the U.K. Border Agency, which was created in 2008.[16]

Last but not least, the State Department, once slimmed down, refocused, and confined to government-to-government diplomacy and some light government-to-public diplomacy, would still need strong leadership to keep employees focused on its mission in the world. Taking a step in the wrong direction, the Obama administration changed the agency's mission statement in 2012 to seek a "world composed of well-governed states that respond to the needs of their people, reduce widespread poverty, and act responsibly within the international system."[17] These laudable but hazy sentiments should rightly be given back to the Peace Corps and replaced with a simple one: advance American interests in the world. The clarity and reinforcement that Shultz provided in reminding U.S. ambassadors who they really served is needed again if an agency that has drifted back and forth between rogue and irrelevant is to be a key part of smart power.

THE CIA

In 1984, one of the longest-running, most successful, government-sanctioned monopolies in U.S. history came to an end. In the earlier part of that century, the Bell System of phones had become what economists call a "natural monopoly," or the condition where the necessity of a large, expensive network precludes more than one choice for consumers. As it would be wasteful and unfeasible for a city to have two competing sewer systems, so too was it improbable at that time to have a country with competing sets of copper phone lines leading to all homes and business that used phones. Thus American Telephone and Telegraph Corporation (AT&T) and the government agreed in 1913 that the company would monopolize nearly all local phone networks and long-distance service between cities. AT&T moved into such other areas as manufacturing and renting individual phones (non-black ones cost more and were a status symbol) and the phone equipment that the company used across the nation. The results were impressive at first. Call quality and network reach in America were superior to that in all other nations.[18]

However, a company without competition has little incentive to innovate. And unlike the sewer business, the telecommunications industry is one where even politicians and lawyers can imagine innovation. A crack in the dam started to appear when the Federal Communications Commission permitted early competitors to AT&T's long-distance monopoly. Soon, they protested the market barriers that AT&T presented to their entry. Washington then began to take notice, and the government brought an antitrust suit against AT&T in 1974. A mere eight years later, the matter was resolved in a settlement that broke up the company, with a divestiture of local service into new "Baby Bells" and with AT&T left to operate in a long-distance market. The Bell System was dead, and the cost of telecommunications soon dropped precipitously with new competition and innovation.[19]

As with "Ma Bell" in 1984, the CIA should be broken up today. The agency's current position and organization prevent innovation in the intelligence bureaucracy and fail to recognize the obvious: what once worked very well is no longer suitable. The agency's numerous flaws and errors, compounded by Congress in recent decades, are outlined in detail in chapter 7. In 2005, in the wake of 9/11 and faulty Iraq-related intelligence, the CIA was technically dethroned as the kingpin of the government's intelligence bureaucracy. Previously, the head of the CIA was also known as the director of central intelligence, signifying that he theoretically sat atop not only his agency but the whole community of sixteen intelligence elements, including, for example, the military services' intelligence branches and those of miscellaneous other agencies.

The 2005 creation of the Director of National Intelligence was supposed to change this hierarchy, replacing the CIA's boss as the head of the broader intelligence community. However, in effect, the DNI — both the new organization and the position of the person in charge — has been weak and unsatisfactory. In 2009, DNI head Dennis Blair issued a directive indicating he might name someone other than the top CIA person in a foreign country — known as the CIA station chief — to be America's top intelligence representative in that country. Blair did not go into details, but one could imagine, for example, that the top U.S. intelligence representative in Colombia might ideally come from the Federal Bureau of Investigation (FBI) or Drug Enforcement Administration rather than the CIA. Similarly, in select friendly countries where spy issues generally center around cooperation on electronic signals intelligence, it would make sense for the top U.S. person to come from the eavesdropping National Security Agency.

The CIA rejected this unflattering logic. Langley was apoplectic about the possibility that its top spook in one or two foreign countries might not outrank a geeky cryptanalyst from Fort Meade. The then-director of the CIA, Leon Panetta, fought the issue at the White House and won.[20] The CIA would continue to name the station chiefs, who would be the bosses. In effect, the CIA remained supreme in the bureaucracy, integrated vertically and horizontally similar to the old AT&T in its industry.

Instead of attempting to restore the supremacy of DNI, though, the organization should be abolished. Its intended function of collating (or centralizing) intelligence from numerous intelligence components can be performed — and in many cases already is performed — by the National Counterterrorism Center, which was set up in 2004. That successful organization's purview in contrasting or harmonizing disparate intelligence could simply be expanded.

The story of the DNI, meanwhile, is a case study in half-baked Washington reforms. Rather than fully think through the intelligence lapses that led to the 9/11 attacks and faulty Iraq-related assessments, and then making painful but necessary changes to various existing intelligence instrumentalities, the Bush administration and Congress decided instead to slap a new layer of bureaucracy on top of the existing dysfunctional structure. Thus, the DNI was born.

In its short life, the DNI has chalked up an impressive list of misleading intelligence and public gaffes from its various directors. The latter category includes an instance where Director James Clapper was caught in an interview unaware of a major terrorist plot days after it was foiled in London. The scheme had led to numerous arrests in the capital of America's closest intelligence partner and had been widely reported in the press.[21]

Three months later, Clapper slipped again in public, predicting errone-ously that Libyan dictator Qaddafi would prevail in his struggle against the rebels on whose behalf the United States was going to war.[22] As out-lined in chapter 7, the DNI was also responsible for the misleading 2007 National Intelligence Estimate on Iran's nuclear program. Rather than dig this hole any deeper, Washington should admit the DNI was a bad idea and terminate the agency.

However, the CIA should not be allowed to retain its supreme posi-tion. The agency remains a jack of all trades and master of none. Other parts of the intelligence bureaucracy generate human intelligence derived from real spies rather than machines but only in limited capacities. For example, the military services' intelligence components and the Defense Intelligence Agency may collect HUMINT and manage human spies, but they generally only do so in relation to existing or possible battlefield situ-ations. The State Department's intelligence bureau is regarded as a joke in the sphere of HUMINT (and most others). The CIA remains basically the monopoly producer of HUMINT on wide-ranging threats to national security or political developments abroad that affect the United States.

This situation is unfortunate. Not only does this antiquated organiza-tional design resemble the old AT&T but it also fails to take advantage of obvious examples of better management within the federal government. Consider military aviation, for example. Clearly it is the forte of the air force, but aviation is also a big part of the other armed services as well. In fact, one might say the navy has an air force of its own, centered around ten aircraft carriers that cruise the globe with as many as seventy planes each. Some even joke that Marine Corps aviation is the "navy's army's air force." Of course, each service has tailored its planes, drones, and missiles to its own mission, but unarguably some overlap exists. This arrangement actually cre-ates a healthy and all-too-rare feature of government where limited compe-tition is permitted. It also gives America's combatant commanders — and its president — alternatives in the event one of the services fails its mission.

This overlap should be replicated with HUMINT. Clearly the CIA has considerable skill in this area, honed over decades, and the agency or a suc-cessor should continue to have a large role in running HUMINT. It may make sense for a CIA successor to run "legal" spy operations that involve officers operating under official cover at U.S. diplomatic missions abroad, but it should lose its monopoly even in this arena. A new agency should be established to conduct "illegal" spy operations (i.e., away from embassies) that are essential if America wants a first-class intelligence program. Furthermore, it may make sense to bring the Pentagon's Defense Intelligence Agency and the FBI into broader areas of foreign HUMINT in order to give policymakers more options and to create useful bureaucratic tension and competition. This suggestion does not mean reerecting those dangerous walls between intelligence components that existed before 9/11 and were subsequently modified. Rather, it should give those who analyze HUMINT more sources and options.

Other parts of the CIA should be cleaved. In recent years, the CIA has become almost a second air force with its heavy usage of drones, especially to kill terrorists in Pakistan and Yemen. The CIA runs its bombing effort in parallel to that of the military — namely, the Joint Special Operations Command.[23] This duplication is somewhat understandable. Having both organizations involved stems from the earliest days of the war after 9/11 when military special forces and CIA paramilitary operatives left together for the non-Taliban-controlled areas of Afghanistan with $9 million in cold cash to begin coalition building.[24] Furthermore, an air force general ran the CIA from 2006 until early 2009.

The CIA's involvement in drone warfare is also supported by the false presumption of many government lawyers that covert activity (including some drone strikes) can be supported by the military but must be initiated by the CIA or that CIA kill operations have more legal latitude.[25] These views stem from interpretations of different parts of U.S. Code that define the role of the armed forces (Title 10) and intelligence authorities (Title 50, chapter 4). When U.S. Navy SEALs killed bin Laden in 2011, CIA director Panetta was at pains to explain that even though the "real commander" was the admiral in charge of the Joint Special Operations Command, the operation was nonetheless a "Title 50" — or covert CIA mission — that the president ordered through Panetta.[26] But this explanation is problematic and improbable since only two civilians — the president and the secretary of defense — are in the military chain of command, and Panetta was not one of them at the time. More astute government lawyers have noted that this legal interplay — and the role it preserves for the CIA — is less about the law and more about turf issues on Capitol Hill, where intelligence committees want to influence activities that otherwise the Armed Services Committees would oversee exclusively.

Regardless, the real problem is not the legal or ethical issues of having nonmilitary personnel (i.e., CIA employees) carrying out activities that are inherently in the military's purview. The issue is that this business is all very far afield from what real intelligence agencies do. The science of airpower and the art of special operations are capabilities the United States surely must master, but there is little reason to distract indefinitely the organizations that presidents rely on to steal secrets and prevent dangerous surprises with these jobs. All of these tasks likely can be assigned to the military. Virtually none of them are truly covert in that the president could plausibly deny the involvement of the U.S. government after the missions — especially the drone attacks — are undertaken.

The reason the CIA reached this point was out of a desire — admittedly a laudable desire — to be relevant to the deadly conflicts in which America was engaged, but there was a cost. Organizations must focus on their core competencies and core mission. Allowing even an isolated part of the CIA to progress further toward becoming a second air force and a paramilitary organization leads inevitably to its core intelligence mission being neglected. If a small, nonmilitary cadre of drone pilots and paramilitary operatives is required for situations where the presence of the U.S. military would be too politically dangerous, then so be it; but a new, small civilian organization attached to Joint Special Operations Command can perform those functions.

Last and least, the name "CIA" should go. While the C in CIA stands for "central," this meaning is not really true anymore and certainly should not be. Any successful reform would involve ending even the supposition that the agency's role remains as the central clearinghouse for either collecting intelligence or presenting it to policymakers in analyzed form. The whole point is not to have a "center" that allows for a sloppy monopoly or constricts the intake of intelligence owing to risk aversion or calcified ways of doing business. Beyond the name, a clear break is needed to signal real reform — whenever it finally comes.

The CIA's employees and all Americans should be very proud of the agency's accomplishments since 1947. But it is time to recognize the reality that the CIA's acting as the government's "Ma Bell" for intelligence is part of the past, not the future — especially if the United States decides improved intelligence is critical to statecraft.

A POLITICAL WARFARE AGENCY

Even with the breakup of the CIA, the creation of multiple HUMINT-capable agencies with some healthy competition, and the reform of the State Department, the smart power spectrum would still have a large missing part where political warfare should fit. As noted in chapter 7, in the sense that espionage is the pull of information U.S. adversaries do not want Washington to have, political warfare is the push of people, ideas, and events with which America's enemies would rather not contend. Presidents need a tool to do this pushing. Given the decline of the CIA and limitations of the State Department, as well as the shortcomings of "non-agencies" like the National Endowment for Democracy, no instrument is available to presidents to initiate and manage political warfare.

This prospect is especially true if the nature of the political warfare mission requires U.S. involvement to be covert, such as in aiding secular, anti-Islamist reformers in the Middle East. No part of the U.S. government today feels ownership of the job of looking at the historical and political context of important countries, assessing which factors could cause the most difficulty for America's adversaries, and developing options for exploiting the situation. Here again, the lack of HUMINT sources and properly trained analysts to interpret the HUMINT is stunning considering the world today, with its multiplying political forces and contests.

The closest operation the United States ever had to a peacetime political warfare agency was the U.S. Information Agency. As outlined in chapter 7, it was a victim of the success to which it contributed — namely, the demise of the Soviet Empire. After the Cold War ended, the USIA languished and was shuttered in 1999.

Its precursor, more or less, was the Office of War Information in World War II. That agency conducted white, or overt, radio broadcasting and other strategic communications missions during the war. The Office of Strategic

Services, predecessor to the CIA, handled "black," or intentionally deceptive, communications that were often falsely advertised as coming from within an enemy-occupied area. However, when it came to propaganda and information operations, America's Office of Strategic Services paled in scope to the British government's Political Warfare Executive (PWE). London originally created what would become the PWE inside the new Special Operations Executive, whose mission Winston Churchill succinctly described as "to set Europe ablaze."

Churchill's prescience in creating the PWE was remarkable. His military background as a young man was as a cavalry officer, and he participated in history's last major cavalry charge at Omdurman, Sudan, in 1898. He became a British hero shortly thereafter in the Second Boer War in South Africa. In World War I, he was initially the civilian cabinet member who oversaw the Royal Navy. None of these conflicts had an overwhelming political component, having to do instead with issues of nationality and empire. Propaganda played a role in World War I, but its application by both sides was simplistic and crass. It was also far afield from Churchill's area of responsibility. Thus Churchill demonstrated wisdom and clairvoyance unforeseeable from his background when creating the PWE and grasping the political dimension of World War II. He brought to bear political forces of subversion in tandem with traditional military forces to assault German interests.

During its wartime existence, the PWE grew rapidly to host scores of radio services directed at various geographies and groups, especially in occupied Europe. It even had a broadcast so specific that it was tailored to German U-Boat crews at sea that the British hoped to demoralize.[27] Other activities included radio, film, and pamphlet activities in places as obscure as Gambia.[28] London took great care in strategic communications and information warfare to an extent not seen from the United States or its allies since.

However, in the 1950s, the USIA made a strong showing despite the inevitable lapses of any bureaucracy. While technically independent, the USIA took cues from the State Department, especially since its officers abroad worked out of U.S. diplomatic missions, where the ambassadors or consuls general heavily influenced local information activities.[29] USIA products included libraries and exhibitions, as well as educational and other exchanges. USIA officers could be more expansive and flexible than other U.S. diplomats in their contact with local intellectuals and media. They had more latitude to be openly supportive of those groups and people who were potentially friendly to the United States and its allies or at least hostile to Moscow. Occasionally these contacts included characters too eccentric for the tastes of stodgy political officers in the Foreign Service.

The inherent problem with occasional calls in Washington to reconstitute the USIA is that what was reasonably well suited to that earlier era would not be particularly useful today. In most countries, people have ceased to gather much information from traditional libraries or the types of exhibits that the USIA assembled and managed. Since the bombing of two American embassies in Africa in 1998 and especially since the 9/11 attacks, many U.S. diplomatic missions have increasingly come to resemble fortresses and have been moved from downtown areas to more remote parts of foreign capitals. Few foreign nationals wish to visit these buildings unless absolutely necessary for work or travel.

Moreover, in its day, the USIA had its own problems. Along with the kinship it felt for the State Department, it possessed a hostility at times for competitive U.S. government–funded information services. For example, the USIA managed and thus felt ownership for the Voice of America. It was jealous of Radio Free Europe and Radio Liberty, which were independent and, by almost all accounts, more effective politically and more popular with audiences behind the Iron Curtain.

Other ideas to re-create the USIA or an equivalent, while well intentioned, would result in a new organization with considerable problems. In 2008, Senator Sam Brownback introduced legislation to create a National Center for Strategic Communications.[30] The year before, Senator John McCain called for a similar act, saying, "We need to re-create an independent agency with the sole purpose of getting America's message to the world."[31] Both suggestions would undoubtedly have resulted in better public diplomacy than what the State Department conducted, but the proposed legislation involved transferring existing parts of U.S. public diplomacy into the new organization to be created. For example, it would have folded into the new agency the Voice of America, which the Broadcasting Board of Governors oversees, and the State Department's Bureau of Educational and Cultural Exchanges. These actions would have saddled the new agency with a workforce that is ignorant of the political warfare component of the smart power spectrum, as in the case of State Department exchange officials, and that is unionized, as in the case of the Voice of America employees. (In U.S. history no crack national security organization has been unionized.)

Furthermore, without being more transparent and more expansive about the new agency's mission than simply tasking it with strategic communications or public diplomacy, there is no reason to assume a new organization would perform much better than what exists today. The mission of "getting America's message to the world" is too modest and too vague. Washington should wait until it can understand and feel comfortable with delineating the clear strategy of using smart power to undermine America's opponents before creating new agencies.

At that point, a new organization should be constituted specifically to learn about the foreign political forces that pose threats to the United States and its allies, and to implement strategies to undermine them peacefully. This agency should then present options to policymakers for supporting friendly movements against America's adversaries while retarding those movements that are likely to harm U.S. interests. Most important, this new organization needs the ability to act covertly and at times even support political forces that might not want U.S. help but whose progress would advance U.S. interests (e.g., the opposition movement in Iran).

To fully appreciate and influence these foreign political forces, the new agency needs the capability to collect and exploit human intelligence, including through foreign networks run completely independently of U.S. diplomatic missions (i.e., using "illegal" spymasters who forgo the luxury of diplomatic immunity). Last but not least, in creating such an organization national leaders need to comprehend and explain to the public the risks this type of work will involve. As with the CIA, this new organization will make mistakes, at times with deadly consequences for those involved. The public and their elected representatives used to grasp that major national endeavors inevitably involve risk, especially when the United States undertook them in opposition to tyrannical governments and other evil forces.

Sometimes this risk taking resulted in embarrassing failures. Sometimes it resulted in death. These risks can be mitigated but never avoided completely when those who favor a civilized order in the world stand up to dangerous foes.

In 1961, President Kennedy complained to Congress that "no objective supporter of foreign aid can be satisfied with the existing program. . . . Bureaucratically fragmented, awkward and slow, its administration is diffused over a haphazard and irrational structure. . . . Its weaknesses have begun to undermine confidence in our effort both here and abroad."[32] Unfortunately the same could be written of foreign aid today, more than half a century later. Correlating Washington's handouts to foreign governments with clear accomplishments that matter to national security or other U.S. interests is simply not possible. Little evidence shows that pouring money into countries leads to sustained economic growth once the aid is stopped. And there is no evidence that traditional assistance reduces corruption, a fundamental cause of economic decay in any country. In fact, injecting funds into a corrupt economy may actually reinforce corrupt institutions and practices.

The Marshall Plan was not the first time the United States engaged in massive peacetime foreign assistance, but nearly sixty-five years later, it remains the guiding light and most cherished legend for advocates of foreign aid. As the problems of Europe and the stakes of the new Cold War became clear, the United States commenced an effort in 1948 that delivered $13 billion in support over four years to many war-ravaged nations, or about $125 billion in today's dollars when adjusted for inflation.[33] Most historians regard the Marshall Plan as a success, both in demonstrating that Washington was still committed to the alliance, which would become NATO, and in preventing conditions that might have made communism appealing to more people. However, practically since that era, U.S. foreign assistance has failed to advance clear economic or national security goals.

Invariably around budget time each year in Washington, advocates on both sides of the political spectrum who want to maintain foreign aid point to the small total amount spent on assistance when compared to the military budget or overall federal budget.[34] However, this point is irrelevant if assistance is accomplishing little or in fact doing harm to U.S. interests.

In the past decade, two of the biggest recipients of U.S. aid outside of declared war zones have been Pakistan and Egypt. Beginning in 2009, Pakistan's take was increased to $7.5 billion over five years.[35] Egypt fares better, averaging $2 billion in aid each and every year since 1979.[36] Both countries have intensely corrupt economies and populations that routinely profess their hatred of America to pollsters. Egypt now has an Islamist government, and some 70 percent of its population opposes U.S. aid.[37] Pakistan's government is even less appealing. It uses terrorists as instruments of national power, including against American troops and interests.

The arguments for sustaining foreign aid to such countries range from the reasonable to the suspicious. Many in Washington believed that aid to Pakistan was necessary to ensure lines of supply to U.S. troops fighting in Afghanistan. This assumption was reasonable, although Washington probably could have bought the supply line security for a great deal less. Other arguments for aid to Pakistan were weaker. For example, in 2011, Representative Michele Bachmann, a member of the Intelligence Committee who was then seeking the Republican nomination for president, called one of her opponents "highly naive" for urging a cut in aid to Pakistan. She added, "Pakistan is a nation that's kind of like 'too nuclear to fail.'"[38] This comment raised several questions. Was the implication that Pakistan would have used or proliferated a nuclear weapon to the detriment of the United States if Washington cut off aid? Did that assertion not make the aid a form of tribute? Would it not have been better to use traditional deterrence, counterproliferation, and missile defense to neutralize such a threat instead? Or if the threat was that terrorists might steal these weapons, should the message have been instead that a country that can afford to build a nuclear arsenal has an obligation to secure that arsenal with its own resources?

Similar questions arise when one considers U.S. aid to Egypt. When some in Congress suggested halting the aid after the Egyptian government stood by as the U.S. Embassy in Cairo was attacked in September 2012, Senator John McCain remarked, "Only someone who doesn't understand anything about that part of the world would suggest such idiocy."[39]

Throughout the year, McCain had stressed Egypt's importance as a bell-wether in the region as justifying the need for continued U.S. aid.[40] But the question was not whether Egypt was important — it was and is — but whether U.S. assistance advanced U.S. interests there. This presumption seems dubious. Many in Washington think aid to Egypt, most of which is in the form of military assistance, is necessary to maintain peace between Egypt and Israel. While a tacit part of the U.S.-brokered 1978 accord establishing peace between Israel and Egypt involves Washington providing both countries with aid of roughly similar magnitude, there was no agreement to continue this assistance in perpetuity. Military reality and national interests result in peace between the two countries, not handouts from American taxpayers.

Skeptics of foreign aid unfortunately tend to overstate their case. Much should be done to reform U.S. assistance, but it should not be eliminated as it remains an indispensable part of smart power. A smaller program linked more closely to near-term U.S. national security interests would be better. For example, in recent history such a program was pursued after the collapse of the Eastern Bloc, which ended the Cold War. Rather than attempt a direct repeat of the Marshall Plan, the U.S. government launched a number of "enterprise funds" authorized by the Support for East European Democracy Act of 1989. These programs basically amounted to venture capital funds that provided loans or equity for promising businesses in newly free Central European nations. The idea was to jumpstart the private sector. The most successful program was the Polish-American Enterprise Fund, and in an unheard-of turn for a government program, it ended up returning money to the U.S. Treasury. A key prerequisite to the funds' success was their general limitation to economies that had only little corruption and were in the process of reforming. One exception was a fund for Russia, and it was the least successful and most controversial of the funds. Thus a nonnegotiable hurdle for standing up to corruption should be in place for any future U.S. economic assistance. Otherwise, aid can end up making a recipient's economy worse in the long run.

This reason is one of several why U.S. economic assistance should be divided between different cabinet agencies. Most funding can be categorized as either economic or military aid. Economic assistance should be handled by the Treasury Department's Office of International Affairs, where the importance of reducing corruption is better understood. Treasury also has a stronger grasp of U.S. economic interests abroad than does the current paymaster of foreign assistance, the U.S. Agency for International Development. Successive administrations have tried to rein in the agency and force it to configure programs so they advance broader foreign goals — that is, turning it from a Peace Corps–type program with a fat checkbook into a force for smart power. Such efforts have not worked. As with other agencies that date from the Cold War and were once productive but now exist in a state of performance collapse, the service should be shuttered.

With economic assistance handed off to the Treasury Department, the question then becomes how to administer foreign military assistance. Oddly, this job currently falls to the State Department. It should be transferred to the Defense Department, which essentially has its own in-house State Department in the form of the country desks of the Office of the Secretary of Defense. While the Pentagon is consulted on foreign military aid, giving the department more complete control would avail the secretary of defense and America's combatant commanders of more effective smart power tools in an area that involves military expertise rather than diplomatic skill. The move would also enable deeper links between U.S. military officers and their allied counterparts.

TYING IT ALL TOGETHER

Reform of this scope will not be easy in Washington, given the foreign policy establishment's resistance to change and hostility to new ideas. However, the suggested elimination, creation, and redesign of agencies would still be of a smaller scale than that which occurred in 1947 as the Cold War challenge became clear. This reform must happen if the U.S. government wants to be serious about smart power. The reform effort of 1947 is unique in that it happened during a time of shock but not in the wake of a truly massive calamity like the Japanese attack on Pearl Harbor or the 9/11 attacks on the United States. Hopefully such a disaster is not a necessary prerequisite to spark the next surge of reform.

If these or similar reforms are enacted, the question remains of how to tie them together. For example, a historical argument for keeping the CIA has been that overlapping responsibilities — especially with different agencies running multiple spy operations — might result in sloppiness where employees of the same government are working at cross purposes or stepping on each other's operations. This same concern applies more broadly to political warfare in general or, going back further, to the whole spectrum of smart power in U.S. statecraft. Is a center that applies some degree of control required?

Certainly it is. The answer is a revitalized National Security Council to act as a conductor of an orchestra and manage the disparate smart power actions from the White House. To succeed, the NSC should be reworked so that it more closely resembles what it was in the Eisenhower era, with some modifications for the present situation. What the real members of the NSC — the president, vice president, and secretaries of state and defense — control is most important. For simplicity and better management, the president should direct the process while the others, joined by the secretary of treasury, should act as the key facilitators of a whole-of-government approach to statecraft. Other principals in government, similar to today's practice, could serve as advisers to this process when so ordered by the president. This input could involve facts or opinions from the chairman of the Joint Chiefs of Staff or intelligence agency leaders. In this arrangement, the military's individual combatant commanders (e.g., head of Central Command) would retain their direct line of communication to the president if needed, as they have in law since the 1986 Goldwater-Nichols Act. But there should be no ambiguity about their roles as advisers: they are not members of the NSC and have no vote. All responsibility and accountability should lie with actual members.

For that reason, the various new and reformed smart power agencies outlined previously — for spying, waging political warfare, handling inter-government communications, doling out foreign aid, and the like — should report to one of the men and women at the NSC table. The choices among those with a seat on the NSC are the secretaries of state, defense, and treasury.

Putting any new agencies under the secretary of state is problematic. The organization that person oversees has an abysmal record of understanding and practicing smart power. Furthermore, an unfortunate custom in Washington has taken place, with a particularly dovish member of a cabinet being assigned to the State Department and presidents dispatching comparative hawks to the other side of the Potomac River to run the Defense Department or CIA. This norm developed partly because many in Washington believe that diplomacy necessarily involves diffidence and a soft touch not only abroad but at home on managerial issues as well. It also partly mirrors the sentiments of the Senate Foreign Relations Committee, which must confirm all presidential appointees for key positions at the State Department, including assistant secretaries and above, plus all ambassadors.

Unfortunately, Washington's natural instinct would be to place a new political warfare agency, which would be seen as a successor to the defunct USIA, under the secretary of state. Those supportive of political warfare would counter and attempt to make such an agency "independent." However, this category works better in theory than in practice: some independent agencies below the cabinet level theoretically report directly to the president but in effect report to his chief of staff, given the limitations of what any president has time to do. But a White House chief of staff has even less time and capacity for strategic thought than a president does. Others agencies are technically independent but fall under the sway of cabinet agencies — for example, the State Department influenced the old USIA. Such arrangements achieve the worst of all worlds: agencies are left without any direct link to the NSC, while they are also degraded by State Department mediocrity. The Pentagon would be a better home for a political warfare organization.

In fact, placing all of the new intelligence agencies under the secretary of defense may make the most sense. Traditionally, much of the intelligence bureaucracy's funding has been laundered through the Pentagon budget in order to conceal America's true intelligence capabilities from its adversaries. This mechanism has given the secretary of defense leverage over intelligence components that are not technically under his purview. There is no strong reason to deviate from this arrangement, although civilians should probably run the new agencies, especially since their focus areas would be more political than military in nature. Nonetheless, cross-pollination of its workforce with the uniformed military would be beneficial. As evidenced by the military's many advanced schools, the armed services have a commitment to professionalism and continued learning throughout its members' careers. This emphasis is lacking in other agencies, including in those whose bureaucrats look down on the military. To the extent intelligence is a science, the Pentagon can teach its soldiers and civilians to be masters of the trade.

This scenario would empower the Departments of Defense and the Treasury at the expense of the State Department. A radical alternative would be to throw all of the nonmilitary agencies under a drastically reimagined secretary of state. This option would only work if that secretary came from a different background and worldview than has been the norm in recent decades. Furthermore, the secretary would have to sit above and separately from the current State Department. Essentially, one would need to create a new "foreign secretary" who sat atop all of the intelligence and political warfare agencies, as well as a dethroned State Department recast as a new Agency for Intergovernmental Communications. The benefit of this organization would be having a member of the NSC — America's de facto war cabinet — who is the supremo for smart power, with considerable information and operational tools at the secretary's fingertips. The downside is it would entail a drastic scope of change, which would make the reform more sweeping than even that of 1947. It would require not merely the approval of Congress — as would all of these reforms — but a major reform of the many committees and subcommittees of Congress. For people whose notion of a big deal is holding a hearing, that work might be overwhelming.

With these more effective tools at the disposal of a president and his top aides, the United States would be prepared to wage smart power in the most effective way possible. Now all the government needs is a plan for applying these refined principles and tools of smart power to the governments of China and Iran and to Islamists around the globe.

CHAPTER 9

Undermining Iran and Islamists

Many older Americans know Abbas Abdi but not by name. He is etched into memories of those who saw him night after night on the evening news. In 1979, he was one of the leaders of the Islamist militants who invaded the U.S. Embassy in Tehran, taking American diplomats hostage. In conduct unparalleled in modern time, the regime that came to power earlier in 1979 used the hostages as propaganda tools and subjected them to psychological and physical torture. For more than a year, Abdi and the other terrorists paraded the hostages in front of crowds and cameras, presenting compelling images to be broadcast nightly in the United States.[1]

The regime rewarded Abdi with a mid-level job in government. However, by 2003, he was on the outs with those in power and had started a two-year term in an Iranian prison. Abdi was disappointed by the revolutionaries he served and faced a common fate for those who work for the forces of tyranny.

For example, after the French Revolution in 1789, not only monarchists and members of the nobility went to the guillotine in the Reign of Terror but also some of those activists who helped spark the revolution. In Russia, most of the leaders instrumental in bringing down the Romanov Dynasty in 1917 were eventually sent to prison or to their deaths by those whom they empowered. The few thousand Americans who joined the Abraham Lincoln Brigade to fight the Fascist side in the Spanish Civil War beginning in 1936 were unfortunately aiding the Soviet agents who captured the broader movement and would have controlled Spain had they succeeded. Disillusionment with the political side of that endeavor is better known, partly because some of its participants lived to tell the tale. American novelists Ernest Hemingway and John Dos Passos were two of the idealists mugged by reality in Spain.

But Abdi never became a true apostate to the cause he served. He remains an adherent to Islamism, but he would merely like power shifted from one set of regime figures to another. This bottom line represents the West's challenge with Iran: Western diplomats are forever sensing in Tehran's power circles so-called moderates, but many of them are still committed to the same basic form of tyranny. Some even want to take a harder line than the current leaders enforce. Almost all of them despise the United States, want Iran to have a nuclear arsenal, and finally are committed to the ultimate destruction of Israel and its population.

Thus it is no surprise that Abdi opposes efforts the United States has undertaken to curb Iran's nuclear-related activities. A reporter interviewing Abdi summarized: "What is most important, he said, is for the United States to realize that by imposing sanctions on Iran, it has become a domestic player. Iran's leaders fear that the White House is secretly trying to use domestic political factions to engineer a change of government."[2]

If only they did. Unfortunately, it is unlikely that Abdi and his fellow Islamists really fear this possibility. They, as with most anyone, recall the spectacle outlined in chapter 2, where the U.S. government essentially ignored those Iranians in the streets protesting their government in 2009. Regardless, rather than allay any concerns of Tehran's about American meddling, making this fear come true ought to be a top priority for the United States. Helping the Iranian people take back their government not only from the incumbent rulers but also from all advocates of clerical rule should be the overriding, long-term U.S. goal. It is also a natural fit for smart power.

Some will say advocating this effort is calling for regime change in Iran. Indeed it is, but only in the sense of enabling its people to change peacefully and voluntarily a government they despise. This essentially democratic act is a far cry from forcible regime change via military means, which was used to depose the Taliban government in Afghanistan in 2001 and

Saddam Hussein's government in Iraq in 2003. That method, more properly, should be described as "regime destruction." While it is necessary in extreme circumstances, it is not in the case of Iran today.

TEHRAN'S SINS

What has the Iranian government done to warrant U.S. and allied support for the Iranian people in their struggle? While some Americans think of Iran first and foremost in terms of the regime's past taking of U.S. hostages — an obvious act of war in the minds of most people — more recent Iranian activity has been far deadlier. During the Iraqi insurgency after the 2003 U.S.-led ouster of Saddam Hussein, Iran contributed to the deaths of hundreds and perhaps thousands of Americans and easily tens of thousands of Iraqis.

Some of the deadliest weapons that the insurgents used were improvised explosive devices, which were made often of old artillery shells wired to act as mines in roadside attacks. This tactic became much deadlier when Iran supplied insurgents with cutting-edge explosively formed projectiles. These weapons produce a molten bullet capable of penetrating many armored vehicles.[3] Their lethal results in Iraq were tracked with a spike in U.S. casualties.

Furthermore, Tehran went well beyond simply supplying weapons to insurgents. The Iranian government was intimately involved in planning and executing attacks against Iraqis and Americans. As the Bush administration moved to surge forces in Iraq and adopt a counterinsurgency strategy there, the United States took one of its few firm actions against Iran. In late 2006 and early 2007, U.S. forces in Iraq swept Iranian targets and arrested those present, including senior officers of Tehran's terrorist-training units.[4]

The Bush administration and reporters downplayed Tehran's role in Iraq, as have historians writing early histories about the war, but plenty of information about Iran's involvement exists. Concurrent with the sweep, secret cables between Baghdad and Washington show the U.S. ambassador had a frank talk with the Iraqi vice president about "Iranian-sponsored targeting of coalition forces."[5] In a 2007 meeting with Iraqi prime minister Nouri al-Maliki, U.S. commander David Petraeus pressed for action on

Iran's support for the dangerous militia controlled by Muqtada al-Sadr. The prime minister said in turn he had raised it with Iran's supreme leader, who even acknowledged Iran's involvement.[6]

Six months later, a classified State Department cable summarized another discussion between Maliki and Petraeus: "Maliki said he agreed with General Petraeus that the Iranian government leadership probably knew the entire truth about the weapons smuggling since they had also acquiesced to the training of hundreds, maybe thousands, of Iraqi criminals and terrorists by their Quds forces."[7] (The Quds Force is an elite part of the Iranian military charged with exporting the Islamist revolution.) As late as 2009 — well after the insurgency had been defeated — the embassy in Baghdad cabled Washington about the Iraqi government's attempts "to restrict the activities of [Iranian] Islamic Revolutionary Guards Corps Quds Force (IRGC-QF) officers operating under diplomatic cover in Iraq."[8]

Unfortunately, the 2006–2007 detentions of Iranian operatives were an exception. All too often, provocative Iranian actions have been met with only weak U.S. resistance. In announcing the sweeps, Bush said, "Throughout Iraq, operations are currently ongoing against individuals suspected of being closely tied to activities targeting Iraqi and Coalition forces." He did not even name explicitly the chief culprit in killing scores of Americans.[9] So it was throughout the war. Part of this disinclination to attack the Iranians' involvement was a political calculation. After the Democrats dealt Republicans a major setback in the 2006 midterm elections, Bush could not afford to be seen itching for a fight with yet another government. He had to preserve his political capital for the controversial surge of forces in Iraq he had ordered. Whatever the practicality of downplaying Iran's role, a consequence was that the administration never explained to the American people the full truth about Tehran's killing of Americans.

The Iranian regime has also escaped punishment for numerous other aggressive acts in the past. Iranian proxies kidnapped scores of Americans, including the CIA station chief, and other Westerners in Lebanon in the 1980s and killed some. Iranian-backed Islamic Jihad, the precursor of Hezbollah, orchestrated the killing of 241 American servicemen in a 1983 attack in Beirut. The United States took only token actions in response, adding unintentionally to the confidence the Iranian regime has felt since coming to power in 1979. Washington failed to punish Tehran for its role in the 1996 bombing of the Khobar Towers in Saudi Arabia, where U.S. servicemen were quartered. The attack caused the death of nineteen people, and wounded approximately five hundred others.[10]

In addition to backing Hezbollah, which went to war with Israel in 2006, Iran also supports the terrorist group Hamas with weapons and military training.[11] Iran's involvement is noteworthy since Hamas, which is headquartered in the Palestinian Gaza Strip, is a Sunni Islamist group while Iran is a bastion of Shiite Muslims. This cooperation refutes others' claims that the Sunni-Shia divide in Islam means a combined Islamism is impossible and that those who warn of this dangerous unity are simplistic and ignorant of the nuances of Islam. Shiite Iran's support of Sunni terrorist groups shows that radical Islamists can put their differences aside to achieve immediate goals. They are willing to defer the settling of internal sectarian scores to a later time.

Some opposed to using smart power aggressively against Iran note that all of the aforementioned activities, while alarming, occurred in the past. The invasion of the U.S. Embassy in Tehran occurred more than three decades ago, and the Iranian-backed killings of Americans in Iraq ended with the conclusion of that war. Unfortunately Iran has exhibited no indication that it is de-escalating its dangerous conduct or broad political ambitions.

Iran's nuclear weapons program, for example, is proceeding steadily. Once Tehran has a nuclear weapons capability or even has the ingredients of a bomb that can be assembled rapidly, the regime will only grow more brazen. In late 2011, operatives of the regime were caught in Texas attempting to hire an assassin to a kill a foreign ambassador in Washington. One of the conspirators who pled guilty, a man with dual Iranian and U.S. citizenship, had been willing to accept theoretically a hundred collateral American deaths to complete the assassination.[12] His link with Tehran was his cousin, a Quds Force commander whom the U.S. government believes planned a 2007 attack in Iraq that killed five Americans.[13] Clearly, the regime maintains the will and means to act and not only against Israel.

The only people who can topple the Iranian government peacefully are those who live in Iran. Luckily many of them are already highly motivated to do so.

In June 2009, Iranian president Mahmoud Ahmadinejad won reelection by a suspiciously large margin. He supposedly trounced three opponents, including two who were considered to be "reformists." To run for office they had received the necessary clearance from Iran's Guardian Council, which confirmed the candidates' Islamist credentials despite their opposition to some regime policies. Given the lack of a real choice, Ahmadinejad probably would have won anyway, but many Iranians suspected the regime inflated Ahmadinejad's margin though rigged votes. They took to the streets, adopting as their banner the campaign color of Ahmadinejad's chief opponent. The Green Movement was born.

Importantly, the movement evolved beyond voicing only its opposition to Ahmadinejad or its support for his immediate opponent. Those who filled the streets of Tehran and other major Iranian cities opposed the regime altogether. They chanted such slogans as "down with the dictator" and "death to the liar." Some sang a well-known protest song titled "My School Friend."[14] The regime reacted violently, especially the Basij militiamen, who killed scores of peaceful protesters. These types of enforcement thugs, similar to Adolf Hitler's private army of Sturmabteilung (stormtroopers or brownshirts), are common in Islamist regimes. The Basiji likely were responsible for the murder of Neda Agha-Soltan, whose horrifying death was caught on video and broadcast around the world. As were many young Iranians, the twenty-six year-old Agha-Soltan was not particularly political before the uprising, but she was motivated by the protests to stand up to injustice. Regime thugs also broke up her funeral and later desecrated her grave.[15]

Ultimately, the government suppressed the mass protests. However, they continued to flare up intermittently. It seems increasingly clear that anti-regime sentiment has reached a new, higher plateau. This development has to be terrifying for those who populate the senior levels of the regime, remembering as they do the gradually deteriorating political situation of the pre-1979 government in Iran. They were the hunters then. Now they are the hunted.

Furthermore, the opposition appears to be expanding and welcoming new groups of Iranians. Economic malaise has affected a country that should be prosperous given its massive oil and gas reserves. Yet, Iran's economy is increasingly dysfunctional. Iran has about the same population as Turkey, but its economy is less than half as large. Tough times have begun to erode one of the key pillars of support for the regime — namely, the merchant class. In October 2012, merchants upset by economic conditions and a rapidly devaluing currency clashed with police in the streets of Tehran.[16]

While it is still entirely possible that less than a majority of Iranians want to depose the regime, practitioners of smart power should keep this disquiet in perspective. Revolutions put to a popular vote would seldom attract a majority of votes. Many American historians believe that a popular vote taken on July 4, 1776, would not have yielded a result of 50 percent or more in favor of declaring independence from Great Britain. Rather, historians generally believe that about a third of Americans favored independence, another third preferred to continue the union with Britain, and the final third was not sure. Certainly revolutionaries in France in 1789 and Russia in 1917 would have never chanced a fair vote, even if one had been possible.

The key point is that a successful revolution is not necessarily about the biggest mass of people. It is about the most energized and organized mass of people. Those who wish to support radical change from afar should keep this truism in mind. Iran's younger citizens and urban middle class are likely the keys to revolution in that country.

WIELDING THE TRUTH

As in virtually any political movement, spreading information is crucial for the Iranian opposition. Censorship in Iran is not as comprehensive and effective as it was in some communist regimes; however, Iranian authorities block literally millions of websites from viewers in the country.[17] The Iranian government also intermittently jams satellite and radio broadcasts from abroad, including independent and governmental broadcasts from the United States, Great Britain, and France.[18]

Overcoming this blockade of information is key. Facts about what is really happening inside Iran, as well as what is going on in the world at large, are highly useful to motivating would-be dissidents and protesters. The truth is seldom friendly to tyrants; thus, they go to great lengths to prevent the free flow of information.

For example, during the Cold War, information seeping past communist censors into East Germany spoke volumes to the average East Germans living under tyranny. They saw that immediately to their west lived other Germans with a very different and more appealing lifestyle. Even aside from hard news or political messaging, accurate images of free Germans living in comfortable apartments and driving cars proved subversive. Simply seeing late into the winter West Berliners consuming fresh fruit, a rarity in the East at times, was eye opening. Many in the East doubted any people could really live so well until they saw the evidence with their own eyes.

This programming was augmented by numerous other channels of information, including news and commentary shows about what was really going on inside both the Eastern Bloc and the free world. When the authorities censored books and newspapers as well, especially in the Soviet Union, it gave birth to the samizdat, a clandestine network of citizens that distributed banned and often crudely reproduced books, plays, and other publications.

While samizdat material was focused on the intelligentsia, broader audiences consumed cultural fare that also proved subversive in its way. One of my fonder memories from my time at the State Department was seeing middle-aged Czechs suddenly start to disappear from an embassy function in Prague as if on cue. As it turned out, they were off to see the terrible new movie *Rambo* (2008) in an abandoned warehouse. They were reliving the days of old when, as young regime opponents in the former Czechoslovakia, they needed to sneak around to watch banned American films that had been hastily bootlegged and dubbed (including much better iterations of the *Rambo* series). Sylvester Stallone greasing commies was a symbol that transcended culture and nationality.

Meanwhile, all of these sources of information collectively put the lie to what repressive regimes told average Russians and Eastern Europeans. By the end of the Cold War, most of them knew instinctively that their governments were lying to them and misleading them about how they had it better than those living in the West. But this realization was the culmination of years of erosion. First communism had to fail economically. Then this failure — along with the political agony tyranny inflicts on a culture — had to be made known and broadly understood. Furthermore, the regime's lies had to be refuted. While much of the information to do so came from the West, it is important to note that the voices that carried the message were of the nationalities and cultures of those oppressed. Free Russians, Czechs, Poles, Bulgarians, and others formed a lifeline to their countrymen living under repression who, in turn, picked up the information and passed it along. It so happened that the U.S. government and private American organizations and average citizens, including those who understood smart power, funded and organized some of this effort.

So it should be for Iran. As with the Eastern Bloc, the United States and other free countries should place a virtual mirror over Iran and serve as a communications platform that spotlights the truth about the regime and the Iranian people's desire for change. Some are already making such efforts on a small scale. Radio Free Europe, which is funded by the U.S. government, operates the Persian-language Radio Farda. The service sends audio programs into Iran on short- and medium-wave radio, as well as via satellite.

Voice of America also has its own Persian News Network. However, the network has had its share of problems to say the least. Tracking with the overall deficiencies of U.S. government–supported broadcasting described previously, Voice of America seems unable even to comprehend its mission. Critics have pointed out that its Persian News Network actually has pro-regime voices on its payroll and air. Other voices are merely anti-American. During an important spike in protests in Iran in 2010, the broadcaster decided to feature an American Marxist who implied the anti-regime Green Movement was somehow "American imperialism" at work. Over the years, the broadcasts have criticized U.S. involvement in conflicts going back to the Korean War and praised anti-American icons like Hugo Chávez. How any of this reporting advanced U.S. goals in regard to Iran is unclear and unexplained.[19]

A much better communication strategy to counter the Iranian regime would rely on more recent exiles from Iran and hidden anti-regime sources inside Iran. Rather than bring these broadcasters into U.S. government agencies, Congress and private organizations should fund independent media groups through grants and do so covertly if necessary. This proven system has conveyed the most effective messages to encourage freedom movements.

Rather than relying simply on one source, Washington could build a platform for multiple anti-regime voices and views. Dissidents and protest leaders are some of the most creative people in the world. They are best positioned to understand what Iranians need to hear. They are familiar with regime censorship and know how to exploit internal political currents. However, they often are less knowledgeable about the technical aspects of disseminating information, especially when repressive governments use sophisticated censorship means. Dissidents operating on a shoestring budget lack the resources to pay expensive commercial rates for satellite and terrestrial transmitters for TV and radio. The associated expense increases dramatically when targeting a government such as Iran's that is proficient at jamming broadcasts. Dissidents thus need to have multiple, redundant methods of broadcasting. Ideally, they should be able rapidly to change their frequencies and times of transmission, and to use a combination of radio and video over terrestrial and satellite platforms, plus the Internet and other telecommunications networks.

Repressive regimes such as Iran's not only rely on direct jamming but also seek to intimidate private communications companies into dropping objectionable content. For this reason, involving the resources and clout of the U.S. government is useful if dissidents are going to mount a major information campaign against Tehran.

In times of crisis, dissidents and protest leaders inside Iran would need a surge capability to talk to their people directly. The U.S. military already has the right tool for this job: a small number of highly modified transport aircraft designated as the EC-130J Commando Solo. These aircraft are basically flying television and radio transmitters that can position themselves to overcome enemy jamming. The military has used them successfully for psychological operations to demoralize enemy troops in combat. These resources would provide a major boost in using smart power against

Tehran. When a moment of democratic opportunity arises, such as a major bout of unrest, the United States should be ready to hand Iranian protest leaders a microphone to speak to their people without a filter. In the meantime, pro-freedom broadcasters outside of Iran can prepare the information space and erode the regime's support.

This information operation is also an excellent opportunity for traditional diplomacy to augment U.S. efforts. Some European countries that would not ordinarily spring to mind as helpful on Iran-related issues are, in fact, committed to free media and efforts to combat censorship. The Netherlands and the Nordic countries — including neutral Sweden — have a strong history of fighting repression and censorship. Since the end of the Cold War, such formerly captive nations as Poland and the Czech Republic, among others, have joined their ranks. Thankfully, these countries have a self-identity and healthy nationalism that stands apart from Brussels, the de facto European capital and seat of the European Union. Put simply, they share American values on essential freedoms and still think for themselves. While U.S. resolve and resources would be indispensable to a serious smart power effort aimed at the Iranian regime, it need not be a unilateral effort. Turkey and friendly Arab states would have important roles to play as well.

From time to time, some question whether it makes financial sense to continue broadcasts that are jammed by adversarial regimes like the Iranian government. Multiple arguments can be made against bowing to this reservation. First of all, jamming is seldom perfect and especially in Iran's case. The government can shield certain important areas from some messages it does not like, but it cannot stop all broadcasts, particularly if they are carried on multiple formats and frequencies. Second, jamming ties up some of Tehran's attention and resources, which leaves less available for other bad uses. Third, jamming becomes apparent to the public whose access to information is being blocked. This effort by itself arouses curiosity and exposes the regime's fear of its own people. Finally, curtailing strategic communications in the face of enemy jamming is a sign of weakness. When the United States gives in, it encourages despots and discourages reformers.

Dissidents and protest leaders in Iran need help with communications, but they also need assistance more broadly. As demonstrated in the early protests of the Arab Spring, secular liberals who want modernity and non-Islamist government exist in great numbers across the Middle East. They filled the town squares and began the protests. However, they are poorly organized in Iran. This disorder is understandable as the Iranian government systematically persecutes those who oppose the Islamist government. Money is not a sure-fire solution to all problems related to organizing political movements, but it helps. During the Cold War, the United States provided covert financial support to anticommunist political parties in Europe. The calculus was simple: Moscow was supporting communists, so the West had to do its part to level the playing field or, better yet, tilt the playing field to the benefit of the West. The results were impressive in places like Italy and Greece. Trade unions and the Vatican also provided financial assistance to the Solidarity union and opposition movement in communist Poland.[20] Washington should repeat these activities today, adjusting them to fit Iran.

A number of groups outside of Iran oppose the regime. Chief among them in funding and organization is the People's Mujahedin of Iran (Mojahedin-e-Khalq [MEK]). The MEK is a mixed bag. On the plus side, it has all of the right enemies in both Tehran and Washington. They include not only the Iranian government but also the State Department bureaucracy and most of Washington's think tanks and establishment foreign policy press. These American critics claim the MEK has little following inside Iran. However, it is unclear how they can be so certain, given their nearly perfect track record of incorrect perceptions about Iran.

The critics do correctly point out the MEK used to engage not only in political warfare but also in violent acts directed at the Tehran regime. Such activities can undermine nonviolent resistance. The MEK partnered with Iraq against Iran in the 1980–1988 war between those countries. (Of course, so too did the United States indirectly at one point by providing Iraq with the military intelligence necessary to thwart an Iranian surge.) Since then, the MEK has forsworn violence and surrendered its capacity for such activities. President Bill Clinton listed the MEK as a terrorist organization in 1997, however, as part of an effort to reach out to supposed moderates in the Iranian regime. Secretary of State Hillary Clinton dropped the group from the list in 2012 amid a remarkable lobbying campaign by former government officials.

Critics say, as with any well-funded exile group, the MEK is out of touch with those for whom it claims to speak: in this case, those still inside Iran. Indeed, some of the MEK's leaders had to leave Iran not long after the 1979 revolution. However, the group draws tens of thousands of supporters to its gatherings in Europe, including many young supporters. Furthermore, history shows that successful dissent movements, including groups like the MEK, draw on a combination of internal and external political actors. The movements eventually bring foreign pressure and internal resistance to a coordinated crescendo that cracks the regime.

The MEK has other skills. A leaked State Department cable from 2006 suggested the MEK might have important human intelligence sources in the governments of Iran and Iraq.[21] The MEK has also provided the outside world with crucial information on Iran's nuclear weapons program.[22] It is clearly a well-established, resourceful opposition group. For all of these reasons, it would be a mistake to overlook the MEK in designing a smart power approach to weaken or replace the Iranian regime. Prudence dictates that Washington should never rely on any single exile or dissent group, but determining how the MEK could connect outsiders with protesters and dissidents inside Iran is worth exploring further.

THE ETHNIC ANGLE

The United States should take yet another page from dissent movements during the Cold War and apply it to Iran. Not only the did the Soviet bloc include entire captive nations that Moscow placed under its control after World War II, but it also held captive peoples within the Soviet Union from earlier conquests. These groups included, for example, Ukrainians, Lithuanians, Kazakhs, and so forth. The Soviet Union also notably persecuted Jews. The survival and flourishing of ethnic identity and pride apart from the Russian culture that dominated the Soviet Union was important to eroding support for the government.

The same opportunity exists in Iran today. While many think of Iran as overwhelmingly comprising Persians — an ethnicity apart from Arab and other Middle Eastern peoples — the country is only about 60 percent Persian. It has significant pockets of Azeris and Kurds and smaller numbers of Lurs, Balochs, and Arabs.[23] None of these groups is particularly enthralled with the incumbent Iranian regime. In fact, Baloch insurgents have targeted the regime with violent attacks in recent years, seeking a separate homeland carved from Iran and Pakistan.[24] Many ethnic Azeris do not feel at home in Iran either. The neighboring country of Azerbaijan, an underappreciated U.S. ally, has had acrimonious relations with Tehran. In contrast to the Iranian model of government, an aide to Azerbaijan's president noted in mid-2012, "We are proud of the fact that we are Muslims, and we are proud that we are a secular country." Tehran is concerned enough to fund considerable Azeri-language programming to shape the opinions of Azeris within its borders.[25] U.S. smart power should seek to cobble together this diverse, ethnically based angst into a broader movement against the Iranian regime.

This effort should also take into consideration the regime's discrimination against minority Sunni and Sufi Muslims, Baha'is, Zoroastrians, Christians, and Jews. Together, these groups are about 10 percent of Iran's population.[26] Many among these groups would welcome a government that respects unalienable individual rights, which the current regime most certainly does not observe.

CLARITY OF MESSAGE

The American president and leaders of other free nations should publicly call for the peaceful end of the Iranian regime and express support for the anti-Islamists protesting the government. There is strong historical precedent for taking this stance. When Reagan predicted in 1982 that the march of freedom would leave communism "on the ash heap of history," the Soviet government called his statement a "provocation." But it proved a tremendous boost to dissidents. One of them, Natan Sharansky, was in a Soviet prison at the time. News of the speech penetrated even that controlled space, where political prisoners then communicated by talking to each other through drained toilets or by tapping on walls. Sharansky later wrote: "Finally, the leader of the free world had spoken the truth — a truth that burned inside the heart of each and every one of us." Sharansky added, "Reagan's challenge to the Soviets was as much moral as it was economic, which is why the impact of his policies on the lives of Soviet dissidents was no less dramatic."[27]

Re-creating this scenario with Iran could be a powerful element of a smart power campaign. Unfortunately, American presidents have consistently avoided such clarity with Iran. Some have hesitated to encourage populist forces in a nation where mobs historically have been enraged at the West. Some, including President Obama, have heeded the advice of Washington experts who say that protesters and dissidents do not want U.S. assistance or vocal support.

The experts point to instances in the past where the United States has intervened in Iranian political affairs, including CIA activities in the country during the 1950s to restore Iran's monarchy — a sore point for some Iranians. However, the reality is more complex. Most of Iran's population was born after the 1979 revolution; only a tiny portion witnessed the events of the 1950s. Protest leaders may conclude that they cannot ask publicly for U.S. support for fear of appearing to be in cahoots with a foreign power, but their cause is still invariably assisted over the long-term when foreign leaders echo their aspirations and condemn their oppressors. Despotic leaders will always accuse dissidents of being stooges of the United States. If a protest movement is already incurring the downside of this dynamic, then why not incur the upside from it is as well? Furthermore, if a foreign political cause advances U.S. interests, Washington ought to consider supporting the movement, regardless of what its leaders say about the United States in public.

MILITARY POSTURE

Last but not least, knowing how the United States and its allies construct and deploy their militaries is important to a smart power plan, even if the overall point of smart power is to avoid resorting to war. Part of demonstrating that a despotic regime's time has passed involves highlighting not only its economic and political bankruptcy but the futility of its military strategy as well.

When repressive governments get in trouble, they often turn to foreign military adventures to distract people's attention from problems at home. Dictators use tales of imminent foreign threats as standard fare to justify their heavy-handed rule. Supposed dangers from abroad also serve as a convenient excuse for the economic problems that repressive governments actually cause. Soviet dissident Andrei Sakharov succinctly captured the linkage between tyranny and foreign belligerence when he said: "A country that does not respect the rights of its own people will not respect the rights of its neighbors."[28]

Numerous examples are on display around the globe today. Perhaps the most obvious instance is demonstrated by the world's most tyrannical country, North Korea. Hardly a month passes without extremely bellicose language from Pyongyang. In September 2012, the regime's mouthpiece said, "If the U.S. seeks to keep its forces in south Korea, contrary to the unanimous desire of the regional people, it had better get itself ready to taste an all-out war with the DPRK [Democratic People's Republic of Korea]."[29] Two years earlier, the regime's news agency announced: "The south Korean puppet forces, obsessed by hysteria for invasion of the DPRK, committed such reckless military provocation as preempting the firing of shells into the territorial waters of the DPRK."[30]

Did the South Koreans really express any "hysteria for invasion" of North Korea during this time? Actually, the only threat came from Pyongyang itself. The statement was a puffed-up reaction to extremely modest steps South Korea took to defend itself after North Korea sank one of its naval ships and shelled a South Korean island without provocation.

The Iranian government is subtler than Pyongyang's spokesmen. (Actually every leader in history since Genghis Khan is subtler.) However, the Islamist regime's conduct fits the same pattern of belligerence. While Washington downplays Tehran's past killing of Americans, it is played up in select circles inside Iran. The Iranian government also prides itself — and predicates part of its existence — on seeking the ultimate destruction of Israel. Related to this goal, Tehran has had its political tentacles deep in countries like Lebanon, Syria, and Iraq. Further, it essentially has two proxy armies, Hezbollah and Hamas, on Israel's borders waiting to strike when the opportunity arises.

Iran's military strategy also now involves a stronger presence in the land-locked Caspian Sea, where new oil and gas discoveries are turning a relative backwater into a promising economic and strategic opportunity. In 2012, Iran indicated it would put submarines in the Caspian for the first time.[31]

This announcement, however, pales in comparison to the arms race Iran has touched off in the Persian Gulf. All U.S. allies there are concerned with recent Iranian aggression and a prospective Iranian nuclear weapons capability. Saudi Arabia has an agreement to buy $60 billion worth of new weapons systems from the United States over a decade.[32] In late 2011, the United Arab Emirates announced it would spend $3.5 billion on a U.S.-made antimissile defense system.[33] This buildup is a direct response to Iranian military developments. Officials and legislators in Tehran also frequently threaten to forcibly close the Persian Gulf in order to halt oil exports.[34]

Defeating this military strategy needs to be a part of any serious effort to undermine the Tehran regime. When a government starts losing militarily, it almost inevitably faces an internal crisis. For example, Adolf Hitler faced numerous assassination attempts in his life. However, the truly serious ones, backed by some within his own government, occurred only after he began losing on the battlefield.

The collapse of the Soviet Union provides a broader, more recent example. By the end of the 1980s, Moscow's military posture faced challenges on all fronts. The United States was resisting the Soviet Union's occupation of Afghanistan by aiding a proxy army, the Afghan mujahideen. Washington also supported the Nicaraguan Contras against the Moscow-backed government in Managua. At sea, the Reagan administration worked to build a greatly expanded six-hundred-ship navy. The air force and navy fielded new nuclear bombers and missiles. The United States also partnered with the governments of Britain, Italy, and West Germany to station intermediate-range nuclear missiles in those countries. They countered a Soviet advantage in that class of weapons, along with Moscow's superiority in troop numbers. More important, they demonstrated a new allied willingness both to stand up to Moscow and to ignore the domestic, antinuclear peaceniks in Western Europe who were a part of Moscow's own smart power campaign.

Perhaps most crucial of all, Reagan himself championed a ballistic missile defense system called the Strategic Defense Initiative. The idea was to supplement nuclear deterrence, which involved threatening retaliation for any Soviet nuclear strike. Reagan wanted to add to this program a new system that could actually shoot down Soviet missiles. It would have afforded future presidents the option to defend the American people from a nuclear attack rather than merely avenging their deaths with a counterstrike. While ahead of its time, the missile shield would have replaced the "balance of terror" that had marked most of the Cold War. The system as envisioned was expensive and reliant on future technological breakthroughs. Regardless, the Soviets knew they could never compete. The Soviet generals and their political masters lost their confidence.

Thus to the average citizen of the Soviet Union and Eastern Bloc, Moscow was failing on all fronts. People without a voice in their government were being impoverished for a costly military strategy that was belligerent yet obviously ineffective. They also had enough knowledge of the outside world to know that a better way of life was possible. Their economy was lousy, with a common joke summing it up: "We pretend to work, and they pretend to pay us." Everything came together in a perfect storm against the regime.

Re-creating this strategy with Iran today would be much less costly. Saudi Arabia and other Gulf nations are already spending large amounts on their own defense. They need no convincing that Iran poses a serious risk to their security. They have also focused heavily on new fighter aircraft and antimissile defense systems, essentially negating Iranian advances in missiles.

The wild card is Iran's nuclear capability, should the regime acquire one. No other military in the Middle East currently possesses nuclear weapons except Israel. Part of the worry about Iran building a nuclear weapon is that it would prompt other governments in the region to pursue the same capability, spurring proliferation.

Early in the Obama administration, Secretary of State Clinton spoke in public of extending the U.S. nuclear "umbrella" over Middle Eastern nations if Iran builds the bomb.[35] This umbrella has been in place for close American allies in East Asia and Europe since the early part of the Cold

War. Unfortunately, the concept lacks credibility in the context of the Middle East because both Iran and U.S. allies doubt America's commitment. During the Cold War, it was safe to assume an American president would retaliate after a Soviet nuclear attack on Europe. In fact, the United States likely would have initiated a nuclear first strike if the Soviets invaded NATO allies with conventional forces. But this calculus is lacking today in the Middle East, where average Americans perceive less commonality with those who would be victims of an Iranian offensive. Put simply, would an American president really nuke Iran on behalf of Israel or Saudi Arabia? Maybe, but maybe not.

To make this nuclear umbrella real — and to demonstrate to Tehran that its nuclear ambitions are pointless — U.S. nuclear weapons would have to be stationed in the region. This effort would essentially replicate the U.S. deployment of intermediate-range nuclear missiles to Europe in the 1980s. The United States and key Persian Gulf allies should also create the Middle East equivalent of NATO's Nuclear Planning Group. Established in 1966 amid European concern that America's nuclear umbrella was not credibly localized for NATO during that time of rapid Soviet military advances, the Nuclear Planning Group brought other NATO members (minus unhelpful France) into discussions about the arrangement of American and British nuclear weapons in the theater. The members coordinated on how the weapons would be targeted and used in the event of war.[36] The existence of the organization validated deterrence for both friend and foe. This process could be repeated today in the Persian Gulf.

The United States should also work with Israel to ensure that nation's undeclared nuclear arsenal could survive a first strike by a nuclear-armed Iran. This survivability would at least create what is known as "crisis stability" in the parlance of nuclear strategists. It would mean that during a crisis, neither side would feel pressured to strike first with nuclear weapons to gain an advantage.[37] Part of achieving this level of deterrence requires Israel to demonstrate to Iran that a single knockout punch is not possible. Some part of Israel's leadership theoretically would have to be able to ride out any Iranian first strike and order a retaliation. Achieving this capability is a serious concern for a country as small as Israel is.

Luckily, the solution is probably close at hand: nuclear-armed cruise missiles placed on Israeli submarines could survive any Iranian sneak attack. Germany sold Israel the submarines, and the German media has speculated they now carry nuclear-armed cruise missiles that could reach Iran.[38] Washington should ensure that Israel has the resources to deploy this force at sea without interruption. When the United States inevitably must restore its deteriorating nuclear arsenal, testing of which has been suspended voluntarily since 1992, Washington also should offer Israel the option of joint testing its own weapons just as the United Kingdom was allowed to do in the past.[39]

Some say Israel cannot rely on simply deterring Iran, because the regime is crazy and willing to create as many martyrs as required to destroy Israel. Certainly Israel should not rely on deterrence alone. But it is unlikely that even Iran's supreme leader would be willing to trade dozens of Iranian cities for Tel Aviv in a nuclear exchange or as a result of a terrorist group taking an Iranian bomb into Israel. Some onlookers understandably think the Iranian regime is reckless enough to pursue this tactic. After all, this cruel government sent tens of thousands of Iranian children, roped together in groups of twenty, to clear Iraqi minefields in the Iran-Iraq War of the 1980s.[40] Most Iranian actions since the 1979 revolution, however, have actually been calculated and carefully planned. The lack of much serious pushback from the West has encouraged Tehran and led to increasingly belligerent and reckless-seeming behavior. So far, Iran has avoided steps that would be obviously suicidal for the regime, but improving regional nuclear deterrence has become more important.

No one likes to talk about using or even deploying nuclear weapons. In fact, President Obama indicated in his first term that he wanted to go dramatically in the opposite direction. Speaking in Prague in 2009, he said, "So today, I state, clearly and with conviction, America's commitment to seek the peace and security of a world without nuclear weapons."[41] In discussing a nuclear umbrella for an increasingly tense Middle East region, meanwhile, average Americans may also wonder why they should be expected to shoulder any burden of defending with nuclear weapons countries with large pockets of anti-American sentiment.

Saudi Arabia is a particularly difficult subject. Fifteen of the nineteen hijackers who attacked the United States on September 11, 2001, were citizens of Saudi Arabia. According to a Gallup poll in February 2012, only 42 percent of Americans had a favorable view of the country. That finding put Saudi Arabia only slightly above China and lower than Russia in the ranking.[42] While it is possible to fashion a smart power strategy against the Iranian regime without extending the U.S. nuclear umbrella over Saudi Arabia and similar countries, doing so would help and advance two key U.S. interests: First, it would render any Iranian nuclear capability largely pointless, causing average Iranians to wonder why their government wasted so much on the effort. Second, it would discourage additional Persian Gulf countries from obtaining their own nuclear arsenals.

A final step to demonstrate that Iran's military strategy is futile could involve thwarting its proxy armies, especially Hezbollah and Hamas. The November 2012 sustained rocket assault on Israel by Hamas forces that control Gaza actually represented some progress. Hamas achieved none of its major tactical, strategic, or political goals. Israel's Iron Dome missile defense system was so effective — achieving an estimated 85 percent success rate — and Hamas so obviously the instigator of the conflict, that Tehran had little to cheer when it ended.[43] Average Iranians who may have no love for Israel, but nonetheless are primarily concerned with scratching out a living, may have wondered if their government's support for Hamas is a good use of the country's resources.

The other problem is Hezbollah, which is more adept than Hamas at both warfare and smart power. Hezbollah is deeply involved in politics and government in Lebanon, where it is based. To obtain power, its representatives use a combination of carrots and sticks, ranging from providing social services to murdering opponents. Luckily a thriving opposition movement to Hezbollah exists in Lebanon that includes those bitterly opposed to what Hezbollah symbolizes: the foreign domination of Lebanon. Whenever non-Islamist Lebanese prevail over Hezbollah, Tehran loses. Free countries should aid this Lebanese opposition.

UNDERMINING ISLAMISM

The plan outlined previously would use smart power to help Iranians free themselves from an unelected regime. Such an effort should go hand in hand with a strategy to undermine the Islamist political ideology globally.

This proposal makes sense for two reasons: the Iranian regime typifies the Islamist form of government, and many of the smart power tactics that should be used against Tehran would work on Islamism more broadly.

Some senior officials in the U.S. government have been concerned about the Islamist threat for a long time and have considered methods to fight the ideology. Interest naturally spiked after the 9/11 attacks. While this book has outlined numerous U.S. shortcomings in the so-called war of ideas against Islamic extremists, some notable moments of wisdom in government have occurred.

Donald Rumsfeld, the secretary of defense during 9/11 and for the following five years, observed in his 2011 memoir: "While those of us in the Bush administration did not engage in the debate needed to identify the enemy's ideology, we did at least recognize that the challenge we faced was fundamentally ideological."[44]

Rumsfeld had traveled to the Middle East the month after 9/11 with Doug Feith, his undersecretary for political affairs. Feith later wrote about one particularly perceptive analysis from Qaboos bin Said, the sultan of Oman, who received them "on a sweltering afternoon in a large open-sided tent in the middle of the desert." Feith noted:

> Qaboos then fascinated us with a strategic exposition on the war's ideological essence. He spoke of a great contest within the Muslim world — between fanatical Islamists, who inspired the terrorists with visions of a restored caliphate, and their opponents. . . . Qaboos warned us against focusing our attention too narrowly on military objectives, for he thought that the outcome of the war might ultimately be decided in the world of ideas. . . . When Rumsfeld and I left the tent, he told me to make sure to report those thoughts in his personal note for [Bush].[45]

Other parts of the U.S. government were obtaining similar information from a variety of sources. Singapore is a country with a particular interest in Islamism given its minority Muslim population and proximity to large Muslim-majority nations with active terrorist groups. The U.S. Embassy in Singapore cabled Washington after a 2005 visit by Hillary Clinton, then a senator. The cable noted that Singapore's senior-most political figure, Lee

Kuan Yew, in a meeting with Clinton "stressed that moderate Muslims had to be encouraged to stand up and speak out against radicalism. They needed confidence that they could win." While noting that the "problem of Islamic terrorism would not be easily extirpated," he nonetheless believed that "we could get to the tipping point."[46]

However, these insights went nowhere in Washington. Rumsfeld later recollected perceptions he had in government: "We needed to tell the truth about the Islamist extremists — about their brutality, injustice, and totalitarian political ambitions. The best way to communicate that message was not for American political leaders to do it, but to find ways to get more Muslims around the world publicly speaking out against them." Rumsfeld's Pentagon tried to turn these views into action. It included the goal of "countering ideological support" for Islamism in a 2005 draft of the National Defense Strategy, but the State Department objected to its inclusion.[47] While ever vigilant and protective of its bureaucratic turf, the State Department had no real plan or inclination to rally Muslims against Islamism.

Remedying this situation requires not only the previously outlined extensive changes to government organization but also a strategy built on proven tactics. The most important step is establishing the modern equivalent of the Cold War–era Congress for Cultural Freedom. This organization was so effective at staunching the intellectual appeal of communism because it relied on people who could have a plausible voice in the debate. Instead of American diplomats, moralists, and economists preaching the virtues of the West, it rallied social democrats and socialists in the thick of the European debate to oppose the alternative of communism.

A modern Congress for Cultural Freedom need not be a congress at all, nor even an organization centered around in-person confabs. Conceptually, it needs to mix old and new methods of disseminating ideas and news and to create linkages between like-minded people so they can increase their intellectual impact. While the overall concept should be global in scope, different regions of the world will call for different structures.

As with efforts directed at undermining the Iranian regime, anti-Islamist efforts should ideally harness diversity. While an obvious bedrock element of an anti-Islamist effort would be the young, modern secularists who flooded town squares at the beginning of the Arab Spring, the larger body of Muslims should not be ignored. A key argument against Islamism is that it perverts real Islam by conflating it with civil affairs. It seeks to unify mosque and state. The same problem existed with Christianity before reformers in the West began separating church and state. This division not only improved freedom and the performance of government but also compelled clergy to focus entirely on spiritual issues. Both church and state improved. Making this case to rank-and-file Muslims is crucial: real Muslims oppose Islamism.

Most Muslims believe in the separation of mosque and state already, even if only latently. It certainly seems to be the case in Indonesia, the world's most populous Muslim-majority country, which has a secular, democratic government. Muslims from these environments need to be the ones convincing others that their way is best. The United States and its allies, meanwhile, should provide the tools and funding necessary for this mission and have the will to conduct much of it covertly.

Indonesia has decades-old moderate Muslim groups like Nahdlatul Ulama and Muhammadiyah. Increasingly fresher, charismatic, moderate Islamic preachers who espouse tolerance and separation of spiritual and civil matters have gained prominence there.[48] While people think of India as Hindu and Pakistan as Muslim, in fact India has more Muslims — many of whom are supportive of secular democracy — than does Pakistan. Turkey has existed as a secular, Muslim-majority state since immediately after the end of World War I. Some are concerned that its popular incumbent government is taking the country toward Islamism. More likely, Turkey is evolving into a modern secular democracy unafraid of an Islamic cultural flavor and eager to break permanently with its history of intermittent military rule.

Within these and other countries are the seeds of Islamism's destruction. Some would counter that none of these countries are Arab or Persian, the insular cultures of the Middle East and North Africa that have been most fertile for Islamists and their terrorist vanguard. Countering that assertion are the events beginning in 2009 and continuing to this day where thousands of Arabs and Persians have taken to the streets seeking anything but Islamism. The opportunity for change not only exists but is also obvious.

Rather than simply complaining about Saudi money funding radical Wahhabi mosques and madrassas around the world, the United States and its allies should emulate the tactic. Funding a mosque is much cheaper than funding a brigade. America and its allies could find ways to support organizations from these moderate populations willing to advance their views with fellow Muslims. While it may not be any more possible to open a moderate, pro-secular mosque in Tehran or Riyadh today than it would have been to open a stock market in Moscow or East Berlin during the Cold War, the free world can do much more than it does at present in the contested ground between Islamist and non-Islamist states.

Finally, the same independent media-based "mirror" that should be placed over Iran should be replicated across areas with significant Muslim populations. The truth, clearly seen and advocated unapologetically, favors freedom. Almost anywhere in the Middle East, a look around neighborhoods reveals a panoply of satellite dishes and other means of receiving information. The region is awash in media content. What is needed is a stronger regimen of facts and context. The United States has a television broadcasting tool, Alhurra TV, that is supposed to be influencing this space. Unfortunately, as with other government-dominated broadcasting today, Alhurra is expensive and little watched. It actually crowds out broadcasts of more appealing news, commentary, and culture. It has cost U.S. taxpayers nearly $1 billion since it was established in 2004.[49] Other government broadcast tools, such as Radio Sawa, present similar problems. Those nations that want a civilized order in the world — including the United States — should replace such desultory information efforts with ones that stand a chance of working. America and its allies used smart power once before to defeat the dangerous, tyrannical ideology of communism. They can do it again.

Smart power can go a long way in abating threats from Iran and Islamists, ideally without firing a shot. Getting a better handle on those two serious threats to the United States and its allies is critical in order to devote more attention — and smart power — to a looming threat across the Pacific that poses the greatest challenge of all.

CHAPTER 10

Making Life Harder for Beijing

They came for Feng Jianmei early in the morning on June 2, 2012. The twenty-seven-year-old Chinese woman had been desperately trying to buy time and evade authorities. She hid in scrub brush for hours and spent terrifying nights concealed under beds at relatives' houses. Seven months earlier, she had become pregnant with her second daughter.

China has a one-child policy. Feng thought the five-year interim since her last birth and her location in a rural area would win her an exemption. Local authorities thought otherwise. Feng's husband had been scrambling to raise money to pay the $6,300 "fine" for having a second child. But the couple ran out of time.

No fewer than twenty family planning officials came to take Feng away. She was beaten, blindfolded, and forced to sign a document that she could not see. Afterward, she was forcibly restrained and given an injection that would end her pregnancy. Thirty-six hours later, she gave birth to a stillborn girl.[1]

Feng's ordeal did not end there. Her sister had been able to snap a photo of the fully formed girl lying dead next to the traumatized Feng. The image spread rapidly before Beijing's censors could act. While forced abortions are common in China, the brutal nature of this one prompted outrage. It even led to an unprecedented apology from the government. But it was simply for show.

Behind the scenes, China's apparatus of repression was shifting into higher gear. Feng was kept at the hospital against her will for a month. As many as a dozen guards patrolled nearby.[2] When Feng's husband first tried to travel to Beijing to meet with journalists, more than a hundred officials descended on him in a dozen vehicles. He was beaten on the spot. Authorities also led local peasants in a parade to denounce the couple and arranged for the mob to hang a banner near the hospital that read, "Severely beat the traitors and expel them."[3] Feng's husband eventually made it to the Chinese capital. He told Western reporters there on June 29, 2012, "I came to Beijing in search of help."[4] After that point, no news of him or his wife has surfaced.

The same government that crushed its own citizens as they engaged in peaceful protest in 1989 in Tiananmen Square and across China remains in power today, unreformed and unrepentant. Virtually every conceivable human right is abridged in China. Many experts in the West predicted that partial economic liberalization in China would inevitably lead to political liberalization. It has not happened. China's economy has grown in size from $350 billion in 1988 to $7.2 trillion in 2011,[5] yet no measurable improvement in human rights has occurred during this time. China continues its ruthless repression in Tibet, and in recent years the brutality has led approximately a hundred Tibetans to self-immolate, one of few forms of protest left open to them. The Dalai Lama noted in 2011 that a "kind of cultural genocide is taking place."[6] The Han Chinese who make up most of the population elsewhere in the country fare better but not by that much, especially if they decide to stand up to their government, fight corruption, or engage in other political activities outside of the Chinese Communist Party.

APOLOGISTS AND FANTASISTS

A government that treats its own people this way can never be a true partner of the United States. Yes, being a world power, Washington has had to work with terrible regimes in the past. The most conspicuous was America's World War II alliance of necessity with Soviet dictator Joseph Stalin. His record of evil and aggression was second only to the man the Allies joined together to defeat, Adolf Hitler. The U.S.-Soviet marriage of convenience lasted no longer than the war. Other U.S. alliances with repressive governments have tended to be with market-based countries where gradual reform was possible, such as South Korea, Spain, and Taiwan. Each transformed from military rule to a full-blown democratic government in the latter half of the twentieth century. Notably, none were communist regimes. History has shown those governments to be irredeemable. They can be cured only by complete replacement.

And yet with China, the Washington foreign policy establishment is forever perceiving incipient reform and imminent partnership. In her inaugural trip to China as secretary of state, reporters asked Hillary Clinton if she would raise China's human rights abuses. She responded that "pressing on those human rights issues can't interfere with the global economic crisis, the global climate change crisis, and the security crisis."[7]

Implicit in this statement was the notion that China was cooperating on these matters, but history shows no such assistance from Beijing beyond vague promises. Certainly China helped on none of the specific matters — especially economics — that Clinton cited. China continues to purchase large amounts of U.S. debt only because China's trade surplus with America provides it with a surplus of dollars that must be parked somewhere. Nearly risk-free U.S. bonds are the only feasible, dollar-denominated option for Beijing at present. Economic reality, not diplomatic charm, is the driver.

The Obama administration was not the first to make faith-based claims about a partnership with the Chinese government. George W. Bush declared that the United States and China were "partners in diplomacy" during the 2003 visit of China's second-ranked official to Washington.[8] Later in Bush's term, my boss in dealing with North Korea issues, Jay Lefkowitz, made a candid statement in public about the lack of promised Chinese cooperation in the six-party talks that included the United States, China, and North Korea, among others. He said, "One key assumption that turned out to be incorrect was that China . . . would apply significant pressure to North Korea to abandon its nuclear weapons."[9] Secretary of State Condoleezza Rice rebuked Lefkowitz publicly for such candor, saying he "doesn't know what's going on in the six-party talks."[10] In fact, however, Lefkowitz knew all too well.

Rice told President Bush at the time that the Chinese were providing crucial assistance in pressuring their ally, North Korea, to uphold its promises to end its nuclear weapons program. A leaked cable indicates Rice's point man on China, Thomas Christensen, discussed the supposed partnership with his counterpart in Beijing. A month before Lefkowitz spoke, Christensen apparently had gushed "that U.S.-China cooperation in the Six-Party Talks is the best example of our bilateral cooperation on international issues." His Chinese opposite wholeheartedly "agreed that bilateral cooperation on this issue has been very good."[11]

Unfortunately, none of this chatter reflected reality. China was not cooperating beyond parroting verbal promises to Washington. It did not apply real pressure to North Korea. China's most readily available tool of coercion over Pyongyang is its export of petroleum; indeed, China supplies fully 90 percent of what North Korea consumes. China provides much of it on credit or for barter essentially in a pay-whatever-you-can handout to ensure North Korea's stability. China halted this flow briefly after North Korea's first nuclear test in 2006 to remind Pyongyang who was boss; however, it never again resorted to the measure, not wanting to destabilize Pyongyang.[12] When Beijing and its friends in Washington were assuring everyone of Chinese cooperation, meanwhile, little actually existed.

Subsequently, the U.S. government and many Asia experts have only further downplayed Beijing's affronts to its own citizens, neighboring countries, and U.S. interests. Whenever the issue of China is raised in discussion, diplomats and experts incant "cooperation" and "partnership" like zombies. In mid-2012, the State Department updated its fact sheet on China to declare that Washington "welcomes a strong, peaceful, and prosperous China playing a greater role in world affairs and seeks to advance practical cooperation with China in order to build a partnership based on mutual benefit and mutual respect."[13] This perspective can only be chalked up to hope divorced from any concrete facts.

Part of this mind-set is also the result of a convenient theory that many China experts and officials in Washington hold: America's treating China as an adversary will make it one. Joseph Nye, bard of Harvard's Kennedy School of Government and the former assistant secretary of defense during the Clinton administration, popularized this theory. In 2011 Nye wrote for Al Jazeera, "If we [treated] China as an enemy, we were guaranteeing an enemy in the future."[14]

Throughout history, this type of conceit has permitted the U.S. government to disregard very real threats. Today, it requires willful ignorance of serious transgressions by the Chinese government that U.S. conduct could not plausibly have caused. Since 2010, China has provoked territorial disputes with almost all of its maritime neighbors. It has targeted Japan and the Philippines most prominently, although it has also placed Taiwan, Vietnam, Malaysia, and Brunei in its crosshairs. Chinese military officials talk openly about establishing dominance over two island chains — the first of which includes the China Seas and Taiwan; the second encompasses southern Japan and all of the Philippines. This territorial expansion would place a massive portion of U.S. trade at the mercy of Beijing, potentially cutting off not only East Asia but also India and the Middle East.

Also, China is increasing its military capabilities by leaps and bounds. It has surprised defense analysts in Washington multiple times, for example, by fielding a new class of attack submarines, a new antisatellite system, and new antiship ballistic missiles.[15] These weapons are intended to deter or defeat the U.S. Navy early in any conflict — first by blinding it, then by sinking the declining number of aircraft carriers it can muster to the region. Courtesy of China, the United States is also set to lose its monopoly on stealth aircraft. In an unexpected and unsubtle surprise move, Beijing conducted the first flight of its J-20 stealth fighter during U.S. defense secretary Robert Gates's visit in mid-2011.[16]

China is also closer to having its first operational aircraft carrier. Defense experts in Washington still dismiss this serious development and stress that it will lack the capabilities of U.S. carriers. But that declaration misses the point. Beijing has little interest in a fair carrier fight reminiscent of the Battle of Midway. Instead, China will use the flattop as a smart power tool of coercion and intimidation against others. It will fill a vacuum in the Pacific that the atrophying of the U.S. Navy is gradually creating.

However, the scariest emerging Chinese capability of all is in the realm of cyber war. The next 9/11- or Pearl Harbor–style sneak attack on America may not involve blowing things up at all, or at least not at first. Instead, the lights may simply go out. The Internet will stop. Communications will fail.

Banks will shut. Fuel pumps will not operate. Food trucks will not make deliveries. Hospitals and airports will close.

Such an outcome may be within the realm of possibilities of a Chinese cyber attack on America's infrastructure. When former secretary of defense Donald Rumsfeld was asked in 2012 if a cyber attack could cause as much as two months of distress and disturbance in the United States, he responded, "It's much more serious." He noted further the potential of an enemy "to disable a power grid."[17]

Gen. Keith Alexander, the commander of the U.S. Cyber Command who serves concurrently as the director of the National Security Agency, explained in 2010:

> Today, our nation's interests are in jeopardy. . . . America's very wealth and strength make it a target in cyberspace. And one of the pillars of that strength, our military, is at risk, perhaps to an even greater degree. Our military depends on its network for command and control, communications, intelligence, operations and logistics. We in the Department of Defense have more than 7 million machines to protect, linked in 15,000 networks with 21 satellite gateways and 20,000 commercial circuits composed of countless devices and components.[18]

In keeping with the inability of many in Washington to characterize accurately the misconduct of the Chinese government, the general did not mention Beijing in his remarks or in his subsequent testimony on Capitol Hill. President Obama reportedly refused in 2011 to act on options put to him to respond to Chinese cyber attacks with counterattacks and sanctions.[19] He also took no action when a U.S. security response firm reported in 2013 that hackers working for China's People's Liberation Army had compromised 115 American private sector and government targets over the course of seven years.[20]

However, a congressional commission did not pull punches in a report the year before that detailed the Chinese cyber threat. It concluded, "Chinese penetrations of defense systems threaten the U.S. military's readiness and ability to operate." It also zeroed in on new cyber techniques that Beijing uses to improve its long, systematic theft of U.S. technology: "China's cyber capabilities provide Beijing with an increasingly potent tool to achieve national objectives. In a strategic framework that leans heavily on cyber espionage, a diverse set of Chinese hackers use pilfered information to advance political, economic, and security objectives."[21]

In response to the report, the Chinese Foreign Ministry issued a pro forma response: "The relevant commission has not let go of its Cold War mentality."[22] Unfortunately Washington has; it is Beijing that has not.

Furthermore, this contention is not simply a concern for the future. China consistently wages cyber war on the United States today. In September 2012, Chinese hackers even broke into the computer system of the White House military office.[23] Intelligence officials involved complained that the Obama administration failed even to reproach the Chinese about the cyber attack.[24] Some of this activity is high-tech espionage. Some likely is probing and testing for a possible catastrophic assault one day.

The consequences of this nefarious activity are already perceptible on a more modest scale. Take Nortel Networks, for example, the Canadian company whose technology still helps run telecommunications systems around the world. Beginning in 2000, Nortel began a precipitous fall from grace in its core business. Its Chinese competitor, Huawei, was beating it consistently in bidding competitions and other sales efforts. Before going bankrupt and liquidating its business, Nortel discovered that Chinese hackers had infiltrated its systems thoroughly. They even had access to the Nortel chief executive officer's computer. Basically, Chinese infiltrators had had free rein inside the company's network for the last decade that the century-old company would exist.[25]

This conduct is not representative of a government that values peace or a civilized order in the world. All of the indicators related to China and security are pointing in the wrong direction. Its domestic repression remains atrocious. It is undertaking a military buildup despite having no plausible foreign threat to its sovereignty. It is probing the peripheries of its neighbors, be they maritime boundaries in the China Seas or virtual ones in cyberspace. It is systematically stealing the industrial and military secrets needed to challenge the United States and its allies. Finally, it is using aggressive diplomacy and political warfare to blind its would-be opponents and assist its supporters and apologists.

What would a better smart power regimen against China's dangerous government entail? As with other serious adversaries, American and allied statecraft should bring to bear peaceful methods to perturb the regime. Conceptually it should push back on the regime's distortions of truth about itself. Free nations should point out that the Chinese economic model is not as strong as its supporters maintain, that its government is not as legitimate or stable as many experts say, that its belligerent conduct is not really about securing its own sovereignty, and that the "social harmony" it promotes is really a corrupt tyranny.

Internationally, Washington should rally the governments in East Asia and the Pacific region against China. Few would require much convincing. Even its fellow communist nation of Vietnam has much wariness and hostility toward Beijing. Other governments in the region share this concern to varying degrees, but they must calculate the degree to which they are willing to risk Beijing's ire. Countries such as Japan and India have the confidence and strength to stand up to the Chinese regime. At the other end of the spectrum, the current government of Cambodia is Beijing's willing patsy. Taiwan is in-between, but its current president leans toward China. When the United States is strong and clear about its disapproval of Beijing, all of these nations are likely to be tougher toward China as well. They would be less inclined to see China as an inevitable juggernaut with which they must have good relations at all costs if the United States demonstrates the suggestion of its decline and withdrawal from the region is unfounded.

Achieving this standing requires that Washington take not only a different tone but also a different military posture. As with the Soviets a generation before, a key part of a U.S. smart power strategy against the Chinese requires getting hard power right — all in the hope that it is never used.

Some claim incorrectly that this process is already under way. On a two-day trip to Australia in November 2011, President Obama announced what would become known as the "pivot to Asia." Speaking to Australia's Parliament, Obama said: "As we end today's wars, I have directed my national security team to make our presence and missions in the Asia

Pacific a top priority. As a result, reductions in U.S. defense spending will not — I repeat, will not — come at the expense of the Asia Pacific."[26] Beyond that, Obama's aides talked about moving forces and sophisticated weapons to the region. They were vague about details, however, likely because none really existed.

When the rhetoric was peeled back, the only new forces that would be placed in the region as part of the pivot were 250 to 2,500 Marines positioned intermittently in Darwin, Australia. That city is some 3,600 miles from Beijing, or only a little closer than Hawaii is. The small number of Marines is not completely insignificant, but their role is unclear in the massive geography of the Pacific and Asia where naval, air, and nuclear assets are most important. Some also speculated that the Marines sent to Darwin would be drawn from those who would otherwise deploy to Okinawa, the Japanese island that has been that service's northeast Asia stronghold for decades. In other words, the deployment would amount to no new force in the region at all; instead, the minor shuffling would actually place a small number of Marines farther from China than they otherwise would have been.

Obama also pulled punches in explaining the pivot. In a press conference after the speech, he said, "The notion that we fear China is mistaken." His undersecretary of defense for policy, Michèle Flournoy, said the following month, "The U.S. does not seek to contain China; we do not view China as an adversary."[27] However, one of the president's White House spokesmen said of the visit, "It's a part of the U.S. sending a signal that we're going to be present, that we're going to continue to play the role of underpinning security in this part of the region. Part of that context is a rising China."[28]

This statement lacked clarity. Why pivot if there is no real threat and nothing to fear? To the Chinese and others, the Darwin plan was less of a strategic pivot and more of a hazy rhetorical flourish. It also occurred at the same time the United States was withdrawing its final combat troops from Iraq; indeed, the last U.S. soldier leaving Iraq crossed the Kuwaiti frontier thirty-two days after Obama spoke. Skeptics concluded that the pivot was more about covering a general American pullback from the world with a move that included no real military (or economic for that matter) component. In December 2012, after Obama was reelected, a Chinese official said a "senior administration official" told him the whole idea of a pivot could be abandoned in Obama's second term.[29] Obama's second-term secretary of state, John Kerry, criticized the pivot in his confirmation testimony before the Senate.[30]

Worse still, the remaining U.S. force available for securing the Pacific is becoming less capable of deterring China. The U.S. Navy is preparing to shed a number of highly sophisticated cruisers that can engage submarine, surface, and airborne targets at great distances and even incoming ballistic missiles in some instances. Washington will replace some with the new littoral combat ship (LCS), which is a vastly less capable coastal warship. The navy eventually plans to send three to Singapore. The LCS might be handy in fighting Somali pirates or nations without an air force (although existing cruisers and destroyers would be handier still), but a single attack helicopter could theoretically defeat an LCS. A Pentagon report plainly stated that the "LCS is not expected to be survivable in a hostile combat environment."[31] It is as though the ship was chosen specifically not to concern China.

Overall, the navy has shrunk dramatically in recent years. It is half the size it was when Ronald Reagan left office. Its number of capital ships during that time has decreased from nineteen — fifteen carriers and four battleships — to ten (carriers only). The air force has also shrunk. Beijing was heartened when Washington canceled the procurement of the world's most advanced fighter attack plane, the F-22. There are only 182 of the planes in the world. Japan and Australia expressed interest in buying an export version for themselves, and it would have been the next-best option to more American copies of the aircraft in the Pacific. This sale, however, was prevented by pork barrel politics in Washington, which favored the less capable F-35 fighter. Supporters of the F-35 wrote into law a ban on selling the F-22 to allies.[32]

The problem is set to grow worse as Congress and the administration cut the Pentagon's budget. While undoubtedly defense spending has room for savings, especially in the ever-growing bureaucratic "tail" that supports the actual war-fighting "tooth," the navy and air force actually need to grow. In budget negotiations, it is important to keep the size of the defense budget in perspective. In 2012, the U.S. federal budget was $3.8 trillion; only 17 percent was spent on defense. That amount includes the cost of operations in Afghanistan and defense spending outside of the Pentagon at agencies like the Department of Energy.[33] If sacrifices must still be made, then Washington should make a real pivot and move its remaining forces out of Europe and into the Pacific. (Russia will always be a concern to the West and Russian president Vladimir Putin is no friend of the United States, but Washington can retain its defense commitment to NATO while insisting Europeans provide peacetime manpower.)

Restoring hard power and projecting it into the Pacific is a key to smart power. It is crucial that Chinese military and political leaders be made to understand that their dreams of dominating the region will never be realized and will only bring more allied forces to their doorstep. Furthermore, the Chinese people should be made to see their government's misadventure for what it is — a colossal waste of resources at a time when no one threatens China with invasion — and that the region's only major threats are Beijing itself and its stepchild, North Korea.

Beyond restoring its hard power, the Department of Defense could also play other valuable roles in using smart power against China. Specifically, it should embrace the role of "bad cop" in order to give Beijing pause about what might happen if it becomes too belligerent. This effort basically involves turning the occasional musings and provocations of China's own military officers back on China. In 1995, in discussing a possible conflict between Beijing and Washington over Taiwan, the deputy chief of staff of the Chinese military mentioned nuclear weapons. He noted ominously that America should worry more about Los Angeles than Taipei in a thinly veiled threat to nuke Hollywood if Washington chose to defend an ally under siege. In 2005, another top Chinese general appeared to abandon a policy of not striking first with nuclear weapons when he said to reporters, "If the Americans draw their missiles and position-guided ammunition onto the target zone on China's territory, I think we will have to respond with nuclear weapons."[34]

Analysts in Washington typically chalk this belligerent talk to China's military trying to sound scary and believe that their statements do not reflect the actual policy of the Chinese regime. This assessment might very well be true. Regardless, it would be a useful element of smart power for Washington to reciprocate. In other words, American generals and admirals should be at liberty to describe the capabilities at their disposal and the fact that they are intended for use on China's military if China starts a war.

Part of this effort should involve permanently ending the on-again, off-again exchanges between officers of the American and Chinese militaries. These dialogues send precisely the wrong signal both to the Chinese government and to America's own military officers. They basically afford the Chinese golden opportunities to collect intelligence, but, in return, U.S. participants are carefully denied useful information. I am reminded of a time in government when a retired solder recounted how he was approached in the 1980s by a U.S. diplomat tending to members of a visiting Soviet military delegation:

> DIPLOMAT: Would you be willing to come over and talk to my Russian guests?
> SOLDIER: Would you like me to kill them?
> DIPLOMAT: What are you talking about! I'm just asking you to talk to them a little.
> SOLDIER: Talking to them is your job. Let me know when you want me to kill them. That's my job.

While his rejoinder of course comes across as unfriendly and bellicose, there is value in conveying such sentiments to Beijing from time to time. It actually advances security and peace for America and its allies to dispense with misleading happy talk and instead to state clearly the willingness of free nations to defend their interests against Beijing. Washington should disclose that it still has flag officers like Gen. George Patton. Of the outspoken field commander in Europe in World War II, Gen. John Pershing said, "It didn't hurt America to have a general so bold that he was dangerous."[35] Today, it would not hurt for Beijing to believe America has admirals and generals who were itching to cream the Chinese military if necessary and who could not care less about their friendship. Making the use of force seem less appealing to Chinese officials aids smart power. It also works against the common misperception that repressive governments always have of democracies: they are unwilling to fight.

Other elements of a smart power strategy that have been proposed for use with Iran could work with China. A coalition of governments willing to be firm with Beijing could change internal perceptions of the regime, eroding its confidence and support. Democracies now encircle China. Japan, South Korea, and Taiwan are symbols of freedom and economic prosperity. Taiwan is particularly important, given the commonality of its ethnic makeup with that of China. Taiwan took a path to democracy, which is an appealing alternative to the corrupt repression currently on display across China. The mainland's Han Chinese — the majority ethnic group of Taiwan and China — should see in Taiwan's example their potential when they too become free. Part of this effort, however, requires Washington to treat Taiwan as an asset rather than as a liability in U.S.-China interactions. The freedoms of speech and worship that exist in Hong Kong should also be highlighted to the mainland Chinese, with the goal of prompting them to ask, "Why not here?"

Tibet presents another opportunity. While the Dalai Lama no longer calls for a restoration of Tibet's pre-1949 independence, seeking instead a cultural autonomy and preservation within China, the desire for full independence still burns strongly in the hearts of many Tibetans. This yearning is the natural result of Chinese repression, which is more onerous in Tibet than in other places under Chinese control. To the extent that Beijing has to worry about political stirrings in Tibet — or the growing military capabilities of neighboring India for that matter — it diverts China's attention and resources from causing problems for the United States in the Pacific.

Similarly the Uyghurs of far western China are a group whose goals ought to be seen as in line with those of the U.S. government. They are a predominantly Muslim people with a history of being relatively tolerant. As with the Tibetans, Beijing treats the Uyghurs as second-class citizens and perversely creates conditions for their radicalization. Washington should support the Uyghurs' aspirations for independence or autonomy. Doing so would be consistent with American values and have the added benefit of advancing U.S. interests.

China also abuses Falun Gong practitioners. The latter do not consider themselves to be part of a religion per se, but they incorporate elements of Buddhism in meditative exercises and deal with some spiritual issues. Fear-ing any movement that cannot easily be controlled, China banned Falun Gong in 1999 after it enjoyed seven years of rapidly expanding membership. The crackdown and subsequent repression have failed to eliminate the clandestine practice inside China. Some estimate it may have tens of millions of adherents.

Beijing suppresses Christians as well. They have long been a small but important group in China. Rather than ban their religion outright, Beijing permits some registered church activity, which it tightly regulates through the Three-Self Patriotic Movement, the China Christian Council, and the Chinese Patriotic Catholic Association. The latter has disavowed the pope and is considered schismatic by other Catholics. Meanwhile, an underground church movement persists, despite intense persecution, and may be growing. The Chinese government estimates 16 million Christians worship in the country. A 2008 study by a university in Shanghai put the number at 40 million, although the actual number may be far higher. It also estimated that 31 percent of Chinese are religious.[36]

The Vatican has been divided over whether to resist Beijing more aggressively — for example, by excommunicating those priests who collaborate — or to seek a peace with the Chinese government that would inevitably leave Beijing in control of church activities. In a lucky break for those willing to fight, Pope Benedict XVI in 2006 elevated Joseph Zen, the bishop of Hong Kong, to the position of cardinal and spokesman for all Catholics in China. The cardinal is outspoken on human rights and critical when the Vatican acquiesces to Beijing's selection of officials for its pretend church.[37] This openness matters to smart power because Zen's path, if followed, would rally the underground church in China and breathe new life into Catholics who have been demoralized by past Vatican appeasement. One way to measure the prospective success of this approach is to note Beijing's vituperative condemnations of Zen. When I recently met the humble, soft-spoken man, now in his eighties, I was reminded of an irony common to dissidents throughout the ages: these meek men and women make some of the world's powerful and corrupt people tremble in fear. China's abused groups of faith, as well as the abused ethnic minorities, can be an important part of any smart power effort to undermine Beijing internally.

Another factor is the multiplying number of Chinese upset with the intense and increasingly ostentatious corruption that is endemic in China. Its magnitude is unprecedented in human history. In a single example that came to light in 2011, a Chinese railway official had squirreled away $2.8 billion in foreign bank accounts and paid bribes amounting to $160 million to China's railway minister.[38] That any public official thought he could hide or make use of such pelf on this scale shows the degree to which China has become a kleptocracy. This malfeasance is not lost on the average Chinese, who stage a surprising number of protests against corruption each year, despite the risks involved in questioning the government. To date, Beijing has managed to keep the public's disgruntlement under relative control, but it may last only until the next economic downturn.

The challenge for American smart power strategists is how to channel these diverse currents of discontent: abused ethnic groups and people of faith, Chinese angry about corruption, intellectuals, and artistic types. Surprisingly little communication and coordination exists among the various groups. At a minimum, they could compare best practices in conducting dissent. Publicity and greater planning could multiply their impact. An allied effort to aid in combining these forces could simply involve clandestinely providing resources for them to gather and compare notes. They could form a key internal piece of a broad smart power strategy that would also include building up international military and diplomatic fortitude to resist China's aggressive actions.

Communications are also crucial to accelerating the rot from within China's regime. Through its censorship of the Internet and other means of obtaining news and information, Beijing augments its control over the people and warps their perceptions of their own country and the rest of the world. Of course, many see through this suppressive effort. Augmenting the flow of information, meanwhile, can help foment political turbulence more often in China. Washington expends some modest resources on this need, especially through its funding of Radio Free Asia, which was established in 1996. A full "open window" on China would be better still. Washington and its allies should create a platform for independent media to penetrate China while using multiple means such as the Internet plus satellite and terrestrial broadcasts. One method is as simple as telling satellite operators that if they wish to have any contracts with the U.S. government, they need to ignore Beijing's requests to drop objectionable content. The concentration of China's population on its eastern seaboard presents the opportunity for airborne and seaborne transmissions that are harder to jam. Satellites could carry independent broadcasts targeting China's interior populations while terrestrial broadcasts could come from free nations around China, including Mongolia and Kyrgyzstan. Instead of propaganda, media content in the open window should consist of news, opinion, and cultural fare that appeals to a broad audience but has an unapologetic political point. It should essentially present journalism with a cause.

One of the many benefits of this overall smart power strategy is that it would not cause economic harm to America or other democracies; thus, allies in East Asia would find it a much more viable option than any other kind of sanctions. Specifically, it does not require any real interruption of trade between China and the rest of the world. China will continue to manufacture inexpensive goods that benefit consumers. Other nations, including the United States, will continue to buy them. Allies such as Australia can continue to sell to China commodities like coal and iron ore. Middle Eastern countries can sell it oil. China will still buy a part of the unfortunately large amount of debt the U.S. Treasury issues to fund deficit spending. Washington should crack down on U.S. companies that transfer any useful technology to Beijing, but this restraint need not impact the broader trade dynamic.

Ultimately, this strategy takes the advice Ronald Reagan gave Americans in his farewell address as president: "Don't be afraid to see what you see." Clearly, China is not a partner of the United States. Contrary to statements of senior U.S. officials, China's unelected government is obviously an adversary in the midst of a major military expansion and aggressive program of intimidating its neighbors. It is also a country with a great deal of internal problems and unrest. Successful smart power would simply recognize these realities and exploit the opportunity of discontent. Doing so would advance U.S. security and reflect the American people's morality and customary support for freedom abroad.

When the people of China see that their government's military buildup and bellicosity have failed and brought the nation more harm than good, they will see the seemingly invincible regime more as the hollowed-out hulk it has become. If combined with international pressure — especially clearer words from Washington and allied capitals — plus internal dissent and protests brought to a higher plateau, major change will come to China.

CHAPTER 11

Leading America's Pacific Century

"You may fire when you are ready, Gridley." That order, issued to his flagship captain by Commodore George Dewey, commander of the U.S. Asiatic Squadron, preceded the near-total destruction of the Spanish fleet in Manila Bay. That day, May 1, 1898, marked the real beginning of the Spanish-American War and the end of Spain's three-hundred-year control of the Philippines.

The war was supposed to be a primarily Atlantic affair. The Spanish occupation of Cuba was the main point of contention between the United States and Spain. The destruction of the USS *Maine* in Havana harbor was the most conspicuous trigger of the conflict. After the short and decisive war, President William McKinley had to decide to what extent the United States was willing to become a Pacific (and imperial) power. He summed up his conundrum: "When I next realized that the Philippines had dropped into our laps I confess I did not know what to do with them. . . . I walked the floor of the White House night after night until midnight; and I am not ashamed to tell you, gentlemen, that I went down on my knees and prayed to Almighty God for light and guidance more than one night. And one night late it came to me . . ."[1]

The next morning, McKinley called the War Department's chief engineer and told him to add the Philippines to the official map of the United States. A more reluctant Senate concurred with the decision but only by a tie vote that McKinley's vice president had to break in his favor.[2]

McKinley's successor in the White House lacked even his minimal reticence in envisioning America's fate in Asia and the Pacific. As on other topics, Theodore Roosevelt was ahead of his time. At the dawn of the twentieth century, about a year before he succeeded the assassinated McKinley as president, Roosevelt stated with his trademark singularity: "I wish to see the United States the dominant power on the shores of the Pacific Ocean."[3]

It was not a fleeting thought. Perhaps more than anyone, Roosevelt's fingerprints were found prominently on Washington's venture beyond the Americas. The journey had not been easy. Roosevelt had been assistant secretary of the navy earlier in the McKinley administration, working under the cautious John D. Long. The position was a vastly more important job in that day and the number-two civilian position in America's most important service, decades before there was a unified Department of Defense under a single secretary of defense. Rural Massachusetts enticed Long away from Washington's typically unpleasant summers for the steamier parts of August and September. Roosevelt encouraged this practice, professing his concern for Long's health. Coincidentally, it also left Roosevelt as acting secretary of the navy.

During one absence, Roosevelt managed to see the president multiple times, cut red tape in building new battleships and cruisers, arranged for unfit Navy Department bureaucrats to be fired, and proposed an invasion plan for Cuba. But most important of all was Roosevelt's positioning of George Dewey to become commander of the Asiatic Squadron in lieu of a more timid flag officer Long had preferred but whom Roosevelt had deemed "irresolute." This bureaucratic maneuver required the interception and slight delay of a letter bound for Long, the enlistment of a senator to lobby Roosevelt's boss in the White House, and other operational sleights of hand that were considered ungentlemanly by standards of the day. The result was having the right man in the right place at the right time when war came to the Pacific. A more timid man may have delivered a more modest victory or perhaps none at all, making subsequent U.S. expansion into the Pacific far less likely. Instead, Dewey, who shared Roosevelt's vision and his daring, performed precisely as Roosevelt had planned.[4]

Thus a major turning point in U.S. history was accomplished without a national consensus or even much of a national debate. Instead, a small number of highly motivated men exploited a change in the calculus of statecraft — in this case, the terminal weakening of what was left of the Spanish Empire. In so doing, they changed the course of history.

But Roosevelt's vision would have to wait. The early decades of the new century commanded little American attention. Not until the 1944 defeat of the Imperial Japanese Navy in the Battle of Leyte Gulf did the United States truly fulfill Roosevelt's vision of being the dominant power in the Pacific. Furthermore, the region remained a comparative backwater to Europe through the twentieth century's two world wars and subsequent Cold War. The modern era Roosevelt helped initiate would be an over-whelmingly Atlantic-focused period for the United States.

A century later, this focus obviously has changed, and this shift is one of the most crucial assumptions that must be considered in any strategy for statecraft and its smart power component. Indeed, one of the biggest arguments for improving its handle on threats posed by Islamism and Iran is so the United States can turn its attention from seemingly endless crises in the Middle East to Asian-Pacific threats and opportunities. Asia matters more in the long run.

In 2012, the United States had a total trade of $536 billion with China, which was second only to Canada in the ranking of U.S. trading partners. Japan was in fourth place and South Korea was in seventh. At times during the year, Taiwan was in tenth place, with strong showings by India and Singapore.[5]

Further, in 2012, as Europe continued to stumble economically and politically, the economies of Burma, Cambodia, India, Indonesia, Laos, Mongolia, Papua New Guinea, the Philippines, Thailand, and Vietnam all grew by 5 percent or more.[6] When one considers the likely trajectory of these economies, it is easy to envision a time when the vast majority of U.S. trade will take place with North America and East Asia plus India.

Europe will continue to matter to the United States, but less each year. While one can point to several factors that show why much of Asia is rising — a young workforce, declining corruption (outside of mainland China), a pro-business environment, simple tax and business laws, and so forth — the most compelling metric cannot be quantified. It is a quality that can only be felt. Step off a plane in Jakarta, Hong Kong, Taipei, Denpasar, or Bangkok and you can feel the buzz instantly. These people are looking to make the next step up the economic ladder. It is the polar opposite of the decadent decline that Old Europe has chosen for itself. Even in more staid Asian cities such as Tokyo, one finds an industriousness and self-reliance that is no longer the norm in Europe.

Between these two worlds lies the United States. America faces serious economic and political challenges in the years ahead. It is not out of the question that matters will deteriorate further. A detriment to U.S. smart power strategy is that many around the world believe America is past its prime and destined for decline — a belief that oddly seems to find its most vocal adherents among the ranks of the elite in American culture and government itself.

Drawing parallels between the United States and historical empires such as those of Britain and Rome that became overextended and fell into terminal decline would be easy but still wrong. Those who tout America's decay do not give enough weight to the fundamentals of American greatness that remain relatively strong, including the size of its economy, its financial and physical capital, its culture, and its military. But trumping even all of these factors is America's historical refusal to accept decline or mediocrity. American voters force reform and restoration sooner or later. Historians who bet against this recurring feature of U.S. history — and many have done so in the darker periods of America's past — have consistently been proven wrong. Little evidence indicates that enough has changed to make them right this time.

Ultimately the United States will find its way out of its current economic, fiscal, and political doldrums. As Winston Churchill once observed, "Americans can always be counted on to do the right thing, after they have exhausted all other possibilities."[7] Further, when a turnaround becomes apparent, it will increase the power of American statecraft and smart power significantly. In the meantime, today's international economic and political turbulence presents opportunities, including for a real pivot to Asia unlike the more rhetorical one that the Obama administration announced in 2011.

Specifically, the United States has an opportunity for new alliances. Shocks to the international system change the system. World War I was the impetus for the League of Nations. World War II gave rise to the only slightly less-flawed United Nations. The onset of the Cold War led to NATO. More relevant to today, the collapse of the Bretton Woods monetary system, first oil crisis, and prolonged recession in the early 1970s gave rise to the Group of Seven (G7). The grouping included the seven most significant rich democracies at the time. The idea was to bring their leaders together in an informal setting and work through challenging issues while also building relationships between the leaders.

All good things come to an end. So it was with the G7. The group invited Russia to join in 1997, making it the Group of Eight (G8). Some of the countries, especially Italy, declined in relative wealth and their ability to wield economic resources. Poor and developing nations were invited as mini-participants to form such ancillary groupings as the G8 Plus Five in a typical feel-good diplomatic move that undermined the model's original intent of gathering a small group of people who can actually solve problems. This development foreshadowed the unfortunate Group of Twenty, which emerged in 2008 as yet another international confab. When the number next to the G grows larger, any gathering starts to resemble the UN General Assembly, with similar, farcical results.

It will soon be time again for change. The Washington foreign policy establishment, terrified as it is of new ideas and reform, has not yet recognized this necessity. The boldest idea this decrepit elite champions at present is having America join the UN Convention on the Law of the Sea, which has been around since the 1970s. The Clinton administration signed the convention in 1994, but its supporters have never quite obtained the two-thirds support they need for Senate ratification.[8] The treaty would "solve" problems that do not actually exist and allow the UN to tax American companies directly for the first time. This convention is what passes for reform in the minds of the Washington establishment today.

But the trajectory of economic and political turbulence around the globe suggests a time of reckoning will come and will be followed by real change. This opportunity to create international groupings and other constructs that work for America's national interests and values could differ from recent experience, where knee-jerk inclusiveness and diplomatic protocol have prevailed over sound strategy and competent execution.

Washington should strive for the Pacific-century equivalent of NATO and the G7, which worked, and not the UN and the League of Nations, which did not.

Successful groupings of allied governments can have some political and economic diversity, but the members must have overwhelmingly overlapping national interests and national values. The governments involved must also want to accomplish a goal rather than simply meeting for the sake of meeting. These factors are why the G7 and NATO succeeded in the last century. Two similar groupings that make particular sense would be among countries willing to contain the governments of Iran and China and make life difficult for them.

The United States should also seek a full free trade area for free nations of the Pacific Rim, one that goes much further than any measures Washington and allied capitals are currently contemplating. Manufacturing-based economies would benefit from both the elimination of tariffs and a free flow of investment capital. Knowledge-based economies would benefit by the harmonization of laws to protect intellectual property. Both groups would benefit by the exclusion of China from the trade pact until Beijing has a government that respects its neighbors and the rule of law and recognizes the unalienable rights of its citizens.

Whether dealing with trade or security issues, choosing the objective of an international construct before selecting the groups' members is the best recipe for success. Furthermore, those members need not all be democracies, but they should all be committed to a civilized order where the rule of law prevails and the world's most disruptive and dangerous authoritarians are viewed and treated as adversaries.

The seeds of these reforms — and of the other radical changes outlined in this book — exist today in the United States. As with other key turning points in U.S. history, they will not come from an entrenched establishment. Instead, determined men and women will recognize that the world has changed drastically and see to it that the United States is prepared to take advantage of the situation, to survive, and to excel.

Tomorrow's Deweys and Roosevelts exist among the ranks of young Americans willing to struggle for freedom and prosperity. They too are peering out at the vast expanse of Asia and the Pacific in search of America's destiny and a lasting and prosperous peace. This time they have the century right.

The Trumans, Eisenhowers, Kennedys, and Reagans of the next era are out there somewhere in America as well. If the past is a guide, American voters will find them eventually. These future leaders' challenge will be to frame and implement a foreign policy that revives America's past pragmatism and idealism and promotes its success in the world. The key to this scenario will be rediscovering smart power and putting it to use.

Acknowledgments

James Rosen, author and chief Washington correspondent for Fox News, was the first person to suggest I write this book. He said it was my "lacuna." After looking up that word, which apparently means "a missing part," I began to give his advice serious consideration. James had asked what I thought my ideal job in government would be. I replied that the government today was not even pursuing the courses of action that I believed were essential for our national security and that were of greatest interest to me. James suggested this topic could fill that lacuna of mine. He was a great help as I refined the idea for this book and began drafting.

I owe a particular debt of gratitude to Stephen Yates, my mentor and colleague in business and political matters. A veteran of the pivotal policy fights at the White House during the first term of George W. Bush, Steve has provided me invaluable insight and wisdom over the years on everything from writing a coherent analysis to organizing a White House to interpreting events in the Middle East and Asia. His grasp of the failing politics of our era has also deeply influenced my opinions.

I am forever grateful to Paula Dobriansky, who wrote this book's foreword. Paula brought me in to the Bush administration. I worked on her direct staff and then in part of her broader area of responsibility for the rest of the administration. Together with Jay Lefkowitz, whom I served when he was the president's special envoy for North Korean human rights issues, these two afforded me a vantage from which to form many of the impressions I present in this book.

John Fox is another person whose guidance and insight over the years are reflected in my writing. His wisdom on freedom movements and the role of independent media therein are unparalleled in Washington or anywhere. Through John, I also had the privilege of knowing the late Mark Palmer, whose proven ideas on undermining dictators have influenced this book greatly.

James Farwell, Allen Roth, Jeff Gedmin, Kathy Lubbers, Richard Grenell, David Patterson, and Greg Jenkins were key resources to me in the formative stages of production. In particular, they aided in refining the book concept and in finding the ideal publisher for this work.

Paul Bonicelli was an early collaborator on the scope of the book. Robert O'Brien offered generous amounts of his time to comprehensively review my manuscript. Claudia Rosett and Tim Wilson have been sources of inspiration and provided crucial feedback on portions of the book related to both China and Islamism.

Bill Creedon provided extensive help, especially in editing. Others aided me throughout this effort, or in related research, with contributions ranging from posing thought-provoking questions to serving as a sounding board for ideas and to providing specific facts and line edits. They include: Robert Andrews, Jeff Berkowitz, David C. Clark Jr., Halah El Sokari, Kate Friedrich, Kristofer Harrison, Adrian Hong, William Inboden, Kevin Knoblock, Barak Lurie, Michael Magan, Lynne Jordal Martin, Alan Mendoza, Robert McNally, Dennis Mulhaupt, Nadia Schadlow, Keith Urbahn, Robert Wells, Matthew Wendel, and Enders Wimbush.

Numerous friends on Capitol Hill helped with the ideas and research that went into this book. As with others, including in the U.S. executive branch and among the ranks of officials in allied governments, they are best served here by anonymity. However, they should know their contributions over the years have been invaluable — to me, to this book, and to the causes they serve.

I am also indebted to my family. My mother, Pamela; father, Herman; brother, Henry; and sister-in-law, Josie, have been sources of inspiration and support. My partner, Marco McClees, has been a great and constant pillar of encouragement. My uncle and aunt, David and Emelyn Patterson, have provided a home base away from home too many times to count, as well as a stimulating environment to ponder the issues of the day.

Hilary Claggett saw the early potential of this book and helped shape its direction. Without her interest and support, this book would not have been possible.

Finally, I owe a debt of gratitude to the team at Potomac Books, including Sam Dorrance, Kathryn Owens, Laura Briggs, Vicki Chamlee, and Elizabeth Demers.

Notes

Introduction

1. Charles Fenyvesi, Victoria E. Pope, Warren P. Strobel, and Christian Caryl, "Cold Warriors' Untold Tales," *U.S. News & World Report*, October 10, 1999, http://www.usnews.com/usnews/news/articles/991018/archive_002128.htm (accessed August 16, 2012).

2. "The Nations: How to Hang On," *Time*, April 19, 1948, http://www.time.com/time/magazine/article/0,9171,798374,00.html (accessed August 16, 2012).

3. Associated Press, untitled wire report issued from Milan, May 24, 1978.

4. "Cold War, Episode 3: Marshall Plan, 1947–1952," CNN, October 11, 1998.

5. William F. Buckley Jr., *Up from Liberalism* (New York: McDowell, Obolensky, 1959), 18.

6. Michael R. Beschloss, *The Conquerors: Roosevelt, Truman, and the Destruction of Hitler's Germany* (New York: Simon & Schuster, 2002), 190.

7. Francis Fukuyama wrote *The End of History and the Last Man* (New York: Free Press, 1992), indicating that the clash of political ideologies was basically ending, classical liberalism having won. The events of the subsequent twenty years have not supported his thesis.

8. This point of view is advocated by Robert D. Kaplan, especially in *The Revenge of Geography: What the Map Tells Us about Coming Conflicts and the Battle against Fate* (New York: Random House, 2012).

9. "China Tells U.S. to Drop 'Cold War' Mindset on Military," Reuters, March 26, 2009, http://www.reuters.com/article/2009/03/26/us-china-usa-idUSTRE52P1XM20090326 (accessed May 1, 2013).

10. Carol Leonnig, "Iran Held Liable in Khobar Attack," *Washington Post*, December 23, 2006, http://www.washingtonpost.com/wp-dyn/content/article/2006/12/22/AR2006122200455.html (accessed May 1, 2013).

1. The False Choice

1. The North Korean Human Rights Act of 2004, Public Law 108-333, 22 USC 7801 et seq., 108th Cong., October 18, 2004.

2. See United Nations General Assembly Resolution 429(v) for the 1951 Convention and Resolution 2198(XXI) for the 1967 Protocol Relating to the Status of Refugees.

3. Matt Kempner and Cameron McWhirter, "Has Sam Nunn's Time for VP Spot Arrived?," *Atlanta Journal-Constitution*, July 13, 2008, http://www.ajc.com/news/content/news/stories/2008/07/12/nunn_0713.html (accessed November 15, 2012).

4. "Abrams Dims Contra Aid Prospects, Nunn Says," Associated Press, June 15, 1987.

5. Donna Cassata, "Cheney, Nunn Clash over Effectiveness of Sanctions," Associated Press, December 4, 1990.

6. Ibid.

7. Sara Fritz and William J. Eaton, "Congress Authorizes Gulf War," *Los Angeles Times*, January 13, 1991, http://articles.latimes.com/1991-01-13/news/mn-374_1_persian-gulf (accessed July 9, 2012).

8. Ibid.

9. United States Information Agency, *USIA: An Overview* (Washington: USIA, October 1998), 35, http://dosfan.lib.uic.edu/usia/usiahome/overview.pdf (accessed April 29, 2013).

10. George W. Bush, "Remarks to the American Association for the Advancement of Science, February 15, 1991," in Gerhard Peters and John T. Woolley, *The American Presidency Project*, http://www.presidency.ucsb.edu/ws/index.php?pid=19306 (accessed April 3, 2013).

11. "Saddam's Iraq: Key Events, Uprisings, March 1991," BBC News, http://news.bbc.co.uk/2/shared/spl/hi/middle_east/02/iraq_events/html/uprisings.stm (accessed July 9, 2012).

12. For example, Paul Wolfowitz, then undersecretary of defense for political affairs, argued that American passivity amounted "to idly watching a mugging." Rick Atkinson, *Crusade: The Untold Story of the Persian Gulf War* (New York: Houghton Mifflin, 1993), 490.

2. Arab-Persian Spring

1. "How a Slap Sparked Tunisia's Revolution," CBS News, February 20, 2011, http://www.cbsnews.com/stories/2011/02/20/60minutes/main20033404.shtml (accessed July 29, 2012).

2. "Profile: Zine al-Abidine Ben Ali," BBC News, June 20, 2011, http://www.bbc.co.uk/news/world-africa-12196679 (accessed July 29, 2012).

3. "How a Slap Sparked Tunisia's Revolution."

4. Josh Rogin, "Feltman: 'What Happened in Tunisia Strikes Me as Uniquely Tunisian,'" *Foreign Policy*, January 26, 2011, http://thecable.foreignpolicy.com/posts/2011/01/26/feltman_what_happened_in_tunisia_strikes_me_as_uniquely_tunisian (accessed July 29, 2012).

5. "Biography: Jeffrey D. Feltman," U.S. Department of State, http://www.state.gov/r/pa/ei/biog/120440.htm (accessed April 3, 2013).

6. CIA, "Egypt," *World Factbook* (online and updated weekly), https://www.cia
.gov/library/publications/the-world-factbook/geos/eg.html (accessed July 24, 2012).

7. Henry J. Reske, "Egypt's Poverty, Unemployment, Push Youths to Breaking Point,"
Newsmax, January 20, 2011, http://www.newsmax.com/Newsfront/Egypt-poverty
-unemployment-unrest/2011/01/31/id/384555 (accessed July 29, 2012).

8. Transparency International, "Corruption by Country: Egypt," http://www
.transparency.org/country#EGY (accessed April 19, 2013).

9. Jeremy M. Sharp, "U.S. Foreign Assistance to the Middle East: Historical Background, Recent Trends, and the FY2011 Request" (Washington: Congressional
Research Service, June 15, 2010), http://www.fas.org/sgp/crs/mideast/RL32260
.pdf (accessed July 29, 2012).

10. Associated Press, "Brotherhood Shows Strength, Limits in Egypt Chaos," Fox News,
January 31, 2011, http://www.foxnews.com/world/2011/01/31/brotherhood
-shows-strength-limits-egypt-chaos (accessed July 29, 2012).

11. Ken Dilanian, "Overall U.S. Intelligence Budget Tops $80 Billion," *Los Angeles
Times*, October 28, 2010, http://articles.latimes.com/2010/oct/28/nation/la-na
-intel-budget-20101029 (accessed July 29, 2012).

12. Secretary Condoleezza Rice, "Remarks at the American University in Cairo,
Egypt," June 20, 2005, U.S. Department of State Archive, http://2001-2009.state
.gov/secretary/rm/2005/48328.htm (accessed July 9, 2012).

13. "Rice Names 'Outposts of Tyranny,'" BBC News, January 19, 2005, http://news
.bbc.co.uk/2/hi/americas/4186241.stm (accessed July 29, 2012).

14. Embassy Cairo, "Egypt's Political Reform Process: Saad Eddin Ibrahim and the
Muslim Brotherhood," State Department cable, September 19, 2006, classified
"confidential," http://www.cablegatesearch.net/cable.php?id=06CAIRO5865
(accessed July 29, 2012).

15. "Exiled Egyptian Activist Sentenced," Al Jazeera, August 11, 2008, http://www
.aljazeera.com/news/middleeast/2008/08/200882116501543352.html (accessed
July 29, 2012).

16. "President Obama's Speech to the Muslim World at Cairo University," *U.S. News &
World Report*, June 4, 2009, http://www.usnews.com/news/obama/articles/2009/
06/04/president-obamas-speech-to-the-muslim-world-at-cairo-university (accessed
July 12, 2012).

17. George Thomas, "Iran Protesters Rally on Anniv. Despite Risks," CBN News,
February 12, 2010, http://www.cbn.com/cbnnews/world/2010/February/Iran
-Protesters-Rally-on-Anniv-Despite-Risks/ (accessed July 29, 2012).

18. Warren P. Strobel, "As Iran Protests Loom, Obama Sticks to a Cautious Script,"
McClatchy, February 9, 2010, http://www.mcclatchydc.com/2010/02/09/84128/
as-iran-protest-looms-obama-sticks.html (accessed July 29, 2012).

19. Consulate Istanbul (Turkey), "Iranian Politics: Mousvi's Lawyer Requests USG
Help," State Department cable, January 21, 2010, classified "secret," http://www
.cablegatesearch.net/cable.php?id=10ISTANBUL31 (accessed July 24, 2012).

20. Golnaz Esfandiari, "What Does Iran's Green Movement Want from Obama?,"
Radio Free Europe/Radio Liberty, November 6, 2009, http://www.rferl.org/

content/What_Does_Irans_Green_Movement_Want_From_Obama_/1871445
.html (accessed July 29, 2012).

21. Joel Gehrke, "U.S. Treasury Sanctions Iranian Military Leaders," *Washington Examiner*, December 13, 2011, http://washingtonexaminer.com/article/1004151 (accessed July 29, 2012).

22. "U.S. Urges Restraint in Egypt, Says Government Stable," Reuters, January 25, 2011, http://af.reuters.com/article/topNews/idAFJOE70O0KF20110125 (accessed July 29, 2012).

23. Dan Murphy, "Joe Biden Says Egypt's Mubarak No Dictator, He Shouldn't Step Down," *Christian Science Monitor*, January 27, 2011, http://www.csmonitor.com/World/Backchannels/2011/0127/Joe-Biden-says-Egypt-s-Mubarak-no-dictator-he -shouldn-t-step-down (accessed July 29, 2012).

24. Bridget Johnson and Michael O'Brien, "Clinton: 'We're Not Advocating Any Specific Outcome' in Egypt Crisis," *The Hill*, January 30, 2011, http://thehill.com/homenews/administration/141095-clinton-on-egypt-were-not-advocating-any -specific-outcome (accessed July 29, 2012).

25. Harry Schwartz, *Prague's 200 Days: The Struggle for Democracy in Czechoslovakia* (New York: Praeger, 1969), 57–58.

26. Ibid., 130–31.

27. Ibid., 141.

28. Ibid., 212–13.

29. Ibid., 222–23.

30. Sarah El Deeb, "Egypt Revolution Death Toll: Arab Network for Human Rights Information Documents 841 Killed," *Huffington Post*, May 15, 2012, http://www .huffingtonpost.com/2012/05/15/egypt-revolution-death-toll-arab-network -human-rights-n_1519393.html (accessed July 29, 2012).

31. Lolita C. Baldor, "State Department Charters Flights to Evacuate Americans," Boston.com, January 31, 2011, http://www.boston.com/news/world/middleeast/articles/2011/01/31/state_department_charters_flights_to_evacuate_americans (accessed July 29, 2012).

32. David Lerman, "Kissinger Says Mubarak Exit a 'Question of Months,' Urges Muted U.S. Reply," Bloomberg, February 1, 2011, http://www.bloomberg.com/news/2011-02-01/kissinger-says-mubarak-exit-a-question-of-months-urges-muted -u-s-reply.html (accessed July 29, 2012).

33. Hillary Rodham Clinton, "Remarks With Hungarian Prime Minister Viktor Orban," Parliament, Budapest, Hungary, June 30, 2011, U.S. Department of State, http://www.state.gov/secretary/rm/2011/06/167374.htm (accessed July 24, 2012).

34. "Muslim Brotherhood Envoys Met with White House Officials in DC," Fox News, April 5, 2012, http://www.foxnews.com/politics/2012/04/05/muslim-brotherhood -envoys-met-with-white-house-officials-in-dc (accessed July 29, 2012).

35. "Morsi during Elections Campaign," MEMRI TV, May 13, 2012, http://www .youtube.com/watch?v=reLigeHGKzE (accessed July 29, 2012).

36. Caryle Murphy, "Saudi to Codify Sharia 'for Clarity,'" *The National*, July 21,

2010, http://www.thenational.ae/news/world/middle-east/saudi-to-codify-sharia
-for-clarity (accessed July 29, 2012).

37. "Egyptian Cleric Safwat Higazi Launches MB Candidate Muhammad Mursi's
Campaign: Mursi Will Restore the 'United States of the Arabs' with Jerusalem
as Its Capital," MEMRI, May 1, 2012, http://www.memri.org/clip_transcript/
en/3431.htm (accessed July 29, 2012).

38. Josh Rogin, "State Department Training Islamic Political Parties in Egypt," *Foreign
Policy*, November 3, 2011, http://thecable.foreignpolicy.com/posts/2011/11/03/
state_department_training_islamic_political_parties_in_egypt (accessed July 29,
2012).

39. "Muslim Brotherhood–Backed Candidate Morsi Wins Egyptian Presidential Election," Fox News, June 24, 2012, http://www.foxnews.com/world/2012/06/24/
egypt-braces-for-announcement-president (accessed July 29, 2012).

40. Embassy Tripoli, "Senator Lugar's Meeting with Qadhafi August 20," State Department cable, August 31, 2005, classified "secret," http://www.cablegatesearch.net/
cable.php?id=05TRIPOLI221 (accessed July 29, 2012).

41. Embassy Tripoli, "A Glimpse into Libyan Leader Qadhafi's Eccentricities," State
Department cable, September 29, 2009, classified "secret/noforn," http://www
.cablegatesearch.net/cable.php?id=09TRIPOLI771 (accessed July 24, 2012).

42. "Gaddafi's 'Deeply Creepy' Condoleezza Photos," Sky News, August 26, 2011,
http://news.sky.com/story/876551/gaddafis-deeply-creepy-condoleezza-photos
(accessed July 29, 2012).

43. Claudia Rosett, "Dial a Dissident: Why Won't Gadhafi Let Fathi Eljahmi Answer
His Phone?," *Wall Street Journal Opinion Journal*, April 7, 2004.

44. "Longtime Libyan Prisoner of Conscience Fathi el-Jahmi Dies from Medical
Neglect," Committee on Human Rights, accessed July 24, 2012, http://sites.nation
alacademies.org/PGA/humanrights/PGA_052263 (accessed July 29, 2012).

45. "Security Council Authorizes 'All Necessary Measures' to Protect Civilians in
Libya," UN News Centre, March 17, 2011, http://www.un.org/apps/news/story
.asp?NewsID=37808#.UV4p814jFCs (accessed July 29, 2012).

46. Justin Elliott, "Will Obama Violate the Arms Embargo in Libya?" *Salon*, March 28,
2011, http://www.salon.com/2011/03/28/obama_libya_arming_rebels/ (accessed
July 29, 2012).

47. Colum Lynch, "U.N. Sanctions Panel Investigates Reports of French/Qatari Arms
Transfers to Libya's Rebels," *Foreign Affairs*, March 15, 2012, http://turtlebay
.foreignpolicy.com/posts/2012/03/15/un_panel_to_investigate_frenchqatari
_sanctions_busting_arms_shipments_to_libya (accessed July 29, 2012).

48. Peter Wilkinson and Marc Straus, "World Leaders Speak of Gadhafi Victims, New
Era for Libya," CNN, October 20, 2011, http://articles.cnn.com/2011-10-20/
africa/world_africa_gadhafi-international-reaction_1_libyan-people-moammar
-gadhafi-national-transitional-council?_s=PM:AFRICA (accessed July 29, 2012).

49. Tom Cohen, "Obama Pledges U.S. Support for Libya after Gadhafi," CNN, October 20, 2011, http://articles.cnn.com/2011-10-20/us/us_gadhafi-reaction_1_libya
-mission-moammar-gadhafi-libyan-people?_s=PM:US (accessed July 29, 2012).

3. Failed Politics of National Defense

1. "Ronulans," Urban Dictionary, http://www.urbandictionary.com/define.php?term =Ronulans (accessed August 16, 2012).

2. Karen DeYoung and Greg Jaffe, "NATO Runs Short on Some Munitions in Libya," *Washington Post*, April 15, 2011, http://www.washingtonpost.com/world/nato -runs-short-on-some-munitions-in-libya/2011/04/15/AF3O7ElD_story.html (accessed November 15, 2012).

3. Charlie Savage, "2 Top Lawyers Lost to Obama in Libya War Policy Debate," *New York Times*, June 17, 2011, http://www.nytimes.com/2011/06/18/world/ africa/18powers.html?pagewanted=all (accessed November 15, 2012).

4. Vote on House Concurrent Resolution 51, June 23, 2011, Open Congress, http:// www.opencongress.org/bill/112-hc51/actions_votes (accessed August 16, 2012).

5. "In Shift from Bush Era, More Conservatives Say 'Come Home, America,'" *Pew Research Center Publications*, June 16, 2011, http://pewresearch.org/pubs/2027/ foreign-policy-conservative-republicans-isolationism-afghanistan-libya (accessed November 15, 2012).

6. Nancy A. Youssef, Margaret Talev, and Jonathan S. Landay, "Will Talk of Afghan 'Off-ramps' Prompt Taliban to Hang Tough?," McClatchy, November 25, 2009, http://www.mcclatchydc.com/2009/11/25/79568/will-talk-of-afghan-off-ramps .html (accessed November 15, 2012).

7. Elicia Dover, "Gingrich to Afghanistan: 'Live Your Own Miserable Life,'" ABC News, February 27, 2012, http://abcnews.go.com/blogs/politics/2012/02/gingrich -to-afghanistan-live-your-own-miserable-life/ (accessed November 15, 2012).

8. E-mail from Newt Gingrich to Ralph Hallow, *Washington Times* chief political reporter, March 19, 2012.

9. Diary entry of Harry S. Truman, July 25, 1945, Harry S. Truman Library, http:// www.trumanlibrary.org/flip_books/index.php?pagenumber=1&titleid=231&tld ate=1945-07-25&collectionid=ihow&PageID=-1&groupid=3702 (accessed April 20, 2013).

10. John F. Kennedy, "Inaugural Address, January 20, 1961," in Gerhard Peters and John T. Woolley, *The American Presidency Project*, http://www.presidency.ucsb .edu/ws/index.php?pid=8032 (accessed August 16, 2012).

11. Michael Kelly, "The 1992 Campaign: The Democrats; Clinton Says He's Not Lean- ing Left but Taking a New 'Third Way,'" *New York Times*, September 26, 1992, http://www.nytimes.com/1992/09/26/us/1992-campaign-democrats-clinton-says -he-s-not-leaning-left-but-taking-new-third.html (accessed November 15, 2012).

12. Reuters, "British Voters Back Tony Blair for Top Labour Party Post," *New Straits Times*, May 16, 1994, http://news.google.com/newspapers?id=hdxOAAAAIBA J&sjid=rBMEAAAAIBAJ&pg=4688,2026449&dq=tony+blair&hl=en (accessed November 15, 2012).

13. Bill Clinton, "Remarks on the Signing of NAFTA," December 8, 1993, Univer- sity of Virginia Miller Center, http://millercenter.org/scripps/archive/speeches/ detail/3927 (accessed November 15, 2012).

14. Stephen A. Holmes, "The 2000 Campaign: Foreign Policy; Gore Assails Bush on Plan to Recall U.S. Balkan Force," *New York Times*, October 22, 2000, http://www.nytimes.com/2000/10/22/world/2000-campaign-foreign-policy-gore-assails-bush-plan-recall-us-balkan-force.html?pagewanted=all&src=pm (accessed November 15, 2012).

15. "Bush, Kerry Spar on Iraq War," Fox News, October 1, 2004, http://www.foxnews.com/story/0,2933,134151,00.html (accessed November 15, 2012).

16. "Transcript: First Presidential Debate," *Washington Post*, September 30, 2004, http://www.washingtonpost.com/wp-srv/politics/debatereferee/debate_0930.html/#b (accessed November 15, 2012).

17. Paul West, "Arrests May Boost GOP, Analysts Say," *Baltimore Sun*, August 11, 2006, http://articles.baltimoresun.com/2006-08-11/news/0608110260_1_iraq-war-war-on-terrorism-fighting-terrorism (accessed April 20, 2013).

18. "Ted Cruz Says Obama Made 'a Worldwide Apology Tour,'" *Austin American-Statesman*, January 20, 2012, http://www.politifact.com/texas/statements/2012/jan/20/ted-cruz/ted-cruz-says-obama-made-worldwide-apology-tour/ (accessed November 15, 2012).

19. Tony Harnden, "President Barack Obama: America Has Been 'Arrogant and Dismissive' Towards Europe," *Telegraph*, April 3, 2009, http://www.telegraph.co.uk/news/worldnews/barackobama/5101244/President-Barack-Obama-America-has-been-arrogant-and-dismissive-towards-Europe.html (accessed April 22, 2013).

20. David Jackson, "Obama Never Said 'Leading from Behind,'" *USA Today*, October 27, 2011, http://content.usatoday.com/communities/theoval/post/2011/10/obama-never-said-lead-from-behind/1#.UC3RganF4yG (accessed April 22, 2013).

21. Jo Becker and Scott Shane, "Secret 'Kill List' Proves a Test of Obama's Principles and Will," *New York Times*, May 29, 2012, http://www.nytimes.com/2012/05/29/world/obamas-leadership-in-war-on-al-qaeda.html?_r=1&pagewanted=all (accessed April 22, 2013).

22. Jonathan Weisman, "How McCain Stirred a Simmering Pot," *Washington Post*, September 26, 2008, http://www.washingtonpost.com/wp-dyn/content/article/2008/09/26/AR2008092603957_3.html?sub=AR (accessed April 22, 2013).

23. "John McCain: Torture Worked on Me," *Newsmax*, November 29, 2005, http://archive.newsmax.com/archives/ic/2005/11/29/100012.shtml (accessed November 15, 2012).

24. Kevin Robillard, "John McCain: Obama 'Shameful' on Syria," Politico, July 23, 2012, http://www.politico.com/news/stories/0712/78851.html (accessed November 15, 2012).

25. Tom Curry, "A New GOP Foreign Policy Tone: Pessimism," NBC News, March 12, 2012, http://nbcpolitics.nbcnews.com/_news/2012/03/12/10656200-a-new-gop-foreign-policy-tone-pessimism (accessed November 15, 2012).

26. Matt Bradley, "U.S., Egypt Look to Settle Nerves over Aid, Trial," *Wall Street Journal*, February 21, 2012, http://online.wsj.com/article/SB10001424052970204131004577235000880596674.html (accessed November 15, 2012).

27. Byron Tau, "Muslim Brotherhood Delegation Meets with White House Officials,"

Politico, April 4, 2012, http://www.politico.com/politico44/2012/04/muslim
-brotherhood-delegation-meets-with-white-house-119647.html (accessed November 15, 2012).

28. Christopher Marquis, "Satisfied with U.N. Reforms, Helms Relents on Back Dues," *New York Times*, January 10, 2001, http://www.nytimes.com/2001/01/10/world/satisfied-with-un-reforms-helms-relents-on-back-dues.html (accessed November 15, 2012).

29. Defense Threat Reduction Agency, "Fiscal Year 2013 Budget Estimates: Cooperative Threat Reduction Program," February 2012, http://comptroller.defense.gov/defbudget/fy2013/budget_justification/pdfs/01_Operation_and_Maintenance/O_M_VOL_1_PARTS/O_M_VOL_1_BASE_PARTS/CTR_OP-5.pdf (accessed November 15, 2012).

30. "Russia GDP," Trading Economics, http://www.tradingeconomics.com/russia/gdp (accessed August 15, 2012).

31. Ira Iosebashvili, "Putin Pledges More Defense Spending," *Wall Street Journal*, February 20, 2012, http://online.wsj.com/article/SB10001424052970203358704577234960796991408.html (accessed November 15, 2012).

32. David Herszenhorn, "Russia Won't Renew Pact on Weapons with U.S.," *New York Times*, October 10, 2012, http://www.nytimes.com/2012/10/11/world/europe/russia-wont-renew-pact-with-us-on-weapons.html?_r=0 (accessed May 2, 2013).

33. "U.S. Senate Passes Kerry Lugar Bill to Triple Aid to Pakistan," *Press Trust of India*, September 25, 2009, http://articles.timesofindia.indiatimes.com/2009-09-25/us/28101474_1_kerry-lugar-bill-afghanistan-and-pakistan-pakistani-people (accessed November 15, 2012).

34. "Sixty Years of U.S. Aid to Pakistan: Get the Data," *Guardian*, July 11, 2011, http://www.guardian.co.uk/global-development/poverty-matters/2011/jul/11/us-aid-to-pakistan (accessed November 15, 2012).

35. Susan B. Epstein and K. Alan Kronstadt, "Pakistan: U.S. Foreign Assistance" (Washington: Congressional Research Service, April 10, 2012), ii, http://www.fas.org/sgp/crs/row/R41856.pdf (accessed April 29, 2013).

36. U.S. Department of State, *Country Reports on Human Rights: Pakistan*, 2009, http://www.state.gov/documents/organization/160472.pdf (accessed August 16, 2012).

37. Adam Levine, "Pakistan Supports Haqqani Network, Adm. Mullen Tells Congress," CNN, September 22, 2011, http://articles.cnn.com/2011-09-22/us/us_mullen-security_1_haqqani-network-pakistan-s-inter-services-intelligence-kabul-attack?_s=PM:US (accessed April 29, 2013).

38. Sebastian Rotella, "Captured Militant Reaffirms Role of Pakistan in Mumbai Attacks," PBS, *Frontline*, August 9, 2012, http://www.pbs.org/wgbh/pages/frontline/afghanistan-pakistan/david-headley/captured-militant-reaffirms-role-of-pakistan-in-mumbai-attacks/ (accessed November 15, 2012).

39. Frank Newport and Lydia Saad, "Americans Oppose Cuts in Education, Social Security, Defense," Gallup Politics, January 26, 2011, http://www.gallup.com/poll/145790/americans-oppose-cuts-education-social-security-defense.aspx (accessed November 15, 2012).

40. Will Rahn, "Richard Lugar Doesn't Live Here Anymore," *Daily Caller*, January 30, 2012, http://dailycaller.com/2012/01/30/richard-lugar-doesnt-live-here-anymore/ (accessed November 15, 2012).

41. Stephen Hayes, "In the Driver's Seat: Condoleezza Rice and the Jettisoning of the Bush Doctrine," *Weekly Standard*, June 2, 2008, http://www.weeklystandard.com/Content/Public/Articles/000/000/015/145jmmdg.asp (accessed November 15, 2012).

42. Glenn Kessler, "Bolton Book Cites Effort to Halt Powell's Iran Initiative," *Washington Post*, October 22, 2007, http://www.washingtonpost.com/wp-dyn/content/article/2007/10/21/AR2007102101042.html (accessed November 15, 2012).

43. "Staff: Edwin J. Fuelner, Ph.D., Founder," Heritage Foundation, http://www.heritage.org/about/staff/f/edwin-feulner (accessed August 17, 2012).

44. Heritage Foundation, "Return of Organization Exempt From Income Tax, 2011," Guidestar, http://www.guidestar.org/FinDocuments/2011/237/327/2011-237327730-088884a6-9.pdf (accessed May 1, 2013).

45. "Ron Paul's Foreign Policy," *Foreign Policy*, http://www.foreignpolicy.com/ron_paul/profile?page=0,1 (accessed November 16, 2012).

46. Video of Congressman Ron Paul, YouTube, http://www.youtube.com/watch?v=1p9boKTT_lQ, (accessed August 16, 2012).

47. Mike Opelka, "Ron Paul Denies Saying He Wouldn't Have Ordered Bin Laden Raid in Pakistan — but Here's the Video," The Blaze, http://www.theblaze.com/stories/ron-paul-denies-saying-that-he-would-not-have-ordered-bin-ladens-killing/ (accessed November 15, 2012).

48. Lucy Madison, "Ron Paul: Time to Stop Spending Trillions on War," CBS News, September 12, 2011, http://www.cbsnews.com/8301-503544_162-20105161-503544.html (accessed November 15, 2012).

49. Amy Belasco, "The Cost of Iraq, Afghanistan, and Other Global War on Terror Operations Since 9/11" (Washington, DC: Congressional Research Service, March 29, 2011), http://www.fas.org/sgp/crs/natsec/RL33110.pdf (accessed May 2, 2013).

50. See sum of 2002–2011 outlays in "Historical Tables, 1.1 Summary of Receipts, Outlays, and Surpluses or Deficits (-): 1789–2017," Office of Management and Budget, http://www.whitehouse.gov/omb/budget/Historicals (accessed April 2, 2013).

51. Transcript of CNN National Security Debate, CNN, November 22, 2012, http://archives.cnn.com/TRANSCRIPTS/1111/22/se.06.html (accessed April 29, 2013).

4. Smart Power with Chinese Characteristics

1. Simon Sebag Montefiore, "Dynasty of Decadence: Behind the Romanov's Glittering Facade Lay an Epic Saga of Depravity and Unspeakable Cruelty," *Daily Mail*, December 19, 2008, http://www.dailymail.co.uk/news/article-1098889/Dynasty-decadence-Behind-Romanovs-glittering-facade-lay-epic-saga-depravity-unspeakable-cruelty.html (accessed May 1, 2013).

2. David Fromkin, *A Peace to End All Peace: The Fall of the Ottoman Empire and the Creation of the Modern Middle East* (New York: Avon Books, 1989), 242–43.

3. Ibid., 244–46.

4. Frederick Kempe, *Berlin 1961: Kennedy, Khrushchev, and the Most Dangerous Place on Earth* (New York: Berkeley Books, 2011), Kindle edition. See also "RB-47H Shot Down," National Museum of the U.S. Air Force, December 6, 2006, http://www.nationalmuseum.af.mil/factsheets/factsheet.asp?id=1881 (accessed April 22, 2013).

5. Brendan Murray and Kevin Carmichael, "U.S. Officials, Lawmakers Say China's Yuan Move a First Step," Bloomberg, July 21, 2005, http://www.bloomberg.com/apps/news?pid=newsarchive&sid=aDJZOtne94Ss (accessed September 20, 2012).

6. United States Census Bureau, "Foreign Trade: Trade in Goods with China," U.S. Department of Commerce, http://www.census.gov/foreign-trade/balance/c5700.html (accessed September 2, 2012).

7. "Sen. Schumer Revives Threat of Action on China Yuan," Reuters, April 28, 2011, http://www.reuters.com/article/2011/04/28/us-usa-china-currency-idUSTRE73R6D020110428 (accessed September 20, 2012).

8. Jack Torry, "Bill on China Trade Easily Passes in Senate," *Columbus Dispatch*, October 12, 2011, http://www.dispatch.com/content/stories/local/2011/10/12/bill-on-china-trade-easily-passes-in-senate.html (accessed September 20, 2012).

9. "Senate Approves Bill to Punish China for Currency," Reuters, October 12, 2011, http://www.usnews.com/news/articles/2011/10/12/senate-approves-bill-to-punish-china-for-currency (accessed September 20, 2012).

10. Charles Riley, "House Passes Bill Aimed at Chinese Currency," CNN Money, September 30, 2010, http://money.cnn.com/2010/09/29/news/economy/congress_china_currency_bill/index.htm (accessed September 20, 2012).

11. Lewis Lehrman, "The Nixon Shock Heard 'Round the World,'" *Wall Street Journal*, August 15, 2011, http://online.wsj.com/article/SB10001424053111904007304576494073418802358.html (accessed September 20, 2012).

12. Michael Kitchen, "U.S. Industry Groups Lobby against China Yuan Bill," MarketWatch, September 21, 2011, http://articles.marketwatch.com/2011-09-21/news/30829892_1_yuan-currency-issue-china (accessed September 20, 2012).

13. James Risen and Jeff Gerth, "China Stole Design of Atom Warhead, a U.S. Report Finds," *New York Times*, April 21, 1999, http://www.nytimes.com/1999/04/21/world/china-stole-design-of-atom-warhead-a-us-report-finds.html (accessed September 20, 2012).

14. Brian Spegele, James Hookway, and Yuka Hayashi, "U.S. Missile Shield Plan Seen Stoking China Fears," *Wall Street Journal*, August 24, 2012, http://online.wsj.com/article/SB10000872396390444082904577609054116070694.html (accessed September 20, 2012).

15. "2009 Report to Congress," U.S.-China Economic and Security Review Commission, November 2009, accessed August 29, 2012, http://origin.www.uscc.gov/sites/default/files/annual_reports/2009-Report-to-Congress.pdf (accessed April 29, 2013).

16. James Mann, *The China Fantasy: How Our Leaders Explain away Chinese Repression* (New York: Viking, 2007), 59–60.

17. Ibid., 61–62.

18. Robert Woodward and Brian Duffy, "Chinese Embassy Role in Contributions Probed," *Washington Post*, February 13, 2007, http://www.washingtonpost.com/wp-srv/politics/special/campfin/stories/china1.htm (accessed April 22, 2013).

19. Joshua Green, "China Bashing on the Campaign Trail," BloombergBusinessweek, November 17, 2011, http://www.businessweek.com/magazine/china-bashing-on-the-campaign-trail-11172011.html (accessed September 20, 2012).

20. Bryan Bender, "Fallon: US Needs Strategy on China," *Boston Globe*, November 25, 2008, http://www.boston.com/news/nation/washington/articles/2008/11/25/fallon_us_needs_strategy_on_china/ (accessed September 20, 2012).

21. Bryan Bender, "Chief of US Pacific Forces Calls Climate Biggest Worry," *Boston Globe*, March 9, 2013, http://www.bostonglobe.com/news/nation/2013/03/09/admiral-samuel-locklear-commander-pacific-forces-warns-that-climate-change-top-threat/BHdPVCLrWEMxRe9IXJZcHL/story.html (accessed May 1, 2013).

22. Joseph P. Duggan, "What Would Jesse Do?," *The American Spectator*, February 9, 2009, http://spectator.org/archives/2009/02/09/what-would-jesse-do (accessed September 20, 2012).

23. Michael Bristow, "Obama Speech Censored in China," BBC News, January 21, 2009, http://news.bbc.co.uk/2/hi/7841580.stm (accessed September 20, 2012).

24. Joshua Kurlantzick, "Nonstop Party," *Boston Globe*, November 22, 2009, http://www.boston.com/bostonglobe/ideas/articles/2009/11/22/the_surprising_persistence_of_chinese_communism (accessed September 20, 2012).

25. "Not a Pretty Dish," *Wall Street Journal*, March 17, 2005, http://online.wsj.com/article/SB111101769524481719.html (accessed September 20, 2012).

26. Rochard C. Morais, "China's Fight with Falun Gong," *Forbes*, February 9, 2006, http://www.forbes.com/2006/02/09/falun-gong-china_cz_rm_0209falungong.html (accessed September 20, 2012).

27. "European Satellite Operator Eutelsat Suppresses Independent Chinese-Language TV Station NTDTV to Satisfy Beijing," Reporters Without Borders, July 10, 2008, http://en.rsf.org/china-european-satellite-operator-10-07-2008,27818 (accessed September 20, 2012).

28. "Statement from New Tang Dynasty TV Regarding Eutelsat Incident," *Epoch Times*, July 5, 2008, http://www.theepochtimes.com/news/8-7-5/72919.html (accessed September 20, 2012).

29. "China Tried to Halt Falun Gong TV in Canada: Defector," *Ottawa Citizen*, April 5, 2007, http://www.canada.com/story_print.html?id=ea72bae7-f0e2-4fcf-877d-b4b092895288 (accessed September 20, 2012).

30. Manuel Baigorri, "China Investment Purchases Eutelsat Stake from Abertis," Bloomberg, June 22, 2012, http://www.bloomberg.com/news/2012-06-22/china-investment-purchases-eutelsat-stake-from-abertis.html (accessed April 29, 2013).

31. Michael Ciepley and Brooks Barnes, "To Get Movies into China, Hollywood Gives Censors a Preview," *New York Times*, January 14, 2013, http://www.nytimes.com/2013/01/15/business/media/in-hollywood-movies-for-china-bureaucrats-want-a-say.html?pagewanted=all&_r=0 (accessed May 1, 2013).

5. Islamist Political Warfare

1. George W. Bush, "Backgrounder: The President's Quotes on Islam," The White House, http://georgewbush-whitehouse.archives.gov/infocus/ramadan/islam.html (accessed September 4, 2012).

2. George W. Bush, "Address to a Joint Session of Congress and the American People," September 20, 2011, The White House, http://georgewbush-whitehouse .archives.gov/news/releases/2001/09/20010920-8.html (accessed September 4, 2012).

3. Alex Brodie, "Tony Blair Interview: Full Transcript," BBC News, September 19, 2001, http://news.bbc.co.uk/2/hi/uk_news/1552265.stm (accessed October 15, 2012).

4. Eric Schmitt and Thom Shanker, "U.S. Officials Retool Slogan for Terror War," New York Times, July 26, 2005, http://www.nytimes.com/2005/07/26/ politics/26strategy.html (accessed October 15, 2012).

5. Advisory Group on Public Diplomacy for the Arab and Muslim World, "Changing Minds, Winning Peace: A Strategic Direction for U.S. Public Diplomacy in the Arab & Muslim World" (Washington, DC: Advisory Group on Public Diplomacy for the Arab and Muslim World, October 1, 2003), 8, http://www.state.gov/documents/ organization/24882.pdf (accessed October 15, 2012).

6. Barabara Slavin, "Hughes Embarks on 'Listening Tour' to Patch U.S. Image," USA Today, September 22, 2005, http://www.usatoday.com/news/world/2005-09-22 -hughes-listening-tour_x.htm (accessed October 15, 2012).

7. Diana West, "A 'Listening Tour' Turns to Capitulation," Jewish World Review, September 30, 2005, http://www.jewishworldreview.com/0905/west093005.php3 (accessed October 15, 2012).

8. Christopher Marquis, "Promoter of U.S. Image Quits for Wall St. Job," New York Times, April 30, 2004, http://www.nytimes.com/2004/04/30/world/promoter-of -us-image-quits-for-wall-st-job.html (accessed April 2004, 2013).

9. James K. Glassman, "Winning the War of Ideas," New York Sun, July 23, 2008, http://www.nysun.com/opinion/winning-the-war-of-ideas/82438 (accessed October 15, 2012).

10. James K. Glassman, Foreign Press Center Briefing: "U.S. Public Diplomacy and the War of Ideas," State Department, July 15, 2008, http://2002-2009-fpc.state .gov/107034.htm (accessed October 15, 2012).

11. Tara Sonenshine, "The State of American Public Diplomacy: Remarks to the American Security Project," State Department, June 28, 2012, http://www.state .gov/r/remarks/2012/195947.htm (accessed October 15, 2012).

12. Art Moore, "U.S. Muslim Lobby Fights Measure to Protect Jews," World Net Daily, September 7, 2012, http://www.wnd.com/2012/09/u-s-muslim-lobby -fights-measure-to-protect-jews/ (accessed October 15, 2012).

13. John Hinderaker, "CAIR: Unindicted, but Still a Co-Conspirator," Power Line (blog), November 28, 2010, http://www.powerlineblog.com/ archives/2010/11/027781.php (accessed October 15, 2012).

14. "Muslims Train FBI in 'Sensitivity,'" *World Net Daily*, December 2, 2004, http://www.wnd.com/2004/12/27816/; and Andrew C. McCarthy, "Singing CAIR's Tune, on Your Dime," *National Review*, January 2, 2007, http://www.national review.com/articles/219624/singing-cairs-tune-your-dime/andrew-c-mccarthy# (accessed October 15, 2012).

15. Kenneth Timmerman, "Obama Administration Pulls References to Islam from Terror Training Materials, Official Says," *Daily Caller*, October 21, 2011, http://daily-caller.com/2011/10/21/obama-administration-pulls-references-to-islam-from -terror-training-materials-official-says (accessed October 15, 2012).

16. Wajahat Ali et al., "Fear, Inc.: The Roots of the Islamophobia Network in America," Center for American Progress, http://www.americanprogress.org/issues/religion/ report/2011/08/26/10165/fear-inc (accessed September 18, 2012). See also "2010 IRS Return of Private Foundation, The Lynde and Harry Bradley Foundation," Guidestar, http://www.guidestar.org/FinDocuments/2010/396/037/2010 -396037928-07b43b33-F.pdf (accessed September 18, 2012).

17. Donald Rumsfeld, *Known and Unknown: A Memoir* (New York: Sentinel, 2011), 353.

18. T. E. Lawrence, *Seven Pillars of Wisdom*, ed. Brad Berner (Apostrophe Books, August 24, 2010), Kindle edition.

6. Five Deadly Illusions

1. Jay Lefkowitz, "North Korean Human Rights after the Six-Party Talks," remarks, Heritage Foundation, Washington, DC, April 19, 2007, http://seoul.usembassy .gov/nkhr_042307.html (accessed October 15, 2012).

2. Glenn Kessler, "From Video to Terrorist Attack: A Definitive Timeline of Administration Statements on the Libya Attack," *Washington Post*, September 27, 2012, http://www.washingtonpost.com/blogs/fact-checker/post/from-video-to-terrorist -attack-a-definitive-timeline-of-administration-statements-on-the-libya-attack/2012/ 09/26/86105782-0826-11e2-afff-d6c7f20a83bf_blog.html (accessed October 15, 2012).

3. Shepard Smith's interview with the author, Studio B, Fox News, September 12, 2012, http://www.youtube.com/watch?v=oUYTmXB3rQw (accessed October 15, 2012).

4. "Libyans Storm Ansar Al-Shariah Compound in Backlash after Attack on US Consulate," Fox News, September 21, 2012, http://www.foxnews.com/ world/2012/09/21/libyans-storm-ansar-al-sharia-compound-in-backlash-attack -on-us-consulate (accessed October 15, 2012).

5. Roula Khalaf, "Radical Islamists Unite under Fresh Name," *Washington Post*, September 27, 2012, http://www.washingtonpost.com/world/middle_east/radical -islamists-unite-under-fresh-name/2012/09/27/7a168fb0-08ca-11e2-858a -5311df86ab04_story.html (accessed October 15, 2012).

6. Associated Press, "U.S. Withholds China Resolution at Rights Conference," *USA Today*, April 11, 2003, http://usatoday30.usatoday.com/news/washington/2003 -04-11-china-us_x.htm (accessed October 15, 2012).

7. Elise Labott, "U.S. Drops China Rights Censure," CNN, March 18, 2005, http://articles.cnn.com/2005-03-17/world/china.humanrights_1_resolution-censuring -human-rights-political-prisoners?_s=PM:WORLD (accessed October 15, 2012).

8. James Morrison, "Embassy Row: Is Jerusalem in Israel?," *Washington Times*, April 10, 2012, http://www.washingtontimes.com/news/2012/apr/10/embassy-row-is -jerusalem-in-israel/?page=all (accessed October 15, 2012).

9. "History of Failed Peace Talks," BBC News, November 26, 2007, http://news.bbc .co.uk/2/hi/middle_east/6666393.stm#campdavid2 (accessed October 15, 2012).

10. Roxana Tiron and Takashi Hirokawa, "U.S. Agrees With Japan on Relocation of Marines From Okinawa," Bloomberg, April 27, 2012, http://www.bloomberg.com/ news/2012-04-27/u-s-agrees-with-japan-on-relocation-of-marines-from-okinawa .html (accessed October 15, 2012).

11. Sachiko Sakamaki and Takashi Hirokawa, "Japan Ends Refueling Ships in Support of War in Afghanistan," Bloomberg, January 14, 2010, http://www.bloomberg.com/ apps/news?pid=newsarchive&sid=aLKi3fb1j9NA (accessed October 15, 2012).

12. Chris Hogg, "N Korea Abductions Hamper Japan," BBC News, March 3, 2008, http://news.bbc.co.uk/2/hi/asia-pacific/7252484.stm (accessed October 15, 2012).

13. Bruce Wallace, "Risking Extradition, Ex-GI Goes to Japan," *Los Angeles Times*, June 19, 2004, http://articles.latimes.com/2004/jul/19/world/fg-jenkins19 (accessed May 1, 2013).

14. Paul Richter, "U.S. Drops North Korea from Terrorism List after New Deal," *Los Angeles Times*, October 12, 2008, http://articles.latimes.com/2008/oct/12/world/ fg-norkor12 (accessed October 15, 2012).

15. "Japan's Next Fighters: F-35 Wins the F-X Competition," *Defense Industry Daily*, September 9, 2009, http://www.defenseindustrydaily.com/f22-raptors-to-japan -01909.

16. "China Officially Labels Senkakus a 'Core Interest,'" *Japan Times*, April 27, 2013, http://www.japantimes.co.jp/news/2013/04/27/national/china-officially-labels -senkakus-a-core-interest/#.UYGX7b83bDU (accessed May 1, 2013).

17. Mark Lander, "No New F-16's for Taiwan, but U.S. to Upgrade Fleet," *New York Times*, September 18, 2011, http://www.nytimes.com/2011/09/19/world/asia/us -decides-against-selling-f-16s-to-taiwan.html?_r=0 (accessed October 15, 2012).

18. "F-16 Fighting Falcon — International Users," Global Security, http://www.global security.org/military/systems/aircraft/f-16-fms.htm (accessed October 4, 2012).

19. Eric Schmitt, "C.I.A. Said to Aid in Steering Arms to Syrian Opposition," *New York Times*, June 21, 2012, http://www.nytimes.com/2012/06/21/world/ middleeast/cia-said-to-aid-in-steering-arms-to-syrian-rebels.html?pagewanted =all&_r=0 (accessed October 15, 2012).

20. Duane R. Clarridge with Digby Diehl, *A Spy for All Seasons: My Life in the CIA* (New York: Scribner, 1997), 111.

21. Ghaith Abdul-Ahad, "Syria Civil War: 'We Expend the One Thing We Have, Men. Men Are Dying,'" *Guardian*, September 25, 2012, http://www.guardian .co.uk/world/2012/sep/25/syria-bloody-stalemate-aleppo-rebels?newsfeed=true (accessed October 15, 2012).

22. Robert F. Worth, "Citing U.S. Fears, Arab Allies Limit Syrian Rebel Aid," *New York Times*, October 6, 2012, http://www.nytimes.com/2012/10/07/world/middleeast/citing-us-fears-arab-allies-limit-aid-to-syrian-rebels.html (accessed October 15, 2012).

23. 50 USC § 413b—"Presidential Approval and Reporting of Covert Actions," Cornell University Legal Information Institute, http://www.law.cornell.edu/uscode/text/50/413b?quicktabs_8=1#quicktabs-8 (accessed October 10, 2012).

24. "CIA Operatives Gathering Intelligence In Libya," NPR, March 31, 2011, http://www.npr.org/2011/03/31/135005728/cia-operatives-gathering-intelligence-in-libya?ps=cprs (accessed October 15, 2012).

25. "U.S. Rescue Chopper Shoots Six Libyan Villagers as They Welcome Pilots of Downed Air Force Jet," *Daily Mail*, March 22, 2011, http://www.dailymail.co.uk/news/article-1368633/Libya-war-US-chopper-shoots-6-villagers-welcomed-Air-Force-F-15-crash-pilots.html (accessed October 15, 2012).

26. Edward Cody, "NATO: Rebels' Use of Tanks May Have Triggered Erroneous Airstrike," *Washington Post*, April 8, 2011, http://www.washingtonpost.com/world/nato-rebels-use-of-tanks-may-have-triggered-erroneous-airstrike/2011/04/08/AFpyYLoC_story.html (accessed October 15, 2012).

27. Viola Gienger and Nicole Gaouette, "NATO Upgrades Libyan Rebel Contact that Was Reliant on Cell Phones, Skype," Bloomberg, April 20, 2011, http://www.bloomberg.com/news/2011-04-21/nato-upgrades-libyan-rebel-contact-reliant-on-cell-phones-skype.html (accessed October 15, 2012).

28. Andrew Sullivan, "The Revolution Will Be Twittered," *The Atlantic*, June 13, 2009, http://www.theatlantic.com/daily-dish/archive/2009/06/the-revolution-will-be-twittered/200478 (accessed October 15, 2012).

29. Lev Grossman, "Iran Protests: Twitter, the Medium of the Movement," *Time*, June 17, 2009, http://www.time.com/time/world/article/0,8599,1905125,00.html (accessed October 15, 2012).

30. Hannah Beach, "You've Got Mail," *Time*, October 16, 2011, http://www.time.com/time/magazine/article/0,9171,2096818,00.html (accessed October 15, 2012).

31. Peter Foster, "China to Force Internet Users to Register Real Names," *Telegraph*, May 5, 2010, http://www.telegraph.co.uk/news/worldnews/asia/china/7681709/China-to-force-internet-users-to-register-real-names.html (accessed October 15, 2012).

32. Priscilla Jiao, "Identity Crackdown Hits SIM Card Sales," *South China Morning Post*, March 30, 2012, http://www.scmp.com/article/723717/identity-crackdown-hits-sim-card-sales (accessed October 15, 2012).

33. Czesław Bielecki, translated by Roman M. Boreyko and André YaDeau, "The Little Conspirator," *Conflict Quarterly*, Fall 1986, 41, http://www.google.com/url?sa=t&rct=j&q=&esrc=s&source=web&cd=2&ved=0CDIQFjAB&url=http%3A%2F%2Fjournals.hil.unb.ca%2Findex.php%2FJCS%2Farticle%2Fdownload%2F14735%2F15804&ei=hqSBUYMfhvyKAvjIgOgK&usg=AFQjCNEVLU_nUXNf-mPckjsb4R2kbU3d8A&bvm=bv.45960087,d.cGE (accessed May 1, 2013).

7. Washington's Broken Institutions

1. Jonathan Lamb, "Captain Cook and the Scourge of Scurvy," BBC News, February 17, 2011, http://www.bbc.co.uk/history/british/empire_seapower/captaincook _scurvy_01.shtml (accessed October 30, 2012).

2. Ibid.

3. Jason Allen Mayberry, "Scurvy and Vitamin C," Harvard Law School, April 27, 2004, http://leda.law.harvard.edu/leda/data/658/Mayberry.html (accessed October 30, 2012).

4. Crispin Burke, "Scurvy, Manpower, and the American Revolution," *Conflict Health*, July 27, 2010, http://conflicthealth.com/scurvy-manpower-and-the -american-revolution/ (accessed May 1, 2013).

5. Ryan Crocker, "Embassy Baghdad: Organization and Staffing," State Department cable, Baghdad, May 31, 2007, http://media.washingtonpost.com/wp-srv/nation/ documents/cable_061907.pdf (accessed October 30, 2012).

6. Karen DeYoung, "Envoys Resist Forced Iraq Duty," *Washington Post*, November 1, 2007, http://www.washingtonpost.com/wp-dyn/content/article/2007/10/31/ AR2007103101626.html (accessed October 30, 2012).

7. Ibid.

8. Alissa J. Rubin and Mudhafer Al-Husaini, "Baghdad Blast Kills Four Americans," *New York Times*, June 25, 2008, http://www.nytimes.com/2008/06/25/world/ middleeast/25iraq.html?_r=0 (accessed October 30, 2012). State Department– related employees killed during the war included either Diplomatic Security officers or temporary employees.

9. Comparison of military and Foreign Service pay in Iraq provided to author by Senate Armed Services Committee staff, June 13, 2012.

10. Ronald W. Reagan National Authorization Defense Authorization Act for Fiscal Year 2005, Department of Defense, Public Law 108-375, 108th Cong., 118 STAT. 1811, October 28, 2004, http://www.dod.mil/dodgc/olc/docs/PL108-375.pdf (accessed October 19, 2012).

11. National Defense Authorization Act For Fiscal Year 2006, Department of Defense, Public Law 109-163, 109th Cong., 119 STAT. 3136, January 6, 2006, http://www .dod.mil/dodgc/olc/docs/PL109-163.pdf (accessed October 19, 2012).

12. Inspector General of the United States Department of Defense, "Management Improvements Needed in Commander's Emergency Response Program in Afghanistan" (Alexandria, VA: Inspector General, Department of Defense, November 21, 2011), 1, http://www.dodig.mil/audit/reports/fy12/DODIG-2012-023.pdf (accessed October 30, 2012). ·

13. Jason Ukman, "Cost of Civilian 'Surge' in Afghanistan: $1.7 Billion," *Washington Post*, September 18, 2011, http://www.washingtonpost.com/blogs/checkpoint -washington/post/cost-of-civilian-surge-in-afghanistan-17-billion/2011/09/08/ gIQARu9qCK_blog.html (accessed October 30, 2012).

14. Geoff Earle, "Obama Leads Romney in Donations from Government Employees," *New York Post*, May 21, 2012, http://www.nypost.com/p/news/national/obama _diplos_ki_up_J1ik9FwN3SisqqGiTr6ZdJ (accessed October 30, 2012).

15. Harry Crosby, "Too at Home Abroad," *The Washington Monthly*, September 1991, http://www.washingtonmonthly.com/features/archives/9109.crosby.html (accessed October 30, 2012). Note that "Harry Crosby" is a pseudonym.

16. Thom Shanker and Eric Schmitt, "The Struggle for Iraq: The Military; U.S. Considering Recalling Units of Old Iraq Army," *New York Times*, November 2, 2003, http://www.nytimes.com/2003/11/02/world/struggle-for-iraq-military-us-considering-recalling-units-old-iraq-army.html (accessed October 30, 2012).

17. Michael Rubin, "Iraq's Electoral System: A Misguided Strategy," *Arab Reform Bulletin*, September 2004, http://www.michaelrubin.org/920/iraqs-electoral-system-a-misguided-strategy (accessed October 30, 2012).

18. Ayad Allawi, "How Iraq's Elections Set Back Democracy," *New York Times*, November 2, 2007, http://www.nytimes.com/2007/11/02/opinion/02allawi.html?_r=0.

19. Rumsfeld, *Known and Unknown*, 528.

20. Mark Mansfield, "Reflections on Service: A Conversation with Former CIA Director Michael Hayden," CIA Center for the Study of Intelligence, July 2, 2010, https://www.cia.gov/library/center-for-the-study-of-intelligence/csi-publications/csi-studies/studies/vol.-54-no.-2/a-conversation-with-former-cia-director-michael.html (accessed April 30, 2013)

21. Gordon Corera, *The Art of Betrayal: The Secret History of MI6: Life and Death in the British Secret Service* (New York: Pegasus Books, 2013), Kindle edition.

22. Allen W. Dulles, *The Craft of Intelligence* (Guilford, CT: Lyons Press, 2006), 114–15.

23. Ibid., 115.

24. Jeff Stein, "CIA Chief Promises Spies 'New Cover' for Secret Ops," *Washington Post*, April 26, 2010, http://voices.washingtonpost.com/spy-talk/2010/04/cia_chief_promises_spies_new_a.html (accessed October 30, 2012).

25. Donald P. Steury, "How the CIA Missed Stalin's Bomb," CIA Center for the Study of Intelligence, April 15, 2007, https://www.cia.gov/library/center-for-the-study-of-intelligence/csi-publications/csi-studies/studies/vol49no1/html_files/stalins_bomb_3.html (accessed October 22, 2012).

26. Jack Davis, "Improving CIA Analytic Performance: Strategic Warning," CIA Sherman Kent Center for Intelligence Analysis, September 2002, https://www.cia.gov/library/kent-center-occasional-papers/vol1no1.htm (accessed October 30, 2012).

27. "U.S. Intelligence Budget Tops $80 Billion," UPI, October 28, 2010, http://www.upi.com/Top_News/US/2010/10/28/US-intelligence-budget-tops-80-billion/UPI-37231288307113/ (accessed October 30, 2012).

28. Fromkin, *A Peace to End All Peace*, 542.

29. Mark Mazzetti, "U.S. Says Iran Ended Atomic Arms Work," *New York Times*, December 3, 2007, http://www.nytimes.com/2007/12/03/world/middleeast/03cnd-iran.html?_r=0 (accessed October 30, 2012).

30. Director General, "Report by the Director General on Implementation of the NPT Safeguards Agreement and Relevant Provisions of Security Council Resolutions in the Islamic Republic of Iran," International Atomic Energy Agency, November 8, 2011, Section 53, http://www.iaea.org/Publications/Documents/Board/2011/gov2011-65.pdf (accessed October 30, 2012).

31. Associated Press, "Bush Warns of 'World War III' if Iran Gains Nuclear Weapons," Fox News, October 18, 2007, http://www.foxnews.com/story/0,2933,303097,00 .html (accessed October 30, 2012).

32. Jay Solomon and Siobhan Gorman, "In Iran Reversal, Bureaucrats Triumphed over Cheney Team," *Wall Street Journal*, January 14, 2008, http://online.wsj.com/ article/SB120027737099687613.html (accessed April 29, 2013).

33. Evan Thomas, *The Very Best Men: Four Who Dared: The Early Years of the CIA* (New York: Simon & Schuster, 1996), 36.

34. Michael Warner, "Origins of the Congress for Cultural Freedom, 1949–50," Central Intelligence Agency Center for the Study of Intelligence, *Studies in Intelligence* 38, no. 5 (1995), https://www.cia.gov/library/center-for-the-study-of -intelligence/csi-publications/csi-studies/studies/95unclass/Warner.html (accessed October 30, 2012).

35. Ibid.

36. Kenneth Osgood, *Total Cold War: Eisenhower's Secret Propaganda Battle at Home and Abroad* (Lawrence: University Press of Kansas, 2006), 303.

37. Thomas, *The Very Best Men*, 35.

38. Warner, "Origins of the Congress for Cultural Freedom."

39. Ibid.

40. Osgood, *Total Cold War*, 29.

41. Ibid., 40.

42. Arnold Beichman, untitled essay, January 14, 1990, http://www.beichman.com/ Articles/RFE.htm (accessed October 30, 2012).

43. Ronald Reagan, "Address to Members of the British Parliament," Ronald Reagan Presidential Library, June 8, 1982, http://www.reagan.utexas.edu/archives/ speeches/1982/60882a.htm (accessed October 30, 2012).

44. Andrey Ostroukh, "Russia's Putin Signs NGO 'Foreign Agents' Law," Reuters, July 21, 2102, http://www.reuters.com/article/2012/07/21/us-russia-putin-ngos-id USBRE86K05M20120721 (accessed October 30, 2012).

45. Matt Bradley and Charles Levinson, "In Standoff, Egypt Blocks Americans from Leaving," *Wall Street Journal*, January 27, 2012, http://online.wsj.com/article/SB1 0001424052970204573704577184751313941924.html (accessed October 30, 2012).

46. Josh Rogin, "State Department Training Islamic Political Parties in Egypt," *Foreign Policy*, November 3, 2011, http://thecable.foreignpolicy.com/posts/2011/11/03/ state_department_training_islamic_political_parties_in_egypt (accessed October 30, 2012).

47. Carl Gershman, "Remarks at the 8th Annual Seymour Martin Lipset Lecture on Democracy in the World," Embassy of Canada, Washington, DC, October 26, 2011, http://www.ned.org/node/2073 (accessed October 30, 2012).

48. See "Advancing the Freedom Agenda" in White House, "Fact Sheet: Promoting Human Rights Worldwide," December 10, 2008, http://georgewbush-whitehouse .archives.gov/news/releases/2008/12/20081210-1.html (accessed April 25, 2013).

49. Department of State, "National Endowment of Democracy: Resource Summary," http://www.state.gov/documents/organization/181143.pdf (accessed April 25, 2013).

50. Testimony of Suzanne Scholte for the Tom Lantos Human Rights Commission Hearing, "North Korea: Ongoing Human Rights Violations in an Era of Change," U.S. House of Representatives, September 9, 2012, http://tlhrc.house.gov/docs/ statements/Suzanne%20Scholte%20-%20Witness%201.pdf (accessed October 30, 2012).

8. Organizing for Victory

1. "Bush: 'I'm the Decider' on Rumsfeld," CNN, April 18, 2006, http://www.cnn .com/2006/POLITICS/04/18/rumsfeld/ (accessed November 14, 2012).

2. Rumsfeld, Known and Unknown, 325–26.

3. Peter W. Rodman, Presidential Command: Power, Leadership, and the Making of Foreign Policy from Richard Nixon to George W. Bush (New York: Alfred A Knopf, 2009), 249.

4. Report of the Preparatory Commission for the Comprehensive Nuclear-Test-Ban Treaty Organization, "The CTBT Verification Regime Put to the Test — the Event in the DPRK on 9 October 2006," 2007, http://www.ctbto.org/press-centre/ highlights/2007/the-ctbt-verification-regime-put-to-the-test-the-event-in-the-dprk -on-9-october-2006/ (accessed November 1, 2012).

5. William Manchester, American Caesar: Douglas MacArthur, 1880–1964 (New York: Dell Publishing, 1978), 229.

6. Rodman, Presidential Command, 24.

7. "Sun Room," White House Museum, http://www.whitehousemuseum.org/floor3/ sun-room.htm (accessed November 4, 2012).

8. "Project Solarium," Eisenhower Memorial Commission, http://www.eisenhower memorial.org/stories/Project-Solarium.htm (accessed November 14, 2012). For NSC 162/2, see Executive Secretary on Basic National Security Policy, "A Report to the National Security Council," Washington, October 30, 1953, http://www.fas.org/irp/ offdocs/nsc-hst/nsc-162-2.pdf (accessed April 29, 2013).

9. "History of the National Security Council, 1947–1997," Office of the Historian, White House, August 1997, http://georgewbush-whitehouse.archives.gov/nsc/ history.html (accessed November 4, 2012).

10. For example, see Karen DeYoung, "Obama's NSC Will Get New Power," Washington Post, February 8, 2009, http://www.washingtonpost.com/wp-dyn/content/ article/2009/02/07/AR2009020702076.html (accessed November 14, 2012).

11. The White House (Clinton administration), "National Security Council Staff," National Archives, January 20, 2001, http://clinton4.nara.gov/WH/EOP/NSC/ html/NSC_Staff.html (accessed May 1, 2013).

12. Alan G. Whittaker, Shannon A. Brown, Frederick C. Smith, and Elizabeth McKune, "The National Security Policy Process: The National Security Council and Interagency System," National Defense University, August 15, 2011, appendix D, http://www.ndu.edu/es/outreach/publications/nspp/docs/icaf-nsc-policy -process-report-08-2011.pdf (accessed May 1, 2013).

13. Thomas L. Friedman, "Baker Brings an Inner Circle of Outsiders to State Dept.," *New York Times*, March 27, 1989, http://www.nytimes.com/1989/03/27/world/baker-brings-an-inner-circle-of-outsiders-to-state-dept.html?pagewanted=all&src=pm (accessed November 14, 2012).

14. Brian Lamb, interview with George Shultz, C-SPAN, April 29, 1993, http://www.c spanvideo.org/program/44051 1 (accessed November 14, 2012).

15. "Source: Terror Suspect's Father Tried to Warn Authorities," CNN, December 27, 2009, http://www.cnn.com/2009/CRIME/12/26/airline.attack/index.html (accessed November 14, 2012).

16. Elliott Abrams, "No More Visas for the State Department," *National Review*, December 29, 2009, http://www.nationalreview.com/articles/228878/no-more-visas-state-department/elliott-abrams# (accessed November 14, 2012).

17. U.S. Department of State, mission statement, November 2012, http://www.state.gov/s/d/rm/index.htm#mission (accessed April 29, 2013).

18. "A Brief History: The Bell System," AT&T, http://www.corp.att.com/history/history3.html (accessed November 7, 2012).

19. Diane S. Katz, "A Telecommunications Policy Primer: What Prompted the Breakup of AT&T?," Mackinac Center for Public Policy, August 16, 2004, http://www.mackinac.org/6769 (accessed November 14, 2012).

20. Walter Pincus, "White House Confirms Primacy of CIA Station Chiefs, Ending Turf War," *Washington Post*, November 13, 2009, http://www.washingtonpost.com/wp-dyn/content/article/2009/11/12/AR2009111210693.html (accessed November 14, 2012).

21. Matt Apuzzo, "White House Defends Intelligence Chief after Terrorism Gaffe: London Plot Wasn't Briefed," Associated Press, December 22, 2010, http://www.cleveland.com/world/index.ssf/2010/12/white_house_defends_intelligen.html (accessed November 14, 2012).

22. Steven Nelson, "Lindsey Graham: Clapper Has Had Three Strikes, Must Resign," *Daily Caller*, March 10, 2011, http://dailycaller.com/2011/03/10/lindsey-graham-clapper-has-had-three-strikes-must-resign/ (accessed November 14, 2012).

23. Adam Entous, Siobhan Gorman, and Julian E. Barnes, "U.S. Relaxes Drone Rules," *Wall Street Journal*, April 26, 2012, http://online.wsj.com/article/SB10001424052702304723304577366251852418174.html (accessed November 14, 2012).

24. Andru E. Wall, "Demystifying the Title 10–Title 50 Debate: Distinguishing Military Operations, Intelligence Activities & Covert Action," *Harvard National Security Journal* 3 (2011): 109, http://harvardnsj.org/wp-content/uploads/2012/01/Vol.-3_Wall1.pdf (accessed April 29, 2013).

25. Ibid., 93.

26. Ibid., 86.

27. David Garnett, *The Secret History of the PWE: The Political Warfare Executive, 1939–1945* (London: St. Ermin's Press, 2002), 207.

28. Ibid., 150.

29. Notably, one of the better sources about life as a USIA officer in the early Cold War comes from chef Julia Child, whose husband, Paul, served in the agency in a num-

ber of Western European cities. See Julia Child with Alex Prud'homme, *My Life in France* (New York: Alfred A. Knopf, 2006), Kindle edition.

30. Craig Hayden, "My 2 Cents on the Brownback Bill: Initial Language and Justifications," *Intermap* (blog), September 30, 2008, http://intermap.org/2008/09/30/my-2-cents-on-the-brownback-bill-initial-language-and-justifications/ (accessed November 14, 2012).

31. Beth Reinhard, "McCain: Bring back the U.S.I.A.," *Miami Herald*, June 20, 2007, http://miamiherald.typepad.com/nakedpolitics/2007/06/mccain-bring-ba.html (accessed November 14, 2012).

32. John F. Kennedy, "Special Message to the Congress on Foreign Aid," in Gerhard Peters and John T. Woolley, *The American Presidency Project*, March 22, 1961, http://www.presidency.ucsb.edu/ws/?pid=8545 (accessed April 29, 2013).

33. "CPI Inflation Calculator," Bureau of Labor Statistics, Department of Labor, http://www.bls.gov/data/inflation_calculator.htm (accessed November 12, 2012).

34. For example see letter from Madeleine K. Albright, Henry A. Kissinger, Colin L. Powell, Condoleezza Rice, and George P. Shultz — all of the U.S. Global Leadership Coalition — to members of Congress, November 14, 2011, http://www.foreignpolicy.com/files/fp_uploaded_documents/111114_Former-Sec-State-Letter-Nov2011.pdf (accessed November 14, 2012).

35. Jane Perlez, "U.S. Aid Plan for Pakistan Is Foundering," *New York Times*, May 1, 2011, http://www.nytimes.com/2011/05/02/world/asia/02pakistan.html (accessed November 14, 2012).

36. Peter Grier, "US Aid to Egypt: What Does It Buy?," *Christian Science Monitor*, February 15, 2011, http://www.csmonitor.com/USA/DC-Decoder/Decoder-Wire/2011/0215/US-aid-to-Egypt-What-does-it-buy (accessed November 14, 2012).

37. Ahmed Younis and Mohamed Younis, "Most Egyptians Oppose U.S. Economic Aid," Gallup World, February 6, 2012, http://www.gallup.com/poll/152471/egyptians-oppose-economic-aid.aspx (accessed November 14, 2012).

38. Lucy Madison, "Bachmann: Perry 'Naive' on Pakistan Policy," CBS News, November 22, 2011, http://www.cbsnews.com/8301-503544_162-57330052-503544/bachmann-perry-naive-on-pakistan-policy/ (accessed November 14, 2012).

39. Scott Wong, "McCain Blasts Conservatives on Foreign Aid," Politico, September 13, 2012, http://www.politico.com/news/stories/0912/81188.html (accessed November 14, 2012).

40. Sarah El Deeb, "McCain: Egypt and US 'Must Remain Friends,'" *Christian Science Monitor*, February 20, 2012, http://www.csmonitor.com/World/Latest-News-Wires/2012/0220/McCain-Egypt-and-US-must-remain-friends (accessed November 14, 2012).

9. Undermining Iran and Islamists

1. Thomas Erdbrink, "Iran Hostage Taker Returns to the Spotlight, with Insight," *New York Times*, November 1, 2012, http://www.nytimes.com/2012/11/02/world/middleeast/spotlight-returns-to-1979-iranian-hostage-taker.html?_r=1& (accessed December 4, 2012).

2. Ibid.

3. Tom Vanden Brook, "U.S. Blames Iran for New Bombs in Iraq," *USA Today*, January 31, 2007, http://usatoday30.usatoday.com/news/world/iraq/2007-01-30-ied -iran_x.htm (accessed December 4, 2012).

4. Robin Wright and Nancy Trejos, "U.S. Troops Raid 2 Iranian Targets in Iraq, Detain 5 People," *Washington Post*, January 12, 2007, http://www.washingtonpost .com/wp-dyn/content/article/2007/01/11/AR2007011100427.html (accessed December 4, 2012).

5. "Ambassador and Abdel Mehdi Discuss New Strategy, Iran, and the Moderate Front," State Department cable, Baghdad, January 9, 2007, http://www .cablegatesearch.net/cable.php?id=07BAGHDAD83 (accessed December 4, 2012).

6. "Maliki Predicts Improved Security Conditions," State Department cable, Baghdad, September 1, 2007, http://www.cablegatesearch.net/cable.php?id=07BAGHDAD 2930 (accessed December 4, 2012).

7. "Maliki on Iran Weapons Smuggling, Current Military Campaigns, Strategic Framework, and Neighbor's Conference," State Department cable, Baghdad, April 28, 2008, http://www.cablegatesearch.net/cable.php?id=08BAGHDAD1315 (accessed December 4, 2012).

8. "Iraq-Iran Diplomacy a Sign of Iranian Influence or Iraqi Resolve?," State Department cable, Baghdad, February 4, 2009, http://www.cablegatesearch.net/cable .php?id=09BAGHDAD289 (accessed December 4, 2012).

9. Wright and Trejos, "U.S. Troops Raid."

10. Secretary of Defense, "The Protection of U.S. Forces Abroad" (executive summary of the Downing Task Force Report on the Khobar Towers bombing and terrorism), *Defense Issues* 11, no. 88 (September 16, 1996), http://www.defense.gov/speeches/ speech.aspx?speechid=937 (accessed April 1, 2013).

11. Richard Boudreaux, "Israeli Official Says Iran Training Hamas," *Los Angeles Times*, March 6, 2007, http://articles.latimes.com/2007/mar/06/world/fg-hamas6 (accessed April 29, 2013).

12. Joby Warrick, "Texas Man Pleads Guilty in Iranian Assassination Plot," *Washington Post*, October 17, 2012, http://www.washingtonpost.com/world/national-security/ texas-man-pleads-guilty-in-iranian-assassination-plot/2012/10/17/b712a022-189a -11e2-a55c-39408fbe6a4b_story.html (accessed December 4, 2012).

13. "U.S. Ties Iran to Assassination Plot against Saudi Diplomat on U.S. Soil," Fox News, October 11, 2011, http://www.foxnews.com/us/2011/10/11/iranians -charged-over-terror-plot-in-us (accessed December 4, 2012).

14. "Iran Witness: Protest Videos," BBC News, November 4, 2009, http://news.bbc .co.uk/2/hi/8342738.stm (accessed December 4, 2012).

15. "Gravestone of Slain Iranian Protester Neda Vandalized," Radio Free Europe/ Radio Liberty, December 11, 2012, http://www.rferl.org/content/Gravestone_Of _Slain_Iranian_Protester_Neda_Vandalized_/1923685.html (accessed December 4, 2012).

16. Ramin Mostaghim and Patrick J. McDonnell, "Iran Police, Demonstrators Clash in Tehran Protests," *Los Angeles Times*, October 3, 2012, http://articles.latimes

.com/2012/oct/03/world/la-fg-iran-economy-protests-20121004 (accessed December 4, 2012).

17. Tarek Bazley, "Iran Internet Plan Ignites Debate," Al Jazeera, September 29, 2012, http://www.aljazeera.com/indepth/features/2012/09/2012927132545740255 .html (accessed December 4, 2012).

18. "Broadcasters Say Syria, Iran Jamming News Info," Associated Press, October 22, 2012, http://bigstory.ap.org/article/broadcasters-say-syria-iran-jamming-news-info (accessed December 4, 2012).

19. Helle C. Dale, "Why America Has Trouble Reaching Iran: VOA's Persian News Network in Dire Need of Reform," Heritage Foundation, March 5, 2012, http:// www.heritage.org/research/reports/2012/03/why-america-has-trouble-reaching -iran-voas-persian-news-network-in-dire-need-of-reform (accessed December 4, 2012).

20. Jeffrey Donovan, "Poland: Solidarity–the Trade Union that Changed the World," Radio Free Europe/Radio Liberty, August 24, 2005, http://www.rferl.org/content/ article/1060898.html (accessed December 4, 2012).

21. "Iraqi Official Betrays U.S. Confidence to Iran," State Department cable, Baghdad, September 22, 2006, http://www.cablegatesearch.net/cable.php?id=06BAGHDAD 3545 (accessed December 4, 2012).

22. Yaakov Katz, "MEK: Tehran Accelerating Its Nuclear Program," Jerusalem Post, May 12, 2012, http://www.jpost.com/IranianThreat/News/Article.aspx?id =269634 (accessed December 4, 2012).

23. CIA, "Iran: People and Society," World Factbook, https://www.cia.gov/library/ publications/the-world-factbook/geos/ir.html (accessed November 25, 2012).

24. "In Depth: Sistan-Baluchestan," Al Jazeera, October 19, 2009, http://www .aljazeera.com/focus/2009/10/2009101813545335456.html (accessed December 4, 2012).

25. David M. Herszenhorn, "Iran and Azerbaijan, Already Wary Neighbors, Find Even Less to Agree On," New York Times, June 5, 2012, http://www.nytimes .com/2012/06/06/world/middleeast/iran-and-azerbaijan-wary-neighbors-find-less -to-agree-on.html (accessed December 4, 2012).

26. CIA, "Iran: People and Society."

27. Natan Sharansky and Ron Dermer, The Case for Democracy: The Power of Freedom to Overcome Tyranny and Terror (New York: Public Affairs, 2004), 138.

28. Ibid., 137.

29. "U.S. Forces' Presence in S. Korea Is Vivid Expression of Hostile Policy toward DPRK: Foreign Ministry Spokesman," Korean Central News Agency, September 7, 2012, http://www.kcna.co.jp/item/2012/201209/news07/20120907-39ee.html (accessed December 4, 2012).

30. "Panmunjom Mission of KPA Sends Notice to U.S. Forces Side," Korean Central News Agency, November 25, 2010, http://www.kcna.co.jp/item/2010/201011/ news25/20101125-01ee.html (accessed December 4, 2012).

31. "Report: Iran to Deploy Submarines in Caspian Sea," Associated Press, June 30, 2012, http://www.foxnews.com/world/2012/06/30/report-iran-to-deploy -submarines-in-caspian-sea/ (accessed December 4, 2012).

32. Mark Lander and Steven Lee Myers, "With $30 Billion Arms Deal, U.S. Bolsters Saudi Ties," *New York Times*, December 29, 2011, http://www.nytimes .com/2011/12/30/world/middleeast/with-30-billion-arms-deal-united-states -bolsters-ties-to-saudi-arabia.html/ (accessed December 4, 2012).

33. Jim Wolf, "U.S. in $3.5 billion Arms Sale to UAE Amid Iran Tensions," Reuters, December 31, 2011, http://www.reuters.com/article/2011/12/31/us-usa-uae-iran -idUSTRE7BU0BF20111231 (accessed December 4, 2012).

34. David Blair, "Iran Threatens to Close Strait of Hormuz over EU Oil Sanctions," *Telegraph*, January 23, 2012, http://www.telegraph.co.uk/news/worldnews/ middleeast/iran/9032948/Iran-threatens-to-close-Strait-of-Hormuz-over-EU-oil -sanctions.html (accessed December 4, 2012).

35. Mark Landler and David E. Sanger, "Clinton Speaks of Shielding Mideast From Iran," *New York Times*, July 22, 2009, http://www.nytimes.com/2009/07/23/ world/asia/23diplo.html?_r=0 (accessed December 4, 2012).

36. "Nuclear Planning Group," North Atlantic Treaty Organization, http://www.nato .int/cps/en/natolive/topics_50069.htm (accessed November 28, 2012).

37. Definition of "crisis stability" from Dean A. Wilkening, Kenneth Watman, Michael Kennedy, and Richard Darilek, *Strategic Defenses and Crisis Stability* (Santa Monica, CA: Rand Corporation, April 1989), 1, http://www.rand.org/content/dam/ rand/pubs/notes/2005/N2511.pdf (accessed December 4, 2012).

38. "Operation Samson: Israel's Deployment of Nuclear Missiles on Subs from Germany," *Spiegel*, June 4, 2012, http://www.spiegel.de/international/world/israel -deploys-nuclear-weapons-on-german-built-submarines-a-836784.html (accessed December 4, 2012).

39. U.S. Department of Energy, Nevada Operations Office, "United States Nuclear Tests July 1945 through September 1992" (Las Vegas: U.S. Department of Energy, December 2000), http://www.nv.doe.gov/library/publications/historical/ DOENV_209_REV15.pdf (accessed April 27, 2013).

40. Milton Viorst and Patt Derian, "Iran Using Children to Clear Minefields," *The Age*, March 23, 1984, reprint of *Washington Post* article, March 22, 1984, http:// news.google.com/newspapers?nid=1300&dat=19840323&id=3kFVAAAAIBAJ&s jid=g5UDAAAAIBAJ&pg=2276,1118583 (accessed December 4, 2012).

41. Kathleen Moore and Brian Whitmore, "Obama, in Prague, Calls for Elimination of Nuclear Weapons," Radio Free Europe/Radio Liberty, April 5, 2009, http://www .rferl.org/content/Obama_Calls_For_Elimination_Of_Nuclear_Weapons_In _Prague_Speech/1602285.html (accessed December 4, 2012).

42. Lydia Saad, "Americans Give Record-High Ratings to Several U.S. Allies," Gallup Politics, February 16, 2012, http://www.gallup.com/poll/152735/americans-give -record-high-ratings-several-allies.aspx (accessed December 4, 2012).

43. Jonathan Marcus, "Is Israel's Missile Defence a Conflict Game-changer?," BBC News, November 26, 2012, http://www.bbc.co.uk/news/world-middle-east -20498971 (accessed December 4, 2012).

44. Rumsfeld, *Known and Unknown*, 722.

45. Douglas J. Feith, *War and Decision: Inside the Pentagon at the Dawn of the War on Terrorism* (New York: Harper, 2008), 94.

46. "Visit by Sen. Clinton to Singapore (July 5–7)," State Department cable, Singapore, July 6, 2005, http://www.cablegatesearch.net/cable.php?id=05SINGAPORE2073 (accessed December 4, 2012).

47. Rumsfeld, *Known and Unknown*, 723.

48. James Hookway, "Moderate Islamic Preachers Gain Followers in Indonesia," *Wall Street Journal*, October 10, 2012, http://online.wsj.com/article/SB1000087239639 0443635404578038541261622144.html (accessed December 4, 2012).

49. Dafna Linzer, "Alhurra's Effectiveness, Expense Criticized in New Senate Report," Pro Publica, June 21, 2010, http://www.propublica.org/article/alhurras -effectiveness-expense-criticized-in-new-senate-report (accessed December 4, 2012). *Note*: Added to the $700 million figure cited in this 2010 article are three subsequent fiscal years in which more than $100 million were appropriated for Alhurra annually.

10. Making Life Harder for Beijing

1. Richard Shears, "China Apologizes to Pregnant Woman Forced to Have Abortion at Seven Months for Breaching One-Child Policy and Suspends Three Officials," *Daily Mail*, June 14, 2012, http://www.dailymail.co.uk/news/article-2159178/ Feng-Jianmei-China-apologises-forced-abortion-child-policy-breach.html (accessed December 9, 2012).

2. "Pregnant Chinese Woman Forced to Abort Baby at Seven Months 'Is Being Kept in Hospital against Her Will,'" *Daily Mail*, June 27, 2012, http://www.dailymail .co.uk/news/article-2165507/Pregnant-Chinese-woman-forced-abort-baby-seven -months-kept-hospital-will.html (accessed December 9, 2012).

3. Associated Press, "China Family in Forced Abortion Case Claims Harassment by Government," CBS News, June 26, 2012, http://www.cbsnews.com/8301-202 _162-57461185/china-family-in-forced-abortion-case-claims-harassment-by -government/ (accessed December 9, 2012).

4. Josh Chin, "Father in One-Child Saga Resurfaces in Beijing," *Wall Street Journal*, June 29, 2012, http://online.wsj.com/article/SB100014240527023048307045770 496550834930224.html (accessed December 9, 2012).

5. CIA, "China; Economy," *World Factbook*, 1989 and 2012. For 1989, see http:// www.theodora.com/wfb1989/china/china_economy.html (accessed December 9, 2012). For 2012, see https://www.cia.gov/library/publications/the-world-factbook/ geos/ch.html (accessed December 9, 2012).

6. "Dalai Lama: 'Cultural Genocide' behind Self-immolations," BBC News, November 7, 2011, http://www.bbc.co.uk/news/world-asia-15617026 (accessed December 9, 2012).

7. PBS, "Should U.S. Pressure China More on Human Rights?," *NewsHour*, transcript, May 1, 2012, http://www.pbs.org/newshour/bb/world/jan-june12/ humanrights_05-01.html (accessed December 9, 2012).

8. David Sanger, "Bush Lauds China Leader as 'Partner' in Diplomacy," *New York*

Times, December 10, 2003, http://www.nytimes.com/2003/12/10/world/bush
-lauds-china-leader-as-partner-in-diplomacy.html (accessed December 9, 2012).

9. Jay Lefkowitz, "North Korean Human Rights & U.S. National Security," remarks, American Enterprise Institute, Washington, DC, January 17, 2008, 3, http://www
.aei.org/files/2008/01/17/20080118_LefkowitzRemarks.pdf (accessed December 9, 2012).

10. Associated Press, "Rice Rebukes Official Critical of North Korea," *USA Today*, January 22, 2008, http://usatoday30.usatoday.com/news/world/2008-01-22-rice_N
.htm (accessed December 9, 2012).

11. "EAP DAS Christensen Presses China on Iran, Burma, Sudan, DPRK, Human Rights," State Department cable, Beijing, December 14, 2007, http://www
.cablegatesearch.net/cable.php?id=07BEIJING7499.

12. Joseph Kahn, "Asia Pacific: China Cut off Exports of Oil to North Korea," *International Herald Tribune*, October 30, 2006, http://www.nytimes.com/2006/10/30/
world/asia/30iht-oil.3334398.html?_r=0 (accessed December 9, 2012).

13. Mary Kissel, "Diplomats for Obama," *Wall Street Journal*, August 22, 2012, http://
online.wsj.com/article/SB10000872396390443324404577595360864041028
.html (accessed December 9, 2012).

14. Joseph Nye, "Should China Be 'Contained'?," Al Jazeera, July 8, 2011, http://
www.aljazeera.com/indepth/opinion/2011/07/2011759113577076I.html
(accessed December 9, 2012).

15. Amy Chang, "Indigenous Weapons Development in China's Military Modernization" (Washington, DC: U.S.-China Economic and Security Review Commission, April 5, 2012), 3, http://origin.www.uscc.gov/sites/default/files/Research/
China-Indigenous-Military-Developments-Final-Draft-03-April2012.pdf (accessed December 9, 2012).

16. Calum MacLeod, "China Confirms Stealth Jet-Test Flight during Gates' Visit," *USA Today*, January 11, 2011, http://usatoday30.usatoday.com/news/world/2011
-01-11-gates-china_N.htm (accessed December 9, 2012).

17. Greta Van Susteren, interview with Donald Rumsfeld, Fox News, June 14, 2012, http://video.foxnews.com/v/1690112886001/rumsfeld-on-intel-leaks-and-the
-need-for-special-prosecutor/?playlist_id=8685 (accessed December 9, 2012).

18. Gen. Keith Alexander, remarks at the "CSIS Cybersecurity Policy Debate Series: U.S. Cybersecurity Policy and the Role of U.S. Cybercom," Center for Strategic and International Studies, Washington, DC, June 3, 2010, http://www.nsa
.gov/public_info/_files/speeches_testimonies/100603_alexander_transcript.pdf
(accessed December 9, 2012).

19. Bill Gertz, "Soft on Cyber Crime," *Washington Free Beacon*, March 11, 2013, http://freebeacon.com/soft-on-cyber-crime/ (accessed April 30, 2013).

20. Andy Greenberg, "The Shanghai Army Unit that Hacked 115 U.S. Targets Likely Wasn't Even China's 'A-Team,'" *Forbes*, February 21, 2013, http://www.forbes
.com/sites/andygreenberg/2013/02/21/the-shanghai-army-unit-that-hacked-115
-u-s-targets-likely-wasnt-even-chinas-a-team/ (accessed April 30, 2013).

21. "2012 Annual Report to Congress" (Washington, DC: U.S.-China Economic and

Security Review Commission, August 13, 2012), 147, http://origin.www.uscc.gov/Annual_Reports/2012-annual-report-congress.

22. Eliza Krigman, "Report Calls China Biggest Cyberthreat," Politico, November 15, 2012, http://www.politico.com/news/stories/1112/83857.html (accessed December 9, 2012).

23. Jana Winter and Jeremy A. Kaplan, "Washington Confirms Chinese Hack Attack on White House Computer," Fox News, October 1, 2012, http://www.foxnews.com/tech/2012/10/01/washington-confirms-chinese-hack-attack-on-white-house-computer/ (accessed April 29, 2013).

24. Bill Gertz, "White House Hack Attack," *Washington Free Beacon*, September 30, 2012, http://freebeacon.com/white-house-hack-attack/ (accessed December 9, 2012).

25. Jameson Berkow, "Nortel Hacked to Pieces," *Financial Post*, February 25, 2012, http://business.financialpost.com/2012/02/25/nortel-hacked-to-pieces/ (accessed December 9, 2012).

26. Dan Lothian and Lisa Jansen, "Obama Pledges U.S. Military Power in Pacific," CNN, November 16, 2011, http://www.cnn.com/2011/11/16/world/asia/australia-obama-trip/index.html (accessed December 9, 2012).

27. Karen Parrish, "Flournoy Terms China Talks 'Very Constructive,'" Armed Forces Press Service, December 9, 2011, http://www.defense.gov/news/newsarticle.aspx?id=66420 (accessed December 9, 2012).

28. David Jackson, "Obama's Asia-Pacific Trip Shadowed by China," *USA Today*, November 16, 2011, http://content.usatoday.com/communities/theoval/post/2011/11/obamas-asia-pacific-trip-shadowed-by-china/1#.UMLM_aW_4yE (accessed December 9, 2012).

29. Bill Gertz, "Inside the Ring: Asia Pivot Questioned," *Washington Times*, December 5, 2012, http://www.washingtontimes.com/news/2012/dec/5/inside-the-ring-asia-pivot-questioned/ (accessed December 9, 2012).

30. Max Fisher, "China Is Happy with John Kerry Because It Thinks He'll Drop the 'Pivot to Asia,'" *Washington Post*, February 27, 2013, http://www.washingtonpost.com/blogs/worldviews/wp/2013/02/27/china-is-happy-with-john-kerry-because-it-thinks-hell-drop-the-pivot-to-asia/ (accessed April 30, 2013).

31. John T. Bennett, "Lawmaker Concerned that Navy Fleet Isn't Ready for Combat," *The Hill*, March 9, 2011, http://thehill.com/business-a-lobbying/148555-moran-concerned-that-navy-fleet-isnt-ready-for-combat.

32. Adam J. Hebert, "Raptor Roulette," *Air Force Magazine* 91, no. 11 (November 2008), http://www.airforcemag.com/MagazineArchive/Pages/2008/November%202008/1108issbf.aspx (accessed April 30, 2013).

33. "National Defense Budget Estimates for FY 2012," Office of the Under Secretary of Defense (Comptroller), March 2011, 6, http://comptroller.defense.gov/defbudget/fy2012/FY12_Green_Book.pdf (accessed December 9, 2012).

34. Joseph Kahn, "Chinese General Threatens Use of A-Bombs if U.S. Intrudes," *New York Times*, July 15, 2005, http://www.nytimes.com/2005/07/15/international/asia/15china.html (accessed December 9, 2012).

35. Department of Defense, *The Big Picture: The General George S. Patton Story,* narrated by Ronald Reagan, 1945, U.S. National Archives, http://www.youtube.com/watch?feature=endscreen&NR=1&v=uYjnWXFTQkM (accessed December 9, 2012).

36. Pew Research Center, "Religion in China on the Eve of the 2008 Beijing Olympics," Pew Global Attitudes Project, May 1, 2008, http://www.pewforum.org/Importance-of-Religion/Religion-in-China-on-the-Eve-of-the-2008-Beijing-Olympics.aspx (accessed December 9, 2012).

37. Mary Shovlain, "Hong Kong Cardinal Warns of 'Schism' within Chinese Church," *Catholic News Service,* February 9, 2012, http://www.catholicnews.com/data/stories/cns/1200545.htm (accessed December 9, 2012).

38. Malcolm Moore, "Chinese Rail Crash Scandal: 'Official Steals $2.8 Billion,'" *Telegraph,* August 1, 2011, http://www.telegraph.co.uk/news/worldnews/asia/china/8674824/Chinese-rail-crash-scandal-official-steals-2.8-billion.html (accessed December 9, 2012).

11. Leading America's Pacific Century

1. "Manifest Destiny, Continued: McKinley Defends U.S. Expansionism," History Matters, George Mason University, http://historymatters.gmu.edu/d/5575/ (accessed December 10, 2012).

2. Steve Tally, *Bland Ambition: From Adams to Quayle — the Cranks, Criminals, Tax Cheats, and Golfers Who Made It to Vice President* (San Diego: Harcourt, 1992), 195.

3. James Bradley, "Excerpt from 'The Imperial Cruise,'" *New York Times,* November 18, 2009, http://www.nytimes.com/2009/11/19/books/excerpt-imperial-cruise.html?pagewanted=all&_r=0 (accessed December 14, 2012).

4. Edmund Morris, *The Rise of Theodore Roosevelt* (New York: Ballantine Books, 1979), 587.

5. "Top Trading Partners — Surplus, Deficit, Total Trade," U.S. Census Bureau, http://www.census.gov/foreign-trade/top/#2012 (accessed April 30, 2013).

6. CIA, "GDP Real Growth Rate 2011," *World Factbook,* https://www.cia.gov/library/publications/the-world-factbook/fields/2003.html (accessed April 30, 2013).

7. N. Gregory Mankiw, "If You Have the Answers, Tell Me," *New York Times,* May 7, 2011, http://www.nytimes.com/2011/05/08/business/economy/08view.html?_r=0 (accessed April 30, 2013).

8. Kristina Wong and Sean Lengell, "DeMint: Law of Sea Treaty Now Dead," *Washington Times,* July 16, 2012, http://www.washingtontimes.com/news/2012/jul/16/demint-says-law-sea-treaty-now-dead/?page=all (accessed April 30, 2012).

Selected Bibliography

Atkinson, Rick. *Crusade: The Untold Story of the Persian Gulf War*. New York: Houghton Mifflin, 1993.

Beschloss, Michael R. *The Conquerors: Roosevelt, Truman, and the Destruction of Hitler's Germany*. New York: Simon & Schuster, 2002.

Buckley, William F., Jr. *Up from Liberalism*. New York: McDowell, Obolensky, 1959.

Child, Julia. *My Life in France*. With Alex Prud'homme. New York: Alfred A. Knopf, 2006. Kindle edition.

Clarridge, Duane R. *A Spy for All Seasons: My Life in the CIA*. With Digby Diehl. New York: Scribner, 1997.

Corera, Gordon. *The Art of Betrayal: The Secret History of MI6: Life and Death in the British Secret Service*. New York: Pegasus Books, 2013. Kindle edition.

Dulles, Allen W. *The Craft of Intelligence*. Guilford, CT: The Lyons Press, 2006.

Feith, Douglas J. *War and Decision: Inside the Pentagon at the Dawn of the War on Terrorism*. New York: Harper, 2008.

Fromkin, David. *A Peace to End All Peace: The Fall of the Ottoman Empire and the Creation of the Modern Middle East*. New York: Avon Books, 1989.

Garnett, David. *The Secret History of the PWE: The Political Warfare Executive, 1939–1945*. London: St. Ermin's Press, 2002.

Kempe, Frederick. *Berlin 1961: Kennedy, Khrushchev, and the Most Dangerous Place on Earth*. New York: Berkeley Books, 2011. Kindle edition.

Lawrence, T. E. *Seven Pillars of Wisdom*, ed. Brad Berner. Apostrophe Books, August 24, 2010. Kindle edition.

Manchester, William. *American Caesar: Douglas MacArthur*. New York: Dell Publishing, 1978.

Mann, James. *The China Fantasy: How Our Leaders Explain away Chinese Repression*. New York: Viking, 2007.

Morris, Edmund. *The Rise of Theodore Roosevelt*. New York: Ballantine Books, 1979.

Osgood, Kenneth. *Total Cold War: Eisenhower's Secret Propaganda Battle at Home and Abroad*. Lawrence: University Press of Kansas, 2006.

Rodman, Peter W. *Presidential Command: Power, Leadership, and the Making of Foreign Policy from Richard Nixon to George W. Bush*. New York: Alfred A. Knopf, 2009.

Rumsfeld, Donald. *Known and Unknown: A Memoir*. New York: Sentinel, 2011.

Schwartz, Harry. *Prague's 200 Days: The Struggle for Democracy in Czechoslovakia*. New York: Praeger, 1969.

Sharansky, Natan, and Ron Dermer. *The Case for Democracy: The Power of Freedom to Overcome Tyranny and Terror*. New York: PublicAffairs, 2004.

Tally, Steve. *Bland Ambition: From Adams to Quayle — the Cranks, Criminals, Tax Cheats, and Golfers Who Made It to Vice President*. San Diego: Harcourt, 1992.

Thomas, Evan. *The Very Best Men: Four Who Dared: The Early Years of the CIA*. New York: Simon & Schuster, 1996.

Index

Hill, Christopher, 105–6
Hindus, 93, 200
Hitler, Adolf, 182, 193, 203
Hollywood, 33, 86, 101, 108–9, 212
Homeland Security Department, 87, 149, 159–60
Hong Kong, 3–6, 214–15
Hoover, Herbert, 56
House of Representatives, 8–9, 44; and China, 71–72; Intelligence Committee of, 171; Pike Committee of, xix
Huawei, 208
Hughes, Karen, 85–88
human intelligence (HUMINT), 130–31, 163–64, 166, 169
Hungary, ix, 22, 25
Hussein, Saddam, xx, 18, 33, 35, 120, 126, 148, 152, 179; 1998 bombing campaign against, 49; invasion of Kuwait, 7–9; uprising against, 12; and WMD, 132–34

Ibrahim, Saad Eddin, 18
Idaho, 41
Incirlik, 110
India, 131, 200, 206, 209, 214, 221
Indian Ocean, 104
Indonesia, 91, 200, 221
intelligence. See Central Intelligence Agency (CIA)
Interim Transitional National Council (Libyan), 38
Internet, 10, 98–99, 115, 206; and China, 79, 114, 216; and dissidents, 115, 186. See also cyber warfare, social media
Iran, xii, xxiv, 6, 15, 16, 61, 103, 221; actions against Americans by, xxiv, 179–81; aftermath of Revolution in, 18, 48, 132, 134, 177; Guardian Council of, 182; and human rights, 93, 182; nuclear weapons program of, 59, 61, 133–35, 149, 163, 178; options for smart power against, xxv, 169, 176, 178–99, 201, 214, 224; smart power by, xxi; unrest in, 19–21, 113–15, 178

Iraq, xxi, 12, 33, 35, 43, 49–50, 52, 76, 91, 210; and Coalition Provisional Authority, 126–28, 148; and Commanders' Emergency Response Program, 123; insurgency in, 100; invasion of Kuwait by, 7–8, 10; and Iran, xxiv, 179, 188, 192, 196; no-fly zone over, 38, 53; Republican Guard of, 12; Section 1206/1207/1208 funding for, 122–23; State Department shortcomings in, 120–23, 127; and WMD, 132–33, 161. See also surge of military forces in Iraq
Iron Curtain, ix, xvi–xvii, xx, 114, 168, 143
Iron Dome, 197
Islam, 82–83, 88, 94. See also Shiites, Sunnis
Islamic Jihad, 180
Islamism, xii, 6, 46, 61, 89, 142, 221; conditions giving rise to, 35; definition of, 83; and East Asia and the Pacific, 77; in Egypt, 15, 18, 28–31, 56, 171–72; in Iran, xxiv, 16, 21, 48, 134, 177–78, 180–82; in Libya, 99; options for smart power against, xxv, 143, 149, 166, 176, 197–201. See also Muslim Brotherhood
Israel, 28, 31, 99, 115, 134, 178, 181, 192, 194–97; and negotiations with Palestinians, 18, 59, 83, 102–03
Istanbul, 20, 67, 110
Italy, xv–xvi, 188, 193

J-20 (aircraft), 206
Japan, 72–73, 102, 104–6, 156, 173, 206, 209–10, 214, 221; use of nuclear weapons against, xviii, 47
Jenkins, Charles, 104
Jerusalem, 6, 31
Jews, 31, 67, 93, 189–90
jihad, 30
jihadism. See Islamism
Joe-1 nuclear device, xvii
John Paul II, xx
Johnson, Lyndon, 23, 25

tion to transnational issues, xii; and
State Department, 160, 169, 174–75
Smith, Chris, 142
social democrats, 138, 199
socialists, 138
social media, 113–16
Solidarity (Polish), 17, 114, 125, 140, 188
Solzhenitsyn, Aleksandr, xi
Somalia, 211
Sonenshine, Tara, 88–89
South Africa, 20, 167
South America, 22
South Korea, 72, 95, 124, 204, 214, 221
Soviet bloc, ix, xi, 22, 141, 151, 166, 189.
See also Eastern Bloc
Soviet Union, 17, 39, 57, 59, 97, 203;
creation of, 67–69, 177, 183; demise of,
xx, 10, 141, 166; dissidents within, 20,
34, 184, 189, 190–92; and espionage,
129; invasion of Afghanistan by, ix,
131; and nuclear weapons, 47, 194–95;
and Prague Spring, 21–26, 131–32;
proxies of, x, 8; use of smart power
against, 139–40, 143, 168, 184–85,
193–95, 209; use of smart power by,
xv–xvii, 48, 137–38, 177–78
Spain, 117–18, 177–78, 204, 219, 221
Spanish Civil War, 177–78
special operations, 164–65, 167
Special Operations Executive (British),
167
Stalin, Joseph, xvi, xviii, 22, 39, 69, 137–
38, 150, 203
State Department, xx, 3, 24, 51–52, 124,
141, 152, 199; author's service at, xxiii,
4–6, 35, 58–59, 95, 119–20, 184, 213;
and China, 77–79, 97, 205; and "clientitis," 101, 158–59; and human rights,
xi, 17, 100, 115; and intelligence, 125,
131, 134–35, 137, 139, 163; and Israel,
102–3; and Jesse Helms 56; management of, 125, 154–60, 173, 174–76;
and Middle East, 14, 18; 19–20, 29,
32–33, 37–38, 120–23, 188–89; and

North Korea, 4, 96–97, 142; and Paki-
stan, 57; and public diplomacy, xxiii,
11, 84–89, 167, 169; and Taiwan, 107;
and visas, 159, 167. *See also* Foreign
Service
stay-behind mission, xvii
Stevens, Chris, 98–99
Stockholm, 68
Strategic Air Command, xvii
Strategic Defense Initiative, 194
Sturmabteilung SA, 182
Sudan, 54, 167
Suez Canal, 28
Sufi Muslims, 190
Sullivan, Andrew, 113
Sunnis, xxiv, 181, 190
surge of military forces in Iraq, 50, 59,
103, 123, 128, 135, 179–80
Sweden, xvii, 187
Syria, 54, 110–11, 192

Taft, William, 151
Taipei Economic and Cultural Represen-
tative Office, 107
Taiwan, 72, 102, 105–8, 206, 209, 212,
214, 221
Taliban, 45, 83–84, 93, 164, 178
terrorism, 35, 50, 60, 63, 82–84, 86,
91, 94, 100, 104, 119, 199. *See also*
Islamism
Texas, 181
Thailand, 221
Thatcher, Margaret, xx
think tanks, 20, 52, 61, 74, 90, 188
third way politics, 48
Three-Self Patriotic Movement, 215
Tiananmen Square, 75, 96, 203
Tibet, 75, 105, 203
trade, x, 70–72, 75. *See also* North Amer-
ican Free Trade Agreement (NAFTA)
trafficking in persons, 4
Transparency International, 14
Transportation Security Administration,
62, 149

About the Author

Christian Whiton is a former diplomat and presidential campaign adviser. He is a prolific commentator on national security issues. From 2003 to 2009, he was a senior adviser and deputy special envoy in the State Department. He is currently a principal at DC International Advisory, a political risk consulting firm. Whiton holds an MBA from the UCLA Anderson School of Management. He frequently appears on Fox News, CNBC, and other networks. He has published articles in the *Wall Street Journal*, *Washington Post*, *Time* magazine, *Daily Caller*, *Huffington Post*, and numerous other publications around the world. Whiton lives with his partner in Los Angeles.